LIVIN' THE DREAM ...

TODAY BECAUSE TOMORROW IS NOT PROMISED

ALEXA GLAZER

DEDICATION

To Dad,
For being world's greatest.
For teaching me what *livin' the dream* means.
For leaving behind a legacy that is worth sharing,
a legacy worthy of the world.

CONTENTS

ACKNOWLEDGMENTS

Dad, I don't have words for how much you have done for me, and for what you continue doing for me. I wish you were here, to have another minute talking to you and hearing you laugh. Until we meet again, stay with me. Move with me.

Mom, thank you for being my mother first and best friend second. For being so strong because we have been dealt cards that have not favored us. For standing by my side through it all. For supporting this journey of mine, even though sometimes it has been difficult. Difficult to have the continued reminders of the past, and my in your face *"livin' the dream"* lifestyle. For doing anything for me, literally. I grow closer to you daily and I am so lucky to have a woman like you in my life.

Nikki, we've have grown closer and closer each day and I am so thankful for the friendship that I have with my older sister. Thank you for always telling me "proud of you Lex" and meaning it, because sometimes it is just the push I need.

Uncle Gus, to the man that reminds me most of Dad. Thank you for taking me under your wing. For taking in another child when you already have three of your own. For taking me to baseball game after baseball game. For calling me to check in on me. For

i

listening to my ideas, my girl drama, and for being a number one fan of everything I have done. Thank you for being like a dad to me, I mean that from the bottom of my heart.

E.T., that unbiological family I talk about so often. You've been hard on me at times I thought I didn't need it. You've been right in the times I wished you were wrong and you have been there on the days I needed someone most. Thank you for taking my dad's request at taking care of me and actually doing so.

My ride or dies, the ones that have stood there, by my side, without flinching. I wanted to make a list and go into everyone specifically, but I could write an entire book of "thank yous" if I did. So y'all know who you are. You are my people. You make my heart dance and my blood pump. You have stood by me through the worst moments of my life. You have held me close when I needed that, you have given me space when that was what I needed, you have wiped my tears and you have made me laugh to my limits.

You have maintained ride or dies with miles and miles of distance. You have done things for me that I wasn't prepared to do, that I felt like I couldn't do, that I didn't want to do. You have listened to me vent, complain, and cry in situations you didn't even know how to respond to, so you didn't respond, you just remained present, which has been exactly what I needed. You have been my hype team. Wow, I have been so lucky on this one. You have listened to me geek out over my ideas, all of them, no matter how big or small they have been. You have listened to chapter after chapter and speech after speech. You have read every blog, liked every post, watched every video, and many times all more than once.

You have believed in me. You have trusted me. You have moved with me and I can't ask for better people to have in a lifetime. You guys are the real deal and I am forever blessed for you all. I appreciate you. I love you. I will continue to thank you all till my day comes. Until then, let's keep thriving together.

Ned Barnett, for seeing the potential in the writer I have become. For long nights, brainstorming ideas, and countless edits, meetings, and emails. Thank you for helping me bring these words together to form a real book. It's my first masterpiece.

The haters, the naysayers, the doubters, the egoists.
The ones who haven't believed. The ones who tried to break me. The ones who revolved our relationship around negativity and hostility. The ones who said they wouldn't read this but have found that they had to anyway. Thank you for the fuel. Thank you for giving me backbone. Thank you for showing me I don't need everyone, and that not just anyone should be on my team. Thank you for that, I sincerely appreciate all that you have done for me.

WHO? ME, THE AUTHOR. DUH. SOMEONE HAD TO WRITE THIS GEM OF A BOOK.

I am a young woman, a passionate, thriving and loving person. I'd like to think I have a heart of gold that is overflowing with love for anything and everyone. My name is Alexa Glazer, but you can call me Lex, Glaze, or Donut. I say this because, since you're reading my book, I now see us as friends, and those are the names my friends and family call me. We are either already friends, or we are about to become friends. And since you're my friend, I am about to pour my heart out to you. I tend to wear it on my sleeve.

In the following pages, as I share with you the experiences life has thrown my way, you're about to get real close to me. You're about to discover that I'm just about as open in what I say as is the book you're holding right now. Too close for comfort? Eh, maybe, but I hope not. I'm writing this with as much candor and open honesty as I can manage, for just one reason. To help you. Though it's kind of frightening – to me, at least – I'm about to get

1

really vulnerable, just so I can help you. You're about to learn my deepest, darkest, more passionate feelings.

Sure, along the way, I'm going to blow off some much-needed steam, but that won't change my candor or the life-lessons I hope you'll find as relevant to you as I've found them relevant to me.

I've reached a point in my life where I am once again having the kind of dreams I had when I was six years old. Each night, I dream of conquering the world, of making this world a better place. My over-riding dream is to help change people's lives ... for the better. The difference between having this dream at age six and having the same dream at age 25 is that, at 25, **I can do it,** and I will.

Call me naïve, but I think I have the power to conquer. In life, we have the power to do anything – and everything – that we truly believe in. All it takes is a two-step process: dreaming, then acting upon those dreams.

December 30, 2017 — The ones that are crazy enough to think they can change the world are the ones that usually do. 2018 goals.

Big dreams or small dreams – these are what make the world go round. **Dreams evolve, stimulate and inspire people from all walks of life, people of all ages, all shapes and all sizes. Dreams don't discriminate – instead, inspiration brings people together.** Whether I touch one person's life, or a million, I will treat each "touch" as a success – and I will use each touch to fuel my fire.

November 15, 2017 — *Intellects don't change the world, people who inspire do.* — **Nikki Glazer Stoicoiu**

You already know a little bit about me, but just wait. Things are about to get a little crazy, a little sad, and – I hope – a little inspirational. I'm about to take you on an emotional roller coaster ride that is going to leave you wanting more, turning these pages like wildfire. You might even dance it out a time or two and maybe cry. I hope you'll laugh – hey, I laugh at my own jokes, and so you should, too, even if it's just to make me feel better. Most important, though, I hope you'll gain some perspective on life. Not just my life – yours.

ALEXA GLAZER

WHAT? THIS IS A BOOK – YOU HAVE TO ACTUALLY READ IT TO FIND OUT.

Along the way, I have faced a few hardships. The one hardship I hold most dear to me is that of losing a parent at a young age. I thought that, for me, this loss was the perfect opportunity to help others, and by others, I mean this entire universe. Some people say this is crazy, to which I say in return, "Then watch me be crazy. This is what I was put on earth to do. A little challenge isn't going to stop me." Not to mention, I think being a little crazy is really just adding to your own personal character.

Of course, I want to help you, my readers, especially those among you who have also lost a parent, a friend, a sibling, a mentor …

But there is also real value here for those who haven't yet suffered a life-altering loss. Don't worry, you will. Everyone, at least those who live long enough, will suffer a crushing loss. I want to help those among you who – on any given day – may find themselves struggling to find some light, or to get out of bed, or to go on living their lives. I want to help the ones who don't yet see their souls' greatest potential, and how suffering a horrific loss can refine that potential.

This book is a compilation of life lessons. Life lessons I have gained on my own, as well as those which came to me from others. These lessons are shaped by the experiences I've been forced to live through, as well as those experienced at second-hand.

My journey involves losing my dad, followed by my continuing journey of day-to-day life as I try – and sometimes struggle – to keep his legacy alive. Most importantly, these lessons include the steps I have taken in the aftermath of that struggle, steps I never dreamed I'd face.

After any hardship, you have a decision to make. Your choices are simple:

A.) Let it break you; or,

B.) Let it build you.

I have chosen B, at least most of the time. Let's be honest: it isn't easy to be positive and bubbly, day in and day out. In this book, I am going to encourage you to embrace the good days, and to survive – and ultimately, to triumph over – the bad days. I want to help you understand that each day is a victory within itself.

Okay, so what should you expect from the rest of this book?

You can expect to read some contradictions – things that may not come out of a cookie cutter or scream out in measures of black-

or-white. You can also expect some sarcasm, along with some giggles, just possibly some crying, and maybe even some thought bubbles that will suddenly appear over your head. I *frickin'* hope you'll also be given some inspiration, as well as a valuable new perspective on life, and death, and life beyond death.

You should take this book for what it is worth. However, I can't promise that you'll buy in to – let alone agree with – everything I have to offer. In fact, I know you won't, and I'm okay with that. I'm not trying to be Gandhi, or Mother Theresa – unlike the great gurus of this life, I don't even pretend to have all the answers. In addition, not all of the answers that work for me will be right for you, let alone for everyone. However, what I can promise you – maybe even a pinky promise – is that, by reading this book, you will gain something of real value. This book was written by a still-young Midwestern girl, one with big dreams and a sometimes-dorky personality – a girl who woke up one day and decided to write this book, just for you.

Although I think I have some answers that you'll value, please don't mistake me for some tenured professor with a string of Ph.Ds.

As you read on, try to imagine that instead of reading, you're hearing me talking to you across a cup of coffee at Starbucks, or in my case, some hot chocolate – so please feel free to narrate what you're reading, using any voice you please … except, please, no Donald Duck. As you read, as you hear me speaking in your head, I hope you'll gain insights into your own character. I know you'll be introduced to a new support system, and I am confident that you'll find in me a friend.

That's important because no one in this world should feel alone. Not even you. Especially not even you!

WHERE? SOMEWHERE BETWEEN HEAVEN AND EARTH.

So my "who," which is me, is still on this Earth. Pinpointed on the map is my base camp in Las Vegas, Nevada, but at any given moment, I am likely to be traveling the globe – which is what I do whenever I can, either for the sheer pleasure of seeing new things and meeting new people, or because I'm on my way to Tahoe to give a talk to people like you – or maybe even to a baseball stadium to knock off my bucket list and to enjoy America's favorite past time with a hot dog in hand. The purpose behind my "why" can be found in Heaven; or, possibly, somewhere between Heaven and Earth. My dad, my "why," is in that unknown and unknowable place we all go when we leave this earth.

That place is the one so many refer to when they tell me he is with me wherever I go. Maybe that's heaven – a heaven that allows its residents to visit their friends back home. It's from this

9

idea that I am getting the sense that Phil Glazer is somewhere between heaven and earth. Because we don't really know – we can't really know. I can't see him in all his glory, so I can't be for sure. I can't find heaven's GPS coordinates or get directions.

I don't see a billboard on I-15 saying: "Welcome to that place you've been looking for. That place you can meet those that have passed over in the flesh. That place located somewhere between Heaven and Earth."

Therefore, my particular "where" is not some GPS coordinate here on earth, or some celestial GPS coordinate between here and Heaven. My "where" is wherever I can make a difference. It's wherever I can put positivity back into people's lives. It's wherever I feel safe.

Right now, my where is inside this book you're holding. When I sit down and write, I jump into my work. I embrace that environment, that place inside myself where I am when I write – that environment is whatever I make of it in my head. It's a place I take myself to. It's where I create and can be anyone. Most importantly though, it's a place where I can be myself. Where I am not what other people think (or insist) I should be – where I am no-one else but the real, honest-to-goodness Alexa Renee Glazer.

How cool is that?

My "where" is someplace where society's ideals and expectations don't matter. Where I can rebel against all the rules while refusing to worry about the consequences. Where I can break the mold, straddle the line, and do whatever my golden heart desires. This "where" is the place I create within myself is my safe haven, my happy place. So, regardless of where I actually am on the map, when I dive into this book, I am always somewhere glorious that can be found between two universes. Between real life and wherever my imagination wants to take me. Somewhere between Heaven and Earth.

ALEXA GLAZER

WHEN? JANUARY 27TH, 2014.

Contrary to what you might think, this is not the date when I started this book. This date has much more value to it. This is the day that changed my life. It was the day that brought me to this book you're holding in your hands, but it by no means was the day I actually started writing. The funny thing is, I am not to someone who had ever dreamt of writing a book, not even once (before this date), not once in all her life. Which probably makes many of my fellow authors – people who've dreamed all their lives about writing a book – upset, and perhaps with good reason. Which probably also makes many journalism majors annoyed, for the same reasons.

However, just because this book didn't start out as the fulfillment of a life-long dream doesn't mean that writing it – and getting it published and in your hands – hasn't been a dream come true. I never pictured myself writing a book. In fact, when I was back in school, I was so allergic to writing that I dreaded writing even short five-page papers in English class, let alone the hundreds of pages I have somehow written, just to place my thoughts and insights into your hands.

Most writers are also readers. I discovered a new-found love for reading when I got in high school, but I was never what you'd call a super book nerd. Until now. Now I run through books, engrossed in each one but eager to finish so I can start the next new book.

Besides not writing books – at least before this one – I also never wrote in journals or had a diary, or in any other way wrote down my deepest, darkest thoughts.

Until now.

Or more accurately, until that awful date, January 27, 2014.

Until my "when" totally changed my life.

Until January 27, 2014, the date my dad, my mentor, my best friend, the closest person to me in the whole world, the day that Phil Glazer died. The day my life changed forever. The day so horrific that I want nothing more than to forget most of its awful details … yet somehow I can't. Because that was the day that led to my purpose in life – the day that gave me my "why."

I can't tell you when your "when" will be – maybe a psychic can, but not me. I don't know when your life will take a turn for the worst, become a little hectic and crazy and when the chaos will begin. I know that your life will take that kind of turn – perhaps more than once – but the "when" remains a mystery until it occurs.

I have a friend who can pinpoint his own "when" – November 17, 1982, at 9 p.m. Central Standard Time – that's the day and the time he hit rock-bottom and swore off drinking, a pledge he finally kept (after several previous aborted attempts to quit). He went through three months of hell, and still fights the demon, but that date is enshrined in his life as the moment when he finally grew up, took control of his life and turned things around for himself.

Your "when" might not be that precise, but I'm willing to bet that it will be. However, friend, you might think your "when" involves taking that turn for the worst and in some "when" moments, that is exactly what happens. But no matter how bad that "when" moment feels, stay calm. When it happens, it can make a dramatic shift – a shift for the better.

Which is why I am using my "when" to write a damn book that I never thought I would write. This book came about due to a moment I never thought I would have to endure. Due to the woman I am today, a woman I became beginning on January 27, 2014.

That's the beauty of your "when"

My "when" is precisely the moment when I suddenly started to feel unlucky – the instant when I finally realized that life is unfair. That my life is unfair. That I no longer believe in luck and fairness. You may feel this way too – and if you don't, not yet, give it time – you will. And when you do, that's okay. Feel it.

But only for a second. Don't dwell on luck, good or bad. Because, ultimately, you create your own luck. You make the

15

most of whatever the hell fate throws your way. Don't loathe life while wallowing in your self-pity. Don't start sending personal invitations to your pity parties.

Although I now find the idea of a pity party pretty hilarious, this is important – we all go through those moments in life. There was a time when I was ready to throw pity parties – to even have them catered! In fact, if you keep reading I will tell you all about these pity parties. I know you've thought these same things, but if you're like me, you don't want to admit it. When you do feel that way, no matter how you feel, fight the urge. Do not send out these invitations. Do not trigger – let alone participate in – those little self-indulgent emotional episodes. Wait until you're ready – and believe me, you'll know when you are ready. Then, instead of a pity party, you'll know it's finally time to throw a "Hey, look at me! Top of the world, ma!" kind of party.

Again, I can't tell you when this is going to happen. In fact, I am beyond glad that I can't tell you when your "when" is going to happen. That I can't give your "when" date and time.

I don't want to be held accountable for something like that. I don't want to be a psychic who can accurately predict the beginning of your momentary dread … no thank you. No one told me; and even if I could, I would not tell you. When it comes … surprise, you're in for a real treat. And that surprise is part of the "when" experience. If you knew it was coming, you'd probably find a way to avoid it. But then where would you be?

Of course, maybe your "when" has already happened. In that case, congratulations. Now, maybe you can write a book about it to and help others like I am trying to do for you.

Regardless of the pain your "when" entails, don't fear "when." If your "when" has already happened, don't hate it. Forgive it, embrace its lessons, and move on. January 27th, 2014 was the worst day of my life, but it has brought me to some of the best days of my life. Your "when" day will, too.

January 29, 2014 – God has been blessed with the most loving, inspiring and selfless angel anyone has ever encountered. I continue to ask myself how he could take away such an incredible person who effected each and every life he touched. From world's best dad, to the most perfect husband for my mother, to the best coach anyone could ever learn from, it's safe to say I have had the best in my life for the past 21 years. My dad has always been my rock, has always kept me level, and has always pushed me to my fullest potential. If he has taught me anything in my life it is to always stay strong, work hard, follow your goals, love endlessly, never give up, find the good, help those that need it, and be proud of who you are. I will live each day for the rest of my life through and for my dad. I know he will continue to be my biggest fan forever and always. I hope to follow in his footsteps and inspire everyone I encounter and become the person he was. The next few days will be the hardest of my life and I pray to my dad that he will keep me strong once again. I love you to the moon and back and promise to you that "I want to succeed as bad as I want to breathe" and I will do just that for you. I will hold you close to my heart and remember everything you taught me "Livin' the Dream." RIP Dad, I love you.

WHY? LIFE HAPPENS. SHIT HAPPENS.

This book is dedicated to anyone and everyone who has lost – or who will lose – someone near and dear to them. It's dedicated to everyone who ever has – or will have – to sacrifice something in life. It's dedicated to people on the search for happiness in their lives, those who savor small victories, and those who know the value of humility. Basically, this book is dedicated to every human being on the face of this earth. Every single person with blood rushing through their veins.

Why? Because we will all lose someone, we all sacrifice, we all need to fight through the grind, we all need to celebrate the smallest of victories and to maintain a sense of humility. Finally, it's important, to find the happiness. To infect each other with the happy bug.

Life is about living until the day that you can't live any longer. For those of us still grateful enough to keep breathing, if we don't already know how, because loss is a reality in this life, we all need to learn to grieve. Because success is a reality, we need to learn to prosper. Because courage is a reality, we need to learn to stand up on our own feet, to maneuver our way through the maze of life. Losing someone or something is like losing a piece of a puzzle. Even missing just that one piece ensures that the puzzle will never quite be complete. Missing one piece means the puzzle is no longer whole, it's damaged goods.

Missing something important in your life will make the way you look at yourself – and the way others look at you – quite different. Losing loved ones before their time feels like walking on broken glass – at any given moment, you'll feel that same intense, gut-wrenching, mind-numbing pain you felt at the moment you first heard the news of that life-shattering loss. You'll once again relive the moment you wish you could forget every detail to. The moment that changed your life forever. The moment that changed you as a person.

This book, these chapters, every page has been written to show you that – in your loss – you are not alone.

Why this, why now? Why did I write this book, and why did I write it now? Those are two quite big questions – and each one has a variety of different answers. Ask me on any given day of the week and you're likely to get a new and different answer every time. The reason is that the *Glazer Formula* – a means I've discovered of dealing with grief which forms the basis for this book – is not a solution, but a process. Each day I – and everyone who has ever suffered a loss – has to work through at least some of those five critical steps, even if they've never heard of the *Glazer Formula*.

This book started out as a very small idea. However, within just a matter of hours, that small concept turned into something much bigger, something much better.

I still remember that epiphany like it was yesterday. It was just another random day, a day when I needed a little guidance, a bit of reassurance, and perhaps more than anything else, some overall perspective. I thought that the best place I could go, and the best person I could talk to, was my biggest mentor in the life department. I marched myself into his office and sat down, then asked for help, for his never-failing words of wisdom. However, I quickly learned that unless they're recorded – or so shockingly memorable you'll never forget them – words can come and words can go.

The first step in any moment of mental chaos and confusion is to ask for help when you need it. So I asked for his helpful wisdom, no matter how hard that pill was to swallow. I learned that it's important to swallow your pride, to humble yourself and by doing so to get the help you need when you need it. However, I want you to remember to only go to those for advice with whom you would be okay with if you were trading places with them. Why ask for their advice otherwise? To get a response you know you won't follow through with or to judge why they thought that was okay advice to give in the first place.

Whatever you do, don't go to someone who is going to give you the advice you want to hear. That's advice that this person already knows will not work, even if it makes you feel better ... for a moment. That's the advice which gets you nowhere. Be picky with those that you reach out to.

So, having asked this guy for wisdom, only to find that it can be difficult to remember even the most powerful answers, I began to write the genesis of what led up to this book. I began writing as a coping mechanism, but it quickly became a way to release pain, to gain inspiration, to talk to my dad (on paper) and to put my thoughts and experiences out there into the universe. Along my path that began by asking him for a bit of wisdom, I've found many ways to release the energy that builds up in my body and mind when someone I loved more than life itself – my dad – left me, departing this world for the next.

When a relationship ends, each of us – you and I – we wind up with an aching void that needs to be filled. When a relationship ends with death, that's even worse – there is no way to patch things up, to re-fill that aching void. In my case, I didn't only write my feelings and insights. Being a dancer, I danced. Being a hiker, I hiked. Being an athlete, I worked out. Being a foodie, I ate chocolate in large quantities. Being a social drinker, I pounded one too many shots of *Ketel One*. One way and another, I did just about everything I could do, just to pass time, just to desperately try to cope.

Having your dad – who also happens to be one of your best friends – pass away at the way-too-young age of 49, to die when you are just 21 years old, still in college and living 2,300 miles away from home – that, my friend, has not been a walk in the park. People keep telling me it gets easier with time. It doesn't. They keep telling me, "Lex, you'll get to the point where you won't think about losing your dad, at least not every single day." But they're wrong – I do. When you lose someone that close, you will, too.

Trying to help – but out of their depth – people will try to help by telling you anything and everything that might make you feel even a bit better. They do this with a sense of desperate helplessness, knowing the worst thing that ever could have happened to you has already happened. Do I blame them? No. It is scary enough for any of us to deal with someone's experience of intimate death, let alone to feel obliged to "cheer up" those suffering from horrific loss. On the receiving side, it's very hard to deal with people trying to tell you the truth about death. Few enough of us are equipped to help someone deal with the aftermath of losing someone so close to them – I know I wasn't.

Who knows though, maybe at least some of them are right. Stranger things have happened. Maybe time really does heal, but four years isn't enough time? Maybe the days do get a little easier, but maybe only after ten or twenty years? But then again, maybe it's all a load of crap. It could be that they these folks are saying these words based on things that happened to them, and the lessons they've learned from their own losses, lessons that don't apply to others. However, in too many cases, the lessons they'd learned themselves – or the lessons they've picked up from others' experience – lack any kind of universality. They were situational lessons, useful only in their own – or in closely parallel experiences.

I've been dealing with my own loss for four years now, which seems like forever, yet those four years also seemed to slip by in the snap of my fingers. Yet, God willing, I will have 60 or more years of life left in which to experience my loss – either struggling through or soaring through life without my dad. That's a trippy, sad and somewhat terrifying thought.

To me, everything about that loss seems awful. I had a hard enough time over these past four years not having my dad to call about my petty girl drama, to ask his help with my school work, to get his advice about old relationships ending or new relationships blossoming, about living arrangements and injuries, shattered cell phones and broken-down cars, old jobs and new jobs, or quitting jobs all together, speaking gigs and blogs – not to mention attending academic dishonesty meetings for cheating, then failing, a college-level course (hey, I did promise honesty here, and not just gold-plated feel-good honesty). I wanted to ask him what should I do about my college graduation, or about how should I go about finding my first "big girl" job – let alone questions, still yet to come, about getting engaged, getting married, having kids. Those same basic "what do you think?" or "what should I do?"

questions touch on every other life accomplishment I have had or hope to have, from making next month's rent payment to publishing the book you're now holding.

With dad gone who do I call the next time my car breaks down? Who should I ask what I should do about putting down a bid on my first home? Who do I turn to in order to figure out something as complex and mundane as life or health insurance? The answers to all of those questions are as simple as they are painful.

Anyone but my dad.

Anyone but the person I used to call in a heartbeat.

Anyone but the person I always called first.

What people forget to tell you when someone really close to you dies is this:

You change. You become a brand new person. Some things that change are, ultimately (if not immediately) for the better; and, of course, some for the worse. At first, everything seems to change for the worse.

You grow. You start to cherish every breath you take. You wake up every morning, then physically wear that day out. You live your life to the fullest, doing anything and everything you can to live for that person you lost because he or she can no longer live it for themselves.

Now, if only life was that simple. If only you could feel that high every day for the rest of your life. The sad truth is you won't. You get tired. You get depressed. You reluctantly wake up, but you don't want to get out of bed. You start to eat less – or at other times, you eat more. A lot more. You don't leave the house unless you have to. The only thing you "wear out" is the same old t-shirt and dirty socks you've been wearing for days.

These feelings and actions are what people don't tell you to expect after someone close to you dies or leaves you for something else. They leave out those gruesome details about not being able to sleep, or about having bruised and swollen eyes from crying so much. You don't learn – not from them, anyway – that you'll wind up looking at yourself in the mirror, staring at your image like you have a limb is missing.

The truth is, after a loss like that, you become someone brand new – and that someone brand new not always for the better.

Everyone deals with death differently. Everyone grieves in a variety of different ways. Absolutely no one feels what you are feeling, or does what you are doing.

Everyone who loses someone close to them has a unique story. Some might not tell you this, but everyone is allowed to feel how they want and need to feel. Your feelings are valid. Death. Sacrifice. Life. They have no rules and no limits.

Death is quite frankly the most damned depressing thing anyone could possibly think about, experience or deal with. However, death is – assuming we live long enough – something we each have to find a way to understand and cope with, in our own minds and in our own lives.

At different points in our lives, good things and bad things happen to us – to each of us. I believe that these horrific life situations in life are not gambles. I believe that good things happen to you when good things need to happen, and that bad things happen to you only when you can handle them. This isn't just me saying that – First Corinthians says: "God ... will not let you be tested beyond your strength, but with the testing, he will also provide the way out so that you may be able to endure it." This testing usually occurs when you have reached a point in your life where you need to be prodded to grow and change. People say "why me?" or "it isn't fair" or "why is it that bad things only happen to good people?" Well, sue me. I've said all of those things too. The truth is, life isn't fair.

Life isn't that unfair if it's unfair to everyone ⋯

The fairness of life lies in the sense that everyone goes through moments that make you ask the question "why me?" With that statement "that's not fair" attached to it. Life is not supposed to be easy. Life will never be easy. Bad things and good things happen to everyone. Trust the process and know that if all is fair in love and war, all is fair in life. This is what makes life so unexpected and beautiful.

Or is it?

I actually believe life is fair because it is unfair to everyone. We all have an even playing field. Bad things happen to everyone. The impact of bad things happening seems magnified when bad things happen to someone who is good. You demand of God or the universe, "Why me?" or "Why them?" Sadly, there is no other answer to that question than "because," or perhaps, "why not?"

In my past, I've been naïve about bad things happening to good people. No matter how good or worthy you are, bad things happen to you when you truly do need something to kick you in the ass.

Thinking back to the time I sat in my mentor's office – he had also become my unofficial therapist for the past five years of my life. He has even become family because family does not need to be biological or so he says so. This has become one of his biggest lessons he taught me, but we will chat about that later. He asked me quite a simple question: "Alexa, tell me, the worst thing that has happened to you?"

My response was naïve because, no matter what was going on in my life just then, I would graciously respond with "Nothing. Minus some stress of school work and overcoming injuries, I have been extremely grateful for the life I have been given." Deep down I not only believed that, I actually felt that it would stay this way. That I was one of those lucky ones.

This was the truth, as far as it went. Sure, I got a detention in 8th grade for having a picture of a friend mooning my camera. And yes, I got my first phone stolen at a school track meet, barely a month after I got it. Once, I had to literally crawl off stage at a dance recital after getting an abnormally painful cramp in my calf. And let's not forget, back when I was about seven, I got spanked in front of my best friend for giving my parents attitude (I deserved it). Of course, there was that time, after being left at the dinner table for an hour by myself because I didn't want to eat any more of my peas, I got yelled at – and probably had to do extra vacuuming – when, out of boredom and frustration, I just happened to carve my name into our wooden kitchen table with my fork and then said it wasn't me.

Clearly, my life had been horrible – everything I had been through was the equivalent of third world, life-or-death problems. But, I don't blame myself for thinking this way. I hadn't faced any major tribulations yet, I didn't know better. That was then.

I now know better. I now know exactly what it's like to be not so lucky – to have the worst thing that's ever happened to you happen. Exactly one college semester after I'd told my mentor that nothing bad has ever happened to me, all of a sudden, a lot of bad things started happening to me. I guess I jinxed myself – the joke's on you, Alexa Renee. Life ain't so perfect after all, you little princess.

Those awful changes began on that "when" date, January 27, 2014 – an instant after I heard the words, "Lex, dad died." Which brings me back to why I'm writing this book. The answer is simple.

I am here. Four years after dad's death, I am still here on earth. I'm still a living, breathing, passionate young lady who is still searching for a way to "be." I can't die physically, mentally, or emotionally, because my dad already did that. Unable to die from the pain, I have to make the best of my situation. I have to remember the life lessons my dad taught, back while he and I still had the time.

In a sense, I have to live for him, to carry his memories forward, to share his wisdom with a world larger than just the Glazer family. While I don't think it is easy to do – after all, I only 21 years of "Big Phil" wisdom under my belt – I still have to do my best to share that wisdom, even as I strive to find ways to learn more than what Big Phil was able to teach me.

This book is going to do exactly that, for both of us. It is more than just a compilation of life lessons intended to benefit you, my reader. This book is also a learning tool. It's a way for me to continue my journey, a way for you and me to get to know my dad even better than I did while he lived and shared his life with mine. My dad may be physically gone, but I continue to search for the ways that I can still connect with him. More than ever before, I want to understand his thoughts and beliefs. I want to hear the old stories that he would have told me, even if I have to learn them through examples from my family and friends. I want to maintain a relationship that feels un-maintainable.

Maintain an unmaintainable relationship.

Here I am trying to maintain a relationship that others think is unmaintainable. Some think you can't maintain a relationship with someone who has died, either physically or mentally, they think this relationship is unmaintainable. To maintain that relationship, you just need to use your imagination more. You can continue learning from those that are gone – you just have to work for it a little harder.

ALEXA GLAZER

HOW? LIVE THE DREAM ...

As you read this book, please maintain an open mind. In doing so, you'll be able to collect all that's in here that offers you some value. As I said earlier, you absolutely will find some contradictions in this book – they are here for a reason. Life is a series of contradictions. Everything in life is situational. Short of the voice of God, or a higher power, there will never be a universally-right answer for ... here we go ... anything.

Call me crazy, (remember, we all need a little bit of crazy, right?) but I believe what I just wrote, and I believe it hard. Deep. Strong. True.

So ... to recap, **"The Who?"** starts with me, Miss Alexa Glazer. I'm the gal who's writing this book, and this is the story of my life, as well as the story of what could be pieces from your life, now or in the future.

"The What?" That is what you're getting from this book:

(1) life lessons

(2) perspective on life struggles and how to get through them

(3) overall gratefulness

(4) and a new kick-ass mindset on what's to come in your life –
and maybe a gentle kick-in-the-ass to get you moving
forward into a new and better life

"The Where?" that place you take yourself to. That safe
haven. The place somewhere between heaven and earth.

"The When?" the moment that gave me my "why." The day
that changed my life forever. January 27, 2014.

"The Why?" That stems from the first real struggle in my life,
from losing my dad. That was my first real struggle, which then
turned into quite a few more struggles. That's when reality
actually set in for me. This struggle is all about striving to survive
life's losses and crises – that's what life is all about, and I'm here
to tell you, life's hard.

Now **"The How?"** ... Drum roll, please ... the how is based on
all the information I just gave you. That is my main, main, main
goal – to help you to move past life's pain, and to begin *Livin' the
Dream ...*

Every. Single. Day.

It is remarkably important, but nonetheless, don't think that
Livin' the Dream is some end all be all. It's our daily life. It was
yesterday, it is today and it will be tomorrow. The good with the
bad. It's every goal you've ever had or ever will have. But I
promise you this – as we dig into what it really means to be *Livin'
the Dream*, I promise you that, by the time you reach the last page

and close this book, you'll feel what *Livin' the Dream* means, deep down to your core.

How do you get there? Is it really easy to be *Livin' the Dream* ...? Nothing that's important is ever really easy, remember that. But I swear it's possible. *Livin' the Dream* can be done. It's being done. So join the club. Because ... why not? The short version of how I think you go about *Livin' the Dream* ... that comes next.

I might be a little early, spilling the beans so soon. This is, after all, just the beginning of my book, and frankly, I want you to continue reading it. Sure, you can try your best to plug and chug this formula, the **Glazer Formula**, but it won't come full circle until you hear what I have to say about each portion. To truly grasp, let alone to benefit from the "**Glazer Formula**" for *Livin'* *the Dream* ... you have to keep turning the pages. At the risk of giving it away all too soon, here is the *Glazer Formula* for a better life, your path to *Livin' the Dream.*

The *Glazer Formula* = *Livin' the Dream* ...

Therefore, The *Glazer Formula* =

Sacrifice + The Grind + Humility + Small

Victories + Happiness =

Livin' the Dream ...

Even if you're a math-phobe who hated high school algebra, I hope you're intrigued by this simple equation to life-long happiness. If not… well, please try to fake it till you make it, damn it. Please don't burst my bubble, at least not till you've finished the book. I just spent four years living this, learning this, writing this – and if I'm any judge of the page count, you still have almost an entire book to read.

So please read on, my *Livin' the Dream* … my go-getter readers. Remember, I want you to try *Livin' the Dream* … **today** because if Big Phil taught me nothing else, tomorrow is not promised.

THE MAN, THE MYTH, THE LEGEND.

The man I am about to talk about, this myth, this legend, is not someone society would honor as a great or extraordinary man. He was never the President. He never walked on the moon. He was never a Major League baseball player, although there was a time in his life when he would have done anything to live that particular dream. He didn't drive a Lamborghini. He never won a Nobel Peace Prize. He didn't have any other extravagant and glamorous life accomplishments – at least extravagant and glamourous in terms of society.

Most would say he was just an average guy. An average guy, living an average life, with an average job, an average family, and average life-goals. I, however, knew this guy, so I beg to differ

37

with society and its judgments, it's silly social standards and expectations.

Phil Glazer was a man full of wisdom, love and high spirits – he was full of life lessons. Among his many accomplishments, he was the most loving husband to my mother, the world's best dad to my sister and me, the hardest but most inspiring coach to his players, and a manager who truly cared for all of his employees. He went beyond that, caring for anyone and everyone with whom he ever built a relationship.

Whether, he was coaching a baseball game, dancing with me on stage while wearing a toga and drinking Ketel One on the rocks, working, bowling in a league with his friends on a Friday night, winning the high school Baseball State Championship at Holy Name, snoring on the couch, being Mr. Social anywhere and everywhere, or cooking sausage and sauerkraut for a family party, he always did everything to its fullest. Nothing was done half-assed. Phil's motto was simple and direct: "do everything with hard work and passion – or don't do it at all." His life can be described as someone who was *"Livin' the dream,"* who wanted nothing more than for other's to live their life this way as well.

Anything my dad set his mind to accomplish, he accomplished. More impressive, along the way to *livin' his dream*, he managed to inspire everyone. That kind of impact in life is what I strive for. That same mentality. That ability to inspire everyone.

It's easy to have a sense of service, discipline, work ethic, and inspiration in your blood when this man is your dad. I grew up with the best. I grew up with structure. Most of all, I grew up with love. When my dad died, it was way too damned easy to feel lost, to feel angry. It was entirely too easy, once I'd lost him, to know what I needed and wanted in my life.

I knew I needed my dad. Knowing that – but living without him – became quite the challenge. One moment he was here, the next instant he was gone. Eventually, I realized that the only way to do this thing we call life, now that he was no longer part of this thing we call life, would be to keep his legacy alive.

From the instant I realized he was gone, I began planning to do exactly that. I vowed to him that I would keep him alive – and not just in my memory. I would make him come alive for all those who were open to transforming their lives – and, for all those who, like you, are reading my book. I knew this would make my dad smile at me from above. I knew that, as I made him come alive in my life – as well as in the lives of others – that he'd beam with pride that I was his daughter.

This book is the story of my journey toward doing just that.

THE FIVE STAGES OF BULL SHIT

"Grief never ends but it changes its passage. Not a place to stay. Grief is not a sign of weakness not a lack of faith. It's the price of love." - Unknown.

The five stages of *bullshit* – I mean *grief* – are presented by the big guys with the fancy degrees and all that book-learning – doctors, therapists, and whoever comes up with these clear-cut definitions – to include these:

1. Denial
2. Anger
3. Bargaining
4. Depression
5. Acceptance

I may not have gone to school for ten plus years, I don't have a Ph.D., nor have I written a thesis on grief and recovery. Yet at the point, I am writing my own insights into the feelings which follow a loss. Which is what gives me some credibility and expertise on this matter, because I am living it. Some may read that and say, "so your point is what, then? Why am I even reading your so-called book? Read the facts. Look at the research and swallow your pride, Alexa."

Well... I'm at times hard-headed and stubborn. So ... that's not going to happen.

According to dictionary.com, the definition of grief is:

"... a multifaceted response to loss, particularly to the loss of someone or something that has died, to which a bond or affection was formed. Although conventionally focused on the emotional response to loss, it also has physical, cognitive, behavioral, social, spiritual, and philosophical dimensions ..."

This seems logical, it appears to make sense – especially when written on a piece of paper – and sure, it's pretty easy to understand. However, the truth to grief, as well as the grieving process – and those five so-called stages people are supposed to go through when they experience loss – well, it's not that simple. Grief isn't easily understood, and each person experiences it differently. Grief is complex, even mind-blowing. In my opinion, having lived with and through grief, it's impossible to come up with a definition to something with so many unknown, variable and fast-changing factors.

Grief is an experience within itself. It fills your whole being. You grieve through every part of your life. Your soul. Your brain. Your heart. Your mind. Your body. Grieving isn't patient. It floods you with any and every imaginable emotion at any given time (sometimes all at once), and those emotions can change – dramatically – in the single beat of your heart.

The contradiction in this grief process is that although the process is not patient, those suffering from grief are told we have to be. Despite what the experts tell us, please understand that grief itself isn't a process of five simple steps. It's not a process that lets you go through stage 1, 2, 3, 4 and 5 and "waaaaalaaaaa," you're "fixed." Now grief is behind you – now you can go back to living your life, free from pain or even memories of those you've lost.

But real life is far different.

For instance, you may go through the steps of grief like this: 1, 3, 2, 2, 1, 5, 1… instead of just 1, 2, 3, 4, 5.

When I began my process of grief I looked at the "official" Five Stages of Grief as a kind of checklist. This was the way it was presented to me as. I looked at this list of five words and said "damn, this list only has 5 stages. I can finish this by Tuesday. Starting today, I'm going back to "normal" and I'll be all better before you know it. I'm going to run through this process fast and smooth, by the book:

Denial, Check.

Anger, Check.

Bargaining, Check.

Depression, Check.

Acceptance, Check.

I looked at that list and confidently said to myself, "this is gonna be easy." HAHAHAHAHAHA. Boy was I wrong. That list turned out to be a hunk of bullshit. Hence the title of this chapter.

When grief strikes, you can count on changing, inside and out. You'll do a better job of dealing with grief if you throw out the "official" book and remember that this is:

Your own process.

Your own journey.

Your own story.

Although you may want your grief-recovery process to go a certain way, life will throw you curve ball after curve ball. You'll learn when you need to take that pitch, and when to swing and when to run.

I look at the grief recovery process as a series of contradictions – one after another. This is something that, in the beginning of the grief process, can be downright depressing – it's overwhelming in the worst possible way. However, as the time goes on, the grief process has the capability to become eye-opening and overwhelming – but this time in the best possible way.

How can something so awful become a positive and somewhat spiritual endeavor at the same time? I agree it doesn't make much sense – at least not at first – but for me, it worked out this way. You have all the power in the world – all the power you need – to do the same thing in your own life.

I think one of the so-called "stages of grief" should involve beginning to feel inspired, uplifted, or motivated. OK, now I really know what you're thinking… "Alexa, are you on crack? Are you out of your frickin' mind?" At times this transformation from soul-searing agony to hopeful joy seems impossible, but trust me. I know firsthand that what I'm telling you is true. You can feel these feelings, deep down in your core. That feeling, once you've achieved it, takes over your entire being.

One thing the experts overlook, their five stages of grief occur forever – they crop up in a different order every day, but they happen, over and over again, for your entire lifetime. So remember that for every day you are angry, as long as you seek out the positive side of grief, you will soon have a happy day. For every day you are in denial, you will have one day that you realize the positive side of grief is, in fact, a part of your reality. For every day you are depressed you will have one that you are absolutely high on life and inspired to do all things that seemed impossible yesterday. For every day you feel like bargaining, you will have a day when you won't blame anyone. You won't blame yourself, nor will you blame a higher power. You'll know there was nothing you could have done to change the situation you are in now. Lastly, for every day you are actually accepting your reality, you will have another day that brings you right back to square one, two, three or four – denial, anger, bargaining or depression. No matter how well and positively you address your grief, you will have days where you're not so happy-go-lucky, days when the last thing you want to do is accept a moment in your life that changed everything. That is quite frankly unfair, unreasonable, and unwarranted. But it is also real. It is life.

When you initially lose someone, your world is turned upside down. I will not sit here and lie to you by saying that your first feeling when you lose someone is inspired.

Hell. Fricken. No!

You will feel like your world is closing in on you or falling apart. You'll feel like shit. You'll be an utter mess. But in time, or at least at times, you'll feel better. This is when the inspiration kicks in.

This is why I have come to realize that the experts' "five stages of grief" is pure, unadulterated bullshit. To me, when something has stages, that very term means you have a start, a mid-point or turning point, and finally a finish.

Wrong.

When someone dies, when a cherished person leaves your life, you do go through denial, then anger, and so on and so forth. But not necessarily in that order, and not necessarily all five stages. You'll find there are days you backslide. You go back to denying that it ever happened – or back to being angry. Once again, you're back to where you started – and if that doesn't trigger its own anger, nothing will. You'll find yourself making excuses. When you think about how it seemed "easier" for a few days, weeks or months, you'll blame yourself for not caring the way you "should."

The truth is, you never really accept the fact that someone in your life is now gone. In my opinion, why should you? Why should you have to accept the fact that someone has left your life too soon? I find that nonsense.

People say they have moved on, that they have accepted the death, the loss, the trauma. They say they'll feel better "in time." I think what they mean to say is that, instead of accepting it, they'll eventually find ways to cope with it. Ways to learn from it and grow as a person.

In time, you get mentally stronger. You cry less. You remember the good times instead of the pain. However, this doesn't mean you become a superhero. I wish it did. I actually have days that I feel I am one. "Super Alexa" coming to the rescue. Those are the days I feel like I can save anyone and everyone – even myself. I can help those who need help. In those moments, on those days, I do have superpowers. Those are the days that you – enjoying an excuse from suffering in your grief – need to get up and grind.

I have lost the person who was closest to me, and I have been around people who have lost those who were closest to them. The one thing I notice about this kind of loss is that grief makes people feel sorry for themselves. That's not on the list of the five stages, but it should be. Grief makes people mope, ask for (even beg for) sympathy. Their instinctive behavior changes for the worse.

Trust me when I say I did and felt all of these things. However, on the days I'm feeling a bit stronger, I remember what my dad always told me and my family: "If anything were to ever happen to me, I want you to be happy. You need to live your life. You cannot be sad forever." If there were ever words to live by, those are the words.

I want people to know that no matter what you are going through, no matter the loss, that thing could be worse. For me, my dad's death was and is the worst thing that has ever happened to me. But if I sit, day in and day, out feeling sorry for myself, I will never see light again. I will have a dark cloud over every bright day. I will forget to smile or to make others smile. That's no way to live the life you are lucky enough to keep living.

The moral of my rant against "the five stages of grief" is that they don't exist as just five stages. Grief is a process. They should call it "the process of grief." It's a process, but it's not always negative. However, it for sure is not always positive. What it is though, is a journey. The lifelong journey of grief. – an unforgiving, unforgettable, and most of the time, unbelievable adventure. The things grief does to you are, in a strange way, beautiful. Grief matures you. Grief gives you perspective and outlook. The process of grief never gets boring or stagnant. It's like binge-watching Netflix. The possibilities are endless.

I was told, as I moved through this process, that people were done being "patient" with me. Told that I was grieving improperly. That I'd hit rock bottom, then I hit it again. And again. Only the second time I hit bottom a little harder, and don't get me started about the third time. These statements – not my grief, but what people who should have cared about me said – that is actually what hit me hard. That people can be so naïve as to think there is a guidebook on grieving. That on day eight I should be doing this, on day 79 that, and in year two I should be something else.

Well, screw that. If only it were so easy (and for those of you who find this "cure" actually works, please let me know).

If I can give any advice to people dealing with people who have lost loved ones it is this: You don't know what they're going through. Even if they lost the same parent you did, or the same friend, or a friend or parent at the same age, in the same way, they're not experiencing what you've experienced. No matter how "similar" the experiences seem to you, frankly, you still don't understand. Worse, you can't. Every situation is different.

So be there. Be present. Make yourself available. Be kind, and most importantly, be grateful for the opportunity to help. Open your heart to love them. Open your ears to listen to them. When they need to feel safe, open your arms to hug them. Have a box of tissues handy for when they feel vulnerable enough to cry. Stash away a carton of ice cream, reserved for when they need to binge. Don't baby them and don't become an enabler.

Remember they may need space and a time to be alone. A time to think and feel. Help them, but as you care for them, don't hurt them. In time, they will find their own strength, but until then – and there is no one-size-fits-all calendar for grief recovery – they just need help getting there. It's all about the process. The process of grief and the adventures that come along with it.

July 23, 2015 — Here I am a year and a half later. Sitting outside, listening to music, watching the stars and writing. More importantly, though, I'm sitting here with every emotion, every "stage of grief", and every bit of me is feeling sorry for myself. This, in turn, just frustrates me, because no matter how hard we try, we can't help but feel sorry for ourselves. You just can't. The point is simple: though we can't help how we feel, we still feel. However, this proves my point that there are not stages to this mess. It just becomes everyday life. It becomes a process until our time comes to leave this place. It becomes part of our daily routine.

PHIL GLAZER RULES: YOU'LL FIGURE IT OUT ON YOUR OWN.

It was made clear to my sister and me that we would figure things out on our own. In time, on our own time. My dad was always ready with a helping hand, an ear that would listen fully, and the voice of reason. However, he never once told me what to do. I thank him for this today because I now know what it feels like to be an adult. Kind of.

I can hold my own. Most of the time. I am my own woman, one who makes her own decisions. Ab-so-fricken-lutley. Thank you, Dad, for leaving me with others who can be that hand, ear, and voice, but a bigger thanks for giving me the courage to make decisions for myself.

I think this lesson, from the perspective of a parent (well, I'm assuming this, as I'm not a parent yet) is a tough one. You're withholding information while realizing that your child may fail. But you do this knowing that they have to fail so they can learn a lesson and, if you've trained them right, to never do that one stupid thing ever again.

As a parent, that's a tough lesson to watch; and as a kid, it's an even tougher lesson to endure. Who wants to be the lead actor in your own play titled "Watch me fail?" However, this lesson teaches you to be more mindful – you know the only reason you're doing what you're doing is because you told yourself to do it. No one else. This concept retired my pull-ups and made me put my big girl panties on. As I look back, I am so grateful for that lesson because:

A. how uncomfortable would it be to still be wearing pull-ups; and,

B. I'm somewhat acting like an adult now. Yay me!

Remembering Phil

"Take one bite out of the elephant at a time. Little chunks, little chunks." – Gma Jo, Mary Jo Grebeck

"I remember him commenting on your dating with your first boyfriend - more than anything he wanted you to be happy - even though he knew he was not the one - he never intervened - his comment was that you would have to figure that out all by yourself - you can't teach love - you just know it when it happens - and when the time comes - Alexa will know. He taught me to let my kids think for themselves and only offer advice if they ask ..." – Niki Tilicki

THE GLAZER FORMULA

This is the most important section in this book; here is where you'll be introduced to the five elements of life that, when embraced, will help you do a better job of *Livin' the Dream*, whatever your dream might be. The Glazer Formula is not a recipe. It's not a step-by-step process. Instead, The Glazer Formula identifies and defines five stages in life we each must address – not in any particular order, or under any kind of time constraints. By embracing and challenging each of these elements, you'll wake up to discover that you're one hell of a lot closer to *Livin' the Dream* than you ever thought possible.

Throughout my days of struggle and my days of celebration, I have tried to search for what the idea of *Livin' the Dream* truly means. I have heard the statement more times than I can count. From my dad, of course, but also from random people I encounter on the street, in grocery stores, or from performers I see on the television screen, hear in songs, and finally, from people who now want to mock a movement I am trying to create.

Initially, I thought *Livin' the Dream* was all about the glitter of life and only applied to those one-in-a-million type of people. I thought *Livin' the Dream* was all about making money. I thought *Livin' the Dream* meant traveling to Europe, eating fancy steak dinners, carrying designer bags, and having everyone know your name. The way I thought you got there was by being a professional athlete, a rock star, an actress. Basically, I thought that if you were famous enough (or infamous enough) to be seen in the tabloids, you were *Livin' the Dream*. Silly girl.

Boy was I wrong. If you're still thinking this ... don't worry – it's okay. I think I can convince you to change your mind. Not because you're wrong, but because this is who I was back when I was close-minded Alexa. Now I am open minded Alexa. Now I understand being a one-in-a-million person is not just about living in the spotlight. It's about being authentic. It's about being you. It's about being passionate about life. Now that I'm open-minded, I know that you can be *Livin' the Dream* regardless of where you came from, how you grew up, or what your current situation might be. Trust in you and love you and you'll be *Livin' the Dream* – your own dream.

Before we go any further, ask yourself a few key questions.

What do you think *Livin' the Dream* means?

What does *Livin' the Dream* mean to you, in your life?

Are you *Livin' the Dream*?

These aren't easy, superficial questions. Take a few minutes to decide how you see this state of grace, and how close you come to it as you define the term. If you said yes, go you – but I still need you to finish reading this book. No matter how close you now come to *livin' your own dream*, this book can still enhance your idea of what *Livin' the Dream* is, and help you do a better job of *findin'* and *livin' your own dream*. If you said no, that you're nowhere near to *livin' your own dream*, don't fret. Honestly, still, go you – being aware of what *Livin' the Dream* means for you, and what you have to do in order to start *Livin' the Dream* is going to help change your life … for the better. Nothing is more exciting than that. Remember, you and I, though we may not have met yet, still, we are friends. I am here for you, whether you like it or not. I can't wait for all of your wildest dreams to become your wildest reality. Just thinking about you *livin' your own dream* makes me feel giddy!

In my own struggle to find and live my dream, I came up with "The Glazer Formula," a five-part formula which defines at least one way you can go about *livin' your own dream*. At various times in your life, this formula will include one or all of the following: Sacrifice, The Grind, Humility, Small Victories and Happiness. But not necessarily in that order, and not all at once.

Here's a bit of good news: you don't have to embrace all of five aspects of The Glazer Formula at once. In fact, you probably won't. You will embrace each of them, not once but many times during the course of your life. Each time you experience one of the five elements that make up The Glazer Formula, your experience will never feel the same way twice. And rest assured, what you experience will never be exactly the same as the way someone else experiences them. Experiencing The Glazer Formula is just one of those things to strive for as you try to make your life fuller, more meaningful and more joyful. Be aware that opportunities to experience the elements found in The Glazer Formula will happen in your life. These are things to welcome – not to be afraid of. Things to try to live your life by. Things to give you perspective on the fact that life is going to go through its ups and downs and plateaus. Best of all, that that is perfectly okay!

This formula is not a checklist. I repeat, it is not a checklist. This formula is not a set steps which you must follow in order, at least if you want to have the best life ever. This formula is not a process you go through once in your life, then bam!, you're *Livin' the Dream.* It is definitely not a formula that, once you've completed it, you will never hit rock bottom again. Life isn't that easy, and it's not meant to be.

This formula is simply an idea, one that works for me. I hope it works for you. I think it can and will work for you, and just between us, I want more than anything for this formula to work for you. I have found that this formula can be a great example of tying together all of life's worst moments with all of life's best moments as you reach out to live your own dreams. If you can trust in your process, then you can trust in this formula. You'll find that even when blending the good, the bad, and the ugly, you can still live an extraordinary life with it all. I am, and you can, too.

Unless you're extraordinarily fortunate, you probably don't have a lot of people in your life who are telling you that:

Your feelings are valid.

Wherever you are in life right now is right where you're supposed to be.

You can still be *Livin' the Dream,* even on your worst day.

You may not have a lot of people telling you those things, but I am. Right here. Right now.

But I'm not telling you these things because I think I'm better than the people in your life, the ones who told you the opposite of these things. No, I'm telling you this because, damn it, I believe in you, and I believe in "The Glazer Formula." Keep an open mind and I swear this will help you lead a better, more fulfilled and joyful life. A life filled with more fun, more love, more satisfaction, and more accomplishment. Who doesn't want to have fun, love, satisfaction, and accomplishment? This is one question to which no one has ever said, "Me – I don't want to have fun, love, satisfaction or accomplishment in my life." So jump on the train, it's never too late. Join the movement and keep the movement moving with me.

Ok, now that you've got a sense of what you're about to get into, let's look at the five elements which form the core of The Glazer Formula. As you explore them, remember that this is not a checklist – you do not have to accomplish each of these in any particular order, nor will you fully accomplish any of them in this life. Instead, as your life changes, grows, soars or crashes-and-burns (for a moment), you'll keep revisiting these elements.

SACRIFICE

Sacrifice is the first major element found in The Glazer Formula. It reflects the need to either give up something or to lose something. To lose someone to death, or to give up a relationship that no longer serves your purpose. To work a few jobs and lose social time because you need that money to pay your bills on time. To giving up candy during Lent. To (maybe) give up drinking alcohol during the week.

The list is long and personal to each of us, but these all reflect something of the nature of sacrifice. Whether you want to or not, you will sacrifice so much in life – and as you do, you'll learn that sacrifice helps you gain perspective, to grow as a person, and to become the strongest you that you can be. Sacrifice is a journey that both helps you and makes you find out who you are as a human. Sacrifice lays out your most important values smack dab right in front of your face.

This is where you find your *"why"* in life, your real and ultimate purpose. Typically, when you make a sacrifice, you give up something you value, something that was – if not now, then at some point in your past – or, in some cases, something that still is worth a lot to you. However, when you sacrifice something or someone, that sacrifice is made because you've decided that something else is more worthy of your time, your energy, and your effort. If you don't sacrifice something in your life that once mattered but now just stands in your way, what you want becomes sacrificed – and that sounds like zero fun to me.

Sacrifice is not just a choice to be made when dealing with grief or loss. My dad, for example, sacrificed his dream of becoming a professional baseball player and big league scout, choosing instead to put his family first. That was a life-changing sacrifice, but he got what he really wanted out of life. For me, the sacrifices I've had to make have been just as life-changing. These include:

Losing my dad

Walking away from an unhealthy relationship with someone who made me lose faith and trust in pretty much everyone

Letting go of a love I wasn't ready to let go of

Giving up on a life-long dream to dance professionally

Quitting my job resulting in losing an income in order to pursue my dreams

Letting go of the family members who became toxic after my dad died

These sacrifices have been the most eye-opening experiences in my life so far. However, despite the pain, I've survived them all, and I did so thanks to something my dad taught me. Sacrifice, he said, will create or make room for something much bigger; but first, you have to learn to let go and let be.

Let go and let be is usually easier said than done. It's an ongoing process of self-talk after self-talk. Of telling yourself to let go, then reminding you that it will all be fine. And then, the next minute, thinking to yourself, *this is definitely not fine.* However, in time, with wisdom, with experience, you do begin to learn to let go. Sometimes letting go does not feel right for you, but in the end, it is. Letting go is part of holding on to that faith that everything does happen for some godly – or, it often feels, godforsaken – reason. Always remember – when you sacrifice what you need to let go of, you will be okay in the end. Once you can finally justify being okay with your decision to let go, then you can begin to let be. Let be means:

Being free. Not being numb anymore. Being okay with situations, or with decisions that have been made by the people you had to let go. Being brave in your own skin. In your own life. In your journey to move forward.

Sometimes the greatest sacrifice can occur at times when you find you have to sacrifice your own happiness for the sake of someone else. This is often the case when sacrifice is something you give up rather than something you lose. Maybe it's letting someone walk away from love because you know it's what they need. Maybe it's watching a friendship change in ways that help the friend but not you. Perhaps it's watching family dynamics change in ways that leave you less secure or less happy. Sometimes it means choosing to remain loyal only to those who stand truly by your side, through thick and thin.

Without sacrifice, you have no victory. Without sacrifice, you can't become a champion of your life – and frankly, that's no way to live the life you were given.

THE PHONE CALL FROM HELL

This day started out the way any other day starts out. It was the second week of my spring semester at UNLV. I woke up at 4 am that Monday morning, ready to make my way to my 5 am boot camp, with my sidekick Maire and our "saaaaweeeetie" of a trainer, Brian.

After we grinded through our workout at the gym, Maire and I had our daily morning before-school nap, snuggling with each other and her stuffed lion at her apartment. These post-workout naps were a necessity to get us through our days. I was swamped this entire year, taking on 18 credits per semester, which translated to nine classes, plus working at my job five days a week, along with waking up at 4 am three times a week for boot camp, and finally, being a member of Rebel Girls, UNLV's national championship dance team.

I was taking on seventeen, eighteen and sometimes even twenty-two hour days of non-stop life. To say the least, I was burnt out, but I'd been taught that when you want something bad enough, your effort will pay off. I was also taught that a little hard work never killed anyone. This kind of frantic schedule is a little thing I like to call "the grind." To thrive under all conditions.

After a full day of school, I went home for the thirty minutes I had to kill before I had to go to work that night. Which I was so looking forward to ... not. I made a quick dinner, then closed my eyes for a power nap (yes, the second one of the day). This was an attempt to get me through the long night ahead of me. However, that long night ahead of me was oh so different than the one I had anticipated. I was thinking it would just be another ten-hour-shift night in my tiny black dress and five-inch stripper heels. I had the joy of working as a hostess on the Las Vegas Strip. I was not expecting the kind of long night that changes your life forever. The kind of night you're never expecting and then ... bam ... that night hits you right in the gut.

While I had been snoozing, I a missed call from my mom. On my way to work, I called her back, but she didn't answer. I didn't know it yet, but this was the night when my mother's life turned into her nightmare.

I got to work, and shortly after that I was told to go on a break, so the other hostess could go home. The crazy thing was, we stopped getting breaks months ago. We typically worked through our shifts, but apparently, tonight was a different kind of night (and thank the Lord for that). When I looked at my phone during my break, I saw I'd two missed calls from my sister-in-law, Mindy. I called her back – her phone rang and rang twice but got no response. I called my mom again, and again I got no response. It looked like it was going to be one of those kinds of nights.

You know the feeling you get when you know something isn't right? When you can't pinpoint "why" because nothing bad has actually happened, yet, but for some odd reason, you just feel uneasy. Well, this is exactly how I started to feel. The stars weren't aligning properly and, to say the least, I felt like something was off. Even from across the country, with no idea of the madness happening back home, I felt like something was terribly wrong.

I made my way over to Starbucks and ordered my hot chocolate to quench my undeniable chocolate addiction and cure the goosebumps I got from the freezing casino. As I was paying, my mom finally called me back. Finally, I thought, the bad case of the phone tag game was over. What I didn't know was that I'd lost the game.

I could tell she was upset, that she had been crying, but she wouldn't give anything away. Between the way she was acting and how the situation had presented itself, as well as because of the phone calls from Mindy, I'm not going to lie, I thought something happened to Nikki, my sister.

I stood there listening to my mom, waiting to figure out some sort of answer as to what the hell was going on. I kept saying, "Mom what is wrong? I can tell something is wrong. Please just tell me."

Because my mom didn't want to blurt anything out, and quite frankly because she couldn't bear to do it, to say the last words any parent ever wants to say to her daughter, she kept replying with "Nothing. What are you doing? Where are you? Are you at work? Are you at home?" I gave it one more shot with her, "Mom, what is going on? I can tell you are upset." There was silence.

The silence had to have lasted just a few seconds but felt like minutes. The longest minutes of my life. Then Nikki's voice was on the phone, "Lex…" My heart immediately sank. I could tell Nikki was crying. Nikki never cries. She's the strong sister. The tough one. I was the crying sister, the more emotional one. In that moment, I could tell something was not only didn't feel right, but it wasn't right.

I wanted to ask where dad was, I wanted to say "give dad the phone," because I knew, whatever was wrong, he would be able to tell me. Instead, I said, "someone tell me what is going on!" While of all these thoughts were racing through my mind, she spoke again. "Lex… Dad died."

My entire world stopped.

My heart dropped.

My stomach hurt.

I felt a sense of dizziness.

Everything felt as if it was moving in slow motion, or worse, not moving at all. However, it didn't feel real. I was completely numb. Dumbfounded. Somewhere inside I already knew I was living in my own personal nightmare.

My dad was 49 years old. He was a healthy, and a beautiful soul. Although I lived on the other side of the country, I'd just seen him – and the rest of my family – just a week before, at my college dance nationals in Orlando, Florida. He was happy and healthy and in his element. He was proudly being my number one fan, cheering me and my teammates on, giving me positive words of encouragement, and, as always, grinning from ear to ear. Just a week ago.

"What could possibly change in one week?" I thought.

The world continued to slow down, and I felt as if everyone was staring at me. Staring at me like there was food on my face. Or that my dress had ripped on my backside. Or that I had just tripped and fell. Were they really staring?

Well, none of those things happened. No one was really staring at me, at least not in as much detail as I thought. But still, it felt as if I had a huge target on my back that said, "Hey, look at me. I just found out my 49-year-old dad just died completely out of nowhere. Please look at me like I am an animal at the zoo."

But the only thing I could say to Nikki was, "What?"

She replied, sobbing her heart out with, "I don't know what we are going to do? How are we going to do this? We need him." The only thing I could say was "Are you kidding me? I have to go."

At this point, I was hyperventilating, but I still didn't understand what was going on. So in that next moment, with nothing to say and unable to believe what I'd just heard, I simply hung up the phone.

I rushed back to work. I stood there in my five-inch heels, on the slippery cobblestone floor, trying to process what was going on, all while trying not to fall face first to the icy floor. I was wondering what my actions were going to be. Wondering what I was going to say and what I was going to do. How I was going to react. How my employees and managers were going to react. I didn't have a clue.

When I got back to work, I told my manager I needed to go home. I didn't want to tell anyone what had just happened. Incredibly, I think part of me was embarrassed. Part of me didn't want to see my manager's reaction. Mostly though, part of me didn't believe any of this was real. I knew I was praying to God it wasn't real.

"I need to go home, I have to go home now," I repeated it over and over.

With glossy eyes, I couldn't bear to imagine – or experience – what my response had to be when my boss asked me what happened and what was going on. So what did I do? After the many "what happened Alexa? Calm down, Alexa? It's okay just talk to me Alexa," I finally blurted out, "I just found out my dad died."

Now saying it out loud, that's tough. That's when things started to become real. When it's now a reality, no longer just a dream. When your body starts to sweat and shake. When your glossy eyes become full-blown streams of tears. When you say it out loud, you become helpless. And I was. My body completely shut down.

This phone call from hell was just that. I didn't get a phone call filled with hopes and future hugs. I got the phone call, "Lex, dad died."

As I said, my dad was 49 years old. He died in three seconds of a massive, unexpected heart attack. He died right there before my mother's eyes, in their bedroom in our home back in Cleveland, Ohio. He and my entire family were there ... and I was in Las Vegas, Nevada ... with not a clue about what my next move was going to be.

Initially, I didn't move, because the room was frozen in time. I was in the daze of my life. I didn't say it out loud because I didn't believe it because my vocal cords wouldn't allow me to say those dreaded words because if I said it out loud it would make it real. I didn't cry because I couldn't. The tears just wouldn't come.

Until the moment I did move.

Until the moment I did say it out loud.

Until the moment I did cry.

That was when my entire world came shattering down. When everything I thought I knew disappeared. When I wanted to collapse to the ground, curl into a ball, and hide for dear life. That was the moment I never felt more alone, more unsure, and more scared of anything in my entire life.

That was the phone call from hell.

IT WAS ALL A DREAM

"The trouble is you think you have time" – Buddha

Just as Biggie Smalls said, "it was all a dream …" This is what it felt like, but it, in fact, wasn't a dream. It was actually the shitty reality I found myself in. Beginning with that phone call from hell, "it was all a dream" is exactly what it felt like as if someone had just picked me up and dumped me in another universe, a nightmare universe. Or even some sunken place that you can't seem to get yourself out of. I felt like a person standing on the outside looking in. Watching the world move slowly. Watching others act as if nothing had happened. Watching life continue on.

After receiving the worst phone call I have ever received – perhaps the worst call I ever will receive – that night, and the next few days and weeks, they were surreal. By surreal I mean chaotic, sad, miserable, shaky, terrible, and overwhelming. It's the type of days you can't prepare for. You don't know how you will react or how others will react. It's a waiting game. It's having a churning

71

in the pit in your stomach and an anxious feeling in your heart –
non-stop.

My at-that-time boyfriend, boyfriend number one, picked
me up from work. However, little did I know that he already knew
what was happening when I called him – or that he was already on
his way. When I didn't pick up her call because I was at work, my
mom was able to get through to him. She asked him to come pick
me up, and to do so fast, to make damned sure I didn't find out
about my dad through social media. She knew that's the age we
live in. Thankfully, social media is not the way I found out my
father had just died, but sadly there are thousands of people who
learn an awful truth in this way every day.

When my now-ex called me to say that he was at the valet
waiting for me, I scurried outside. I literally scurried, so that I
didn't wipe out in my too-tall pair of heels on the too-slippery
casino floor. When I saw him, I started balling and screaming,
"He's gone! He's dead! I don't know what to do."

I remember that moment so vividly. I can still see the
outfit he was wearing, the red zip-up hoodie. I still recall the tan
jacket I had on, the friend that was in his car, and the face of a man
in a car asking if I needed to sit down. "No I don't need to sit
down," I shouted, "I just found out my dad died."

I was confused – I was also irritated by everyone I came in
contact with. I now feel bad for snapping at a man who was just
trying to help, but really, what's a girl supposed to do in a situation
like that?

On our drive home, I texted four people. My four go to people. My mentor, and virtual family member otherwise known as my personal therapist. Maire but I like to call her Moy – my best gal pal from our UNLV dance team. My two best friends from back home, Celia and Sara. I can still vividly remember these conversations – especially how very nonchalant I felt texting them because, let me remind you again … "it was all a dream."

I texted my mentor., "my dad died." He responded with "Send me your address I'll be there in 20 minutes." And he was. Literally in 20 minutes, tops. He's always been that type of person. He's one of those "be there as soon as I can no matter what I am doing" kind of person. Not only did he come to comfort me, as well as to help figure out my plans for the next day, he also took me to the store to buy me a bottle of Ketel One to toast to my dad's life, and to pour some out for him on the pavement.

My text to Moy was the same "my dad died." Her response was "you're joking right?" I said "I wish," and she too was over my house within the next 20 minutes. She was my savior that night. She helped me pack for the trip home. By helping me, I mean she finally said, "You don't need to worry about this. Whatever you already have packed is great – come by my house and I will have the rest for you."

She said this after I had a slight hissy fit (rightfully so), saying "I don't know what to pack for this! Who the hell knows what they want to wear for their dad's wake and funeral?" My emotions were on fire at this point. She hugged me and took care of me. Moy, was also the one who was strong enough to tell the rest of my teammates why I would not be at practice the next day. She was my rock.

Lastly, my dearest Celia and Sara. I texted them in a group text, saying "Hey guys, I am coming home tomorrow, but I don't know for how long. My dad just died. I didn't want you to see everything and think I didn't want to see you guys while I am home."

Like what?!

I honestly thought they would be upset with me if I didn't see them while I was home, or that they wouldn't come to the funeral? This dreamlike stuff makes your perspective a little crazy. Of course, they didn't care. Of course, they made arrangements to drive home from college and be with me this week. Of course, because that's what forever friends do in situations like this.

There were two phone conversations I remember having. First, I called my dance team coach as soon as I got home, telling her that I wouldn't be at practice the next day. Secondly, my Uncle Gus called me. He asked what my plans were. "I will get in the car and drive to you right now and we can figure it out and fly back to Ohio together. You just tell me what to do." Uncle Gus lives in Tucson, about 6 hours from Vegas. He would have left in a heartbeat – I appreciate that more than he will ever know. Uncle Gus really stepped up to the plate, from the moment I moved across the country and lived closer to him than my own parents –

and even more so after my dad passed. I am forever grateful for this man. Forever.

Living in Las Vegas, you can count on having an available red-eye flight out to Cleveland. Always. Except for the day you want to get on that flight more than anything. On the day my dad died, it was not to be. My flight home wasn't until noon the next day. With the time zone change from Pacific time to Eastern Time, I didn't get home until about 8 pm. Talk about the worst and longest four-hour flight of your life. Knowing why you're going home and not knowing what is going to happen is a great and functional definition of hell on earth.

My now-ex-boyfriend's parents picked us up at the airport and dropped us off at my house. When we turned down our street, there were cars everywhere. All of them had brought family and friends to my house. My now-ex's parents pulled their car into the bottom of the driveway. Without saying anything, I jumped out of the car and ran to the garage door. It was snowing, but I still literally ran my ass as fast as I could without falling on the ice.

My sister Nikki was at the door when I opened it. She grabbed me. This was the moment when I officially lost it. Within seconds, my mom was also there. We joined together in on a Glazer Girls group hug. The now three amigos. All three of us felt empty, alone and scared. The rest of my family was standing there, watching us. They didn't know what to do. The house was so quiet, you could hear a pin drop. When I finally walked into the kitchen, everyone was crying as I gave and received my rounds of hugs. Finally, I said, "If dad were here, he'd tell us to strap on a pair, so we all need to stop crying."

This made everyone chuckle for at least a second. More important, it broke the ice and, for a quick moment, things felt normal.

The next few days were hectic. Family was coming to town. Family and friends came over to the house. People gave us food – lots of food. Not knowing what to say, people asked how we were doing. We had little sleep, and despite all the food at the house, no appetite to actually eat any of it.

Then came the wake. For those of you who don't "celebrate" a life in the way we in the Catholic Church do, we had a viewing. This is a time that all the family and friends come and say their final goodbye's to the departed. For me, this was the first time I saw my dad in a completely different form, one with no life left in him. The pressure was on because I had to view him this way in front of my closest family members. The car ride to the funeral home was stressful. My heart had to have been beating 200 beats per minute, and my palms were the sweatiest they have ever been. Still, I got through it. Somehow, I got through it. I had my moment, my tears, and my final goodbye before the rush of people came to give dad their own goodbyes.

The next five hours at the funeral home were strenuous. It was us – my mom, my sister and me – standing at the front of the casket, waiting for everyone to talk to us, to say their apologies, and then for them to go kneel by the casket and talk to my dad.

To thank him.

To say goodbye.

Maybe to reminisce over some shared memories.

To honor his life.

Everyone came. By "everyone," I mean almost 500 people signed the guest book. People my dad went to elementary school with were there, along with baseball players, coworkers, clients, family, friends, high school classmates, anyone and everyone my dad encountered in his life. This was a shining moment for me. By a moment for me, I just mean a realization moment. This was where my dad went from being just my own personal hero to being so many others' hero as well. How cool is that? In that moment, I realized that dad had made an impact so much further than I had actually thought.

My dad's players wore their baseball jerseys under their suit jackets. Talk about the sweetest sight to see. The sweetest sight followed by the saddest. All of these boys were emotional, crying and holding each other. Hands on shoulders. Hugs on hugs. There is something about seeing a group of baseball players cry that's truly heart-breaking. Those were my dad's sons. His adopted family. My adopted baseball brothers. His baseball team was a family, and they had just lost their father figure, coach, and mentor. Their hearts were just as broken as any of ours.

The wake was exhausting. It was a day full of laughter, crying, standing around in business attire and heels, talking, watching videos, looking at pictures, and hugging. Lots and lots of hugs. Lots and lots of tissues. Raw noses from blowing them so many times. Sore feet from our too-tight shoes. Empty stomachs. Tired eyes. Exhausted hearts.

Next up was the funeral. My family and I started out at the funeral home, where we gathered for our official last goodbye, then headed to the church. The entire place was filled with people. I mean filled. The service was honestly a blur. I remember walking in, walking down the aisle, and seeing everyone just staring at me. That's really the only thing I can pick up on. It was one of those from the outside looking in moments, looking but not being able to comprehend anything. Everyone and everything was a blur. The priest's words did not resonate. I went through the motions. I stood when others stood. I knelt when others knelt.

However, one of the most magical moments I do recall was leaving the funeral to go to the cemetery. I still think about this moment from time to time. My mom knew about this but she didn't tell Nikki and me. As we walked out of the church, all of my dad's players, standing there in their jerseys and suits, held up a tunnel of baseball bats as we walked under and out.

This. Was. So. Special.

It was exactly what my dad would have wanted, a moment to remember and to be honest I still get "the feels" when I think about this today. This was the first time since I'd returned I saw one of my dad's players, John. Now, John and I go way back. Back to the years our sisters played softball together while we just ran around getting into mayhem all weekend. We spent softball tournament weekends away together, we went camping in the summer with our families, we had sleepovers, told inside jokes, shared family vacations to Disney World – we did all of this, all together. We were hooligans to say the least. We always said back then that he would be my future hubby one day and to this day I still call him "hubby" when I talk to him or about him.

When our sisters stopped playing softball, that was when my dad transitioned from coaching girls' softball, back to coaching boys' baseball again. That's when he started coaching John. My Johnny boy, my once-upon-a-time one day hubby, was the last one in the tunnel of bats. When I saw him for the first time this week, I just grabbed him and started to ball. I hugged him and held him tight because I knew he was hurting too. He was such a sense of comfort for me in that moment and exactly what I needed.

On our way to the cemetery, we had to have three different cities' police departments follow, lead, and actually stop traffic because we had that many cars in line. That row of cars seemed like it was never-ending. When we got to the cemetery, we waited for what seemed like forever because people just coming and coming. This was another moment that showed my mom, my sister and me how much people cared, how much they wanted to celebrate my dad's life.

The next few days were still filled with more food and more people at the house. My mom and sister and I were all just trying to figure out our new life and what our plans would be. I stayed in Ohio for a week before deciding to go back to Vegas. It was finally time to start a new semester at school, and I very much wanted to get back to dancing. I also wanted to avoid what was really happening at home. A week of that intense pain was enough.

All in all, for me, that week remains filled with details and blurriness. Some things are so vivid and others are barely a memory, a blurred photograph.

PHIL GLAZER RULES: STRAP ON A PAIR

To this very day, "strap on a pair" is one of my favorite dad rules. If at any point my dad caught me complaining about something that wasn't quite valid – or worse, complaining rather than just venting in order to just hear myself talk – it would be "Alexa, strap on a pair." That was one of those sayings that I couldn't help but smile and laugh every time he said it. Strap on a pair was my dad's perfect combination of get it together … with a side of goofiness.

Not only did he say this to my sister and me, but he said it to the baseball and softball players he coached. It was one of his choice terms, most of which were a bit "colorful" but also humorous. For instance, if his players really needed an extra kick in the ass, he would tell them to "soap it up." This kind of statement gave them the sense that – at least in that given situation – they were acting more like girls than any baseball players or guys should be.

I even used this statement when I walked in the door for the first time coming home for my dad's funeral. I walked in and the tears began. The hugs began. The silence. The discomfort in the room. The "oh shit, what's going to happen next" moments. When everyone said their apologies and began with the never-ending streams of tears, I said: "Everyone, if dad was here, he would say strap on a pair … so we all need to get it together." It was a little comedic relief when we all really needed it. Of course, we all knew it was the truth, too.

I find that I use this saying all the time with friends and family. Sometimes I say it to athletes I currently work with. I've found from them that, if you want something bad enough, you won't complain about what you have to experience to achieve your goal. You'll get the work done … and you'll strap on a pair in order to do so. Even today, whenever I need a little reminder, I'll use self-talk and tell myself to strap on a pair.

Remembering Phil

*"Heard this statement when he started coaching Nick. No matter how hard you think the task is, how frightened you might be to do something, do not let fear win. Strap on a pair and face the task. It was better to try and fail then to not try at all." – **Jean DePalma***

"Strap on a pair. This one I heard a few times over the year, and of course, was said to me personally a few times. At first it seemed like he was saying something

*along the lines of "don't be a girl" or "don't be a wimp." I think I got this impression because, I had seen only selective parts of Uncle Phil's personality, like his coaching of baseball. But, when I think back on it, I can't help but think that what Uncle Phil really meant was, "don't be afraid" and was telling us to do what needed to be done. To me, "strap on a pair" as a philosophy means to take an active role in your life and happiness. This can be seen if you take the time to think about all of the people that Uncle Phil affected over the years". – **Nick Glazer***

*"One of Coach Glazer's many famous lessons to his players was S.O.A.P. which stands for Strap on a Pair. That was one of many lessons I will apply to my life today. Back when I was a ball player Coach Glazer, anytime adversity hit or it was a crucial situation in the game he would always tell us to strap on a pair. Don't be afraid to fail and go out there and give it everything you have. Don't be scared of the moment, go out and cease it. I will one day instill this lesson and many more I learned from Coach Glazer to my kids" – **Nick DePalma***

(Final copy)

The crack of the bat, the smell of cut grass, the sun shining in my face, working with my Uncle Phil on grounders and pop ups, One of the best days of my life.

Uncle Phil taught me how to ... hands ...g ... One day after school my brother, my Mom, my uncle ..., my Mom's friend and me went to ... to practice baseball. My Uncle was pushing me really, really hard. I got mad because he was making fun of me. He said things like, "you're playing like ..." He also said ... strap ... and when we were doing the ball I was still mad, After that my mom ... me ride back to my uncle's ... with him. I stopped crying and I was just mad. Then he said, "There is no crying in baseball". Finally we ... cousins and ate hotdogs at his house.

Because he ... and ... the ... I learned ... that ... Another thing he taught me is to never ... when I think of my uncle I ... of ... feeling other people the way you want ...

EVERYTHING HAPPENS FOR A REASON ... THEY SAID

"It takes grace to remain kind in cruel situations" - Rupi Kaur

I can guarantee you that no matter what happens to you, good or bad, someone will say "everything happens for a reason" at some point ... well ... more likely, you'll hear that tired cliché statement at many points in your life. It seems to be something that just rolls off some people's tongues as if that explains everything that seems otherwise inexplicable. Whether something bad or good has happened to you, you can count on being told: "it happened for a reason."

Typically, we tend to agree with these "optimistic" people – at least when something great happens to us. Of course, something good always "happens for a reason." Even something that we worked our asses off for – even something happily unexpected. When the little accomplishments and big miracles give us instant gratification, we like to think "everything happens for a reason" and this reason is a good one.

I got an A in my class… it happened for a reason.

I survived a car accident… it happened for a reason.

I won the lottery… it happened for a reason.

My dad died… whomp, whomp, whomp. Oops.

There's absolutely no way anyone can give me a reason for that – a reason that justifies laying it out for me that: "it happened for a reason…" Don't even bother, because I won't believe you. Don't even bother, because that kind of reason just doesn't exist. Nothing so monumentally "wrong" could ever happen for a reason.

Instead of believing that bad stuff also happens for a reason, we tend to shut ourselves off when something doesn't go as planned. We might even panic. Sometimes we self-destruct. What if I could tell you – and prove to you – that bad things really do happen for a reason? That, for a majority of these happenings, you won't have a definite answer to the madness, but if you look, you can find the clues. I'm basing this on my own personal experience, as well as the "signs" I have been given, so take this section of the book for what it's worth. I'm just trying to give you hope, not to solve any Nancy Drew mysteries.

For the longest time, I was sure there couldn't possibly be a reason that my dad died. He was young. Brave. Inspiring. Fearless and motivating. I questioned his death for a long time. In fact, I still question his death to this day. No matter how much I try to reason out his death, that feeling that will never quite disintegrate. I, in fact, know I'll never find a concrete answer to that oh-so-big question.

Why?

The thing about death is both simple and hard. There isn't always someone to blame. However, even if there is someone to blame, trust me, you'll still question it. But many times, such as in my case, death occurs from some freak accident which occurred on some freak night and changed our freakin' lives forever.

As that one moment in my life changed everything, I began to think – to see things – differently. I started thinking outside of the box. I started looking at life in detail. I started trying to find that "reason" which explains why anything and everything happened in my life – and the lives of others. Quite frankly, it started making me feel a little nuts.

One of many things I have noticed since I began this quest for understanding is that we are fine agreeing with people when good things happen. You know, those blissful, undenyingly-outstanding butterfly-and-rainbow moments. But, when tables are turned, and bad things happen, then – heaven forbid – we are the first ones to disagree with the notion that this shit happened for a reason.

How could it?

Why could it?

Why now?

Why me?

Who would do such a thing to me?

Guilty. My white flag is up and I surrender. I disagreed. I became small – I flat out asked: "Why did this happen to me?" Along with all those other who, what, when, where, why and how questions.

As I questioned the why, I also questioned my faith. Growing up, I'd attended Catholic school. I made all of my sacraments. I attended Sunday Mass every week with my family. With that said, what I am about to say may offend others who share these religious beliefs with me, but hey, I'm just being honest – which, frankly, is something more people should try doing.

Some of my "why me, why now" questions were based on the pedestal we put God on and this applies to whoever, or whatever, you happen to believe in. We've each made our deals with God or a higher power: "I'll believe in you, I'll worship you, I'll be a good girl. All you have to do is deliver me a perfect, pain-free life, and no matter what, you will NOT take away from me those whom I love most deeply."

Overall, you can't help but wonder, how can someone with so much power allow you to go through so many personal hardships? In some cases, going through the hell of a deeply personal loss brings people closer to their faiths. However, in other cases, such as mine, tragedy can take you further from your faith. At least for a time, and sometimes for all time.

In my case, that doesn't mean I don't believe, it just means I now have some unanswered – and apparently unanswerable – questions.

Deep down, I know there is a reason for my dad leaving this life. It's a reason I will never know, a reason that will forever remain unclear. However, in my mind, I do know there must be a reason. I also now believe that: **Traumatic events have the potential to create monumental moments that in turn can create overall happiness.**

Creating that happiness is up to you. Like it or not, you hold onto the keys of success in the happiness department. Look at 9/11 for example. By any measure, it was a horrible event in our World's history, yet it created a national sense of community, of pride and even love for our fellow Americans. These events created inspiration for people to work together as a team, to become more caring, giving and supportive. In fact, many people wanted to join the forces after this happened. People changed their career paths to become teachers, police and firemen. For instance, people 2,000 miles from the tragedy held bake-sales and yard-sales and other fund-raising events to help strangers they'd never meet.

We saw this again, recently, when a madman killed 58 fellow Las Vegans and injured nearly 500 more in a single savage, horrific 20-minute attack that destroyed lives and families, hopes and dreams. Yet "Vegas Strong" became the city's rallying-cry, as people from all over the Valley – and all over the world – pulled together to support the survivors and the victims' families. These kinds of horrific events bring people together time and time again. They gave millions of people perspective on what it really means to cherish the life they are given.

When you start to believe that everything does happen for a reason, you start to look at things in a more positive light. You start to see the truth in the statement that everything, in fact, does happen for a reason, basic or complex. To illustrate this, I'll lay out some of my life for you, the portion of my life when it rained and then poured – when I found myself struggling in a giant tsunami of personal traumas and tribulations.

My life's crazy year started out at the UDA College Dance Team Nationals in January 2014. The previous year, 2013, my team from UNLV won this competition. Hey, we really did it. We became national champions. We each got rings and people cheered. It was a truly shining star moment in our lives. So fast forward a year. We were hungrier than ever. We brought something unique to the competition. We were in the best shape of our lives, we had overcome adversity and we were mentally strong. We were ready to conquer this competition once again.

Well… we came in second.

We did not win.

We did not get another ring.

We were the first runners-up, which meant we were the first losers.

What a gut check this was. In that moment my heart hurt. However, I had no way of knowing that this moment in my life, which at that moment seemed like a heap of pain and a downpour of disappointment, was really just a drizzle. Who knew in just a week, my heart would go from "hurting" to completely broken, shattered and scattered on the floor in a million and one pieces?

Just a week and two days after this dance competition disaster, I got the phone call I spoke about earlier. The "Lex, dad died." phone call. The phone call from hell.

Talk about going from hurt to heartbroken to completely shattered. That call felt like it was the worst of my crushing personal disasters, and it was, but it was also just the beginning of the pain that was to follow.

Picture this:

My national champion dance team gets second

My dad dies

My relationship of seven years ends – and ends badly

I blow the transmission on my car

I was involved with a boy I shouldn't have been involved with

I failed a class because I was caught cheating on an exam – which pushed my graduation back a semester

I gained some unwanted weight (that sure was fun)

I got into a destructive drinking and that party stage

My back injuries turned into fractures and stress fractures, with herniated discs and talk of painful, expensive corrective surgery

I could continue on with this remarkable tale of woe, but I'll spare you the gory details. But I did learn some vital, valuable lessons: For instance, I learned from being the first loser in that dance competition is that your life revolves around what you do after you lose. It's not the loss, it's seeing whether that failure defeats you, or whether it motivates you to work harder the next time.

Do you quit or do you thrive? Do you talk smack or do you accept that maybe a better team won? My answer: I learned that I had to get back on my horse and get on with my life – then work even harder for the next time.

What I learned from the disastrous crash-and-burn end of my seven-year relationship was quite insightful. He'd been my high school sweetheart, my best friend, the man I thought I would marry one day. At the bitter cold end of this relationship, I started to realize something important that eventually made it all worthwhile. If my ex-boyfriend of seven years hadn't had a secret rendezvous with a stripper from back home, I might never have learned the value of a trusting, pure and love-filled relationship.

I would never have learned what it felt like to be heartbroken because of some other person's actions and choices. I wouldn't have learned what I wanted in a man – as well as what I didn't want in a relationship. Finally, I would probably still be a naïve young girl, stuck in her comfort zone and married to a man who had ripped my heart to shreds and made me lose a lot of trust in people.

Eventually, I also learned to forgive. I forgive this person, I really do. I wish no bad blood on him. I just want nothing to do with that past – that relationship had become toxic beyond recovery or redemption.

Here we are almost four years later, still living in the same city. We barely run into each other, only a handful number of times. But, what I now appreciate is that I have maintained a now healthy relationship with him and his family and we reach out when life altering moments happen for one another. That's what you do when "you want to stay in touch with each other." It's what you do when both people decide they will be mature … eventually.

What I learned from blowing the transmission on my car is the importance of car maintenance. I will never miss an oil change again. Enough said.

What I learned from being involved with a boy who other people felt I shouldn't be involved with is that sometimes you have to follow your gut. Sometimes you have to listen to your heart instead of your brain. Things I learned from that crashed-and-burnt previous relationship told me that this guy was something different – my feelings for him were different, too. Sure, in the beginning, we faced some challenges … such as living a secret life. However, some of the memories we created during those six months remain some of my favorites. I learned:

That even when timing doesn't feel right, it always is.

What it's like to fall in love hard and fast.

What it's like to have someone accept you for you.

That in some of your ugliest days, a person can see the beauty inside of you.

I learned all of this because my secret lover accepted me for who I was, and did so less than a year after my dad died, just months after that seven-year relationship ended. He accepted me at a time when I was having to deal with keeping him a secret. That secret was not what I had wanted, but it was what I needed. He loved me when I was broken and filled with loads and loads of baggage, which taught me that I could be loved even with baggage.

I also learned all that from this boyfriend, who ultimately became my best friend, who made me laugh more than anyone, and who then broke up with me. Ouch.

Once again, I'd been involved with a man I thought maybe I could marry. That break-up loss is still raw. It still feels like it happened just last night, and not just because I literally wrote the portion of this book that very night. This break up was different because the emotions were so big.

I don't hate him in any way – I wish I did because it would have made this feeling so much easier to move on from. The problem is, I can't hate him because I still love him, correction, loved him. I loved him with my entire heart. This human, this man was someone I loved more than I thought I could love someone. When it came time for him to say his goodbyes, I crumbled. When he walked out my front door, I hit the floor hard as a rock. I felt my tears run down my face and my fists ram into the tile floor.

I know I sound dramatic, but this is what love does to you. The real kind of love. It's the strongest feeling you'll ever feel. Break-ups aren't always a he-said/she-said, or a he-did this/she-did that situation. Sometimes it's the time and place that doesn't fit when one person needs to go find themselves again, while the other is left behind. I can't say I was happy about it because well … I wasn't. But I cared enough for this person, to let him go and find himself once again. Maybe in another time, in another place. we will meet again, but we won't know until we go there.

This experience finally taught me to be selfish for once. To put me, my goals, and my dreams to the top of my priority list. I think it was time for this. I am now so grateful for it. Having been in a relationship from age 14 until age 25, I realize that I deserve a much-needed relationship with myself. So I learned to let go. To not let myself chase people who choose to not choose me. I learned that it's okay to be young, wild, and free.

What I learned from cheating on an exam is that any form of cheating always gets you in trouble. Even when you think you can "cheat" because that exam happens to be a take-home exam in your finance class, so who doesn't use outside resources and help? But … you still fail because of it. What do you do? You walk all the way across campus balling your eyes out, while on the phone with you mom, as you're in a hurry to go talk to your mentor and have a not so fun conversation with your coach telling her "You're not going to be very happy with me I am just warning you. I did something stupid. I cheated in class. I now failed the class. What do you want to do with me?" Basically, you move backward. You become filled with shame and guilt. From this, I learned that if you need help, ask for it. When you want to do things the quick, fast and easy way, don't. Just don't.

What I learned from gaining weight was that having a round face and zero signs of abs made me very self-conscious. It destroyed my self-esteem, as well as my confidence. Having been a competitive dancer, my body image had a lot to do with my self-image. I learned that I never want to be there again. Finally, I had to learn how to fall back in love with myself, and in doing so, I found myself working out, eating healthy and removing the more wasteful attachments, especially those I had to drinking and chocolate, at least in large quantities.

What I learned from being in that partying stage was that alcohol numbs you, but only for the night. It doesn't mend anything. You sure as hell can have fun, and I had fun alright, but if you can't remember that fun the next morning, what do you have to show for it? Except for a headache and a hangover.

What I learned from my broken back is that I am a young woman in an old woman's body. I learned pain management. I learned how to suck it up. I learned that sometimes you can't push it as hard as you want. I learned that it's going to be like this for the rest of my life, so I might as well deal with it and move on. Sometimes you have to listen to your body and not your mind. In listening to your body and not your mind I learned I will need back surgery to fix my problems. That sometimes the worst case scenario is the only scenario that will get you back to the good days. The good days being those when I did not feel like a 95-

year-old woman. I even learned that you can survive surgery and move on from that, too.

When things seem impossible, it's important to remember that things do happen for an un-definite reason. You might as well remove the word impossible from your dictionary – I did, because I no longer believe in that word. It would be a very rare situation in which I would agree with the term. I am not sure if God is the reason, or science, or even pure luck – or un-luck if you believe in that sort of thing. It's unfortunate to know that we need these events to happen in order to maintain grateful and learn new perspective, but it's the hardships we go through as people that bring out the most growth in a person. That's another Phil Glazer lesson I had to learn the hard way.

I challenge you to look at your own hardships as a way to learn life lessons. In moments of sacrifice, ask yourself what you have learned, what you can learn and how far you have come or will go. Sure, life would be easier if these things didn't happen, but we also wouldn't learn a damn thing. We wouldn't grow as people. Honestly, life would be boring if someone didn't shake it up with the bullshit that we call reality. Trust in the process. Know that the process can be beautiful if you just embrace it. Struggle creates warriors – they always come out on top. From the top, you can point your middle fingers straight up and tell the world "I'm ready. Up for the challenge. You ain't ruining anyone's life today. Watch and learn, brothers and sisters." A little self-talk doesn't hurt anyone.

January 27, 2015 — You never know how strong you are until being strong is the only option you have.

PHIL GLAZER RULES: IT IS WHAT IT IS

We've all heard "it is what it is," and we've all said it. We say it whenever we hit some sort of roadblock on the road of life. When control is no longer ours, and times when control never was. In those moments, you have to learn to pivot. Life is all about what comes after "it is what it is." What you do with what that really "is."

My dad's rule on this was simple and direct. Regardless of the bump in the road, even when the bump is completely out of your control, the next step – what you do about that bump – that is in your control. You go to work on that bump, and even though you aren't a construction worker or a gardener, and even though you don't have any sort of tools, you either smash it, drive over it or go the hell around it. And fast! You get to decide what happens next, it is completely on you.

For me, the perfect example of this is my dad dying. Completely out of my control. At that point, it is what it is right? A death. A life lost. However, what I did next was in my control. My response to his death continues to have endless possibilities.

Don't let the roadblock stop you from future greatness. I drove over, went around, hit another "it is what it is" bump (actually, I hit more than a few) and worked hard to come out on top. You can, too.

Remembering Phil

"To me, this means that things don't always work out like you had hoped or planned, but what matters is how you react afterward and where you go from there...so don't beat yourself up over would-a, could-a, should-a's." – Jennifer DeLeva.

PHIL GLAZER RULES: THE BALL FIELD IS WHERE YOU LEARN YOUR LIFE LESSONS

Sports teach you a lot of what you need to know for your future. Done right, sports are more than games, they are lessons. They teach your discipline, a positive work ethic, passion, and teamwork. When you play a sport, an instrument, create art, sing, write books, or own a business, you learn life lessons. You learn these life lessons because you learn how to be respectful to superiors, teammates, bosses, and mentors. How to problem solve and how to rally.

My dad always taught Nikki and me – and his players – life lessons on the ball field, because he knew you had to start somewhere, and where he liked to start was the ball field.

The ball field is different for everyone. If you play basketball, it's your court. If you're a singer, it's your microphone or a stage. If you're an n artist, it's your easel and stool. If you're a business owner, it's your office or your go-anywhere laptop. These places are your own particular ball field. How you learn, how you aim for perfection – or as close to what we think perfection is – it is different on your ball field than it is on mine, but the principles are the same. When we made mistakes on the ball field, we were held accountable for them. That way, when we made mistakes in real life, we are ready to hold ourselves to higher standards, to accept our faults and try to fix them. The discipline you get from your ball field, whatever type of field it may be is, what moves you from being average and mediocre "player" to incredible and outstanding.

Remembering Phil

"We had a common belief, that the ball field was a great place to teach our kids life's lessons. All you really needed to learn about life you could learn on a ball field. I remember when you stopped playing ball and concentrated more of your time and energy on dance, he said from his heart, "the dance floor is her ball field". He was so very proud of the beautiful dancer you became

and had every confidence that you would learn the same life experience on "your ball field". – **Nancy Dzurnak**

HOME SWEET HOME

"Home is not place but a feeling" – Unknown
Hirath (n.) a homesickness for a home in which you cannot return, a home which never was, the nostalgia, the yearning, the grief for the lost places of your past.

As I stated earlier, my dad passed away while I was living 2,300 miles away from home.   Home being "The Land," Cleveland, Ohio.   Then and now, I was – and am – living in Sin City, Nevada, and although the weather here is much nicer, Vegas will never quite be home to me.   My life in Las Vegas consists of me, myself, and I.   What I mean is that I have no family here.   By no family, I mean no biological family.   Lacking blood relatives here, I have formed my own family.   For quite some time, Vegas held no traditions for me, no home-cooked meals, no "homey" feeling when I came back from a long day of school or work.   Despite that, I am learning to become quite domesticated, so please, someone wife me up.   I've learned how to cook dinners, make my own traditions, and my house is the homiest it has ever felt.

I will always proudly say I am from the Midwestern state of Ohio, and praise the fact that I am from "Believeland."   That I am, along with the rest of the city, a die-hard, loyal Cleveland Cavs, Indians, and yes, even Browns fan. Miracles happen. We are in fact, not "the mistake on the lake." We will (eventually) win a World Series. Even more miraculously, we will win the Super Bowl one day, though not this year, and probably not next year. With all of its greenery, flat land, friendly people and seasons that actually change, Ohio is what home feels like to me. Or so I thought.

From the moment I left that green, humid, rainy, snow-covered and slushy place, I counted down the days till the next time I would step off the airplane and smell Ohio's sweet air again. I always felt a sense of warmth being home and being surrounded by the people who I love the most, who love me the most – the ones who made me who I am today.

I remember the first time I came home. I returned after being tucked away in the Mojave Desert for 168 days. Not that I was counting or anything. After starting dance team, living on my own, attending a university, making new friends, and overall putting my big girl pants on, I'd become a young lady in all my glory – though I admit, on some days, I was not so glorious. It was Christmas break, and I knew I'd only be able to return home for a few days – if for no other reason than that my dance team was in the midst of competition practices, practices that were going to make us national champions. Regardless, I was happy and content, confident that I'd make the best of those few days. I flew a red-eye from Vegas to Detroit, but I was too excited to get any shuteye. The moment I saw my dad at the bottom of the escalator, and my mom in the front seat of the car, I had a rush of emotions, including instant butterflies. I remember even getting somewhat teary-eyed. My parents, they were home to me. In that moment, I couldn't have been happier.

It's moments like this when you learn that home isn't just a place. All this time, I thought my home was a physical place, a house on Timberlake Drive in Strongsville, a suburb on the outskirts of Cleveland. However, during this Christmas break, I quickly learned I was quite wrong. This revelation taught me that dictionary.com definitions aren't always the answer to all of our questions.

Home is people.

Home is family.

Home is love.

Home is a place or a thing that makes you feel comfortable, warm, accepted, loved.

Home is a place you go to when you need to just be you.

Home is a feeling.

For me, family is my home. My mom and my sister are home. My dad is home. Or he was until January 27th, 2014. That was the day when my comfort zone became uncomfortable. The day my actual, physical home didn't feel like my home anymore. The day a huge part of "home" went missing, never to return. This was the day I officially changed the definition of home from being a physical place to being a feeling, or a person.

That was the day I went from counting down the days until I'd go back home again to counting the number of times I refused to make my next trip. Losing my dad brought fear into my life, leaving me feeling isolated and alone in a world filled by billions of strangers. The day I lost confidence in making my own decisions. The day I started trying so hard to be the strong daughter my dad raised me to be, even though most of the time I felt weak. I became afraid to get close to people, fearful that one day I'd lose them, too. The day I realized that tomorrow is promised to no one.

There are any number of reasons people can lose a home. Whether it is from a fire, a flood, an eviction, a job relocation – or an overwhelming need to get the hell out of the city they are in. Sometimes people just need a change, and the best way to do that is pack up all of your things and leave.

When you lose your home – or decide that you're going to leave your home because it no longer feels like home – there is a process you take in order to find a new home. You want to find the perfect place. You need to love it. This new home must fit your personal needs – or the needs of your family. if you have one. Despite your best efforts, chances are this new home will be missing something – something that demands a compromise

The same thing happens when your home is a person and this person leaves you – for another life, or, in my case, for an afterlife. You have to find a new person. Or a new home. That's impossible though, right? That person you lost became your home for a reason. They were your special place. They gave you all the warm and fuzzies. I have learned throughout my experience in losing my home, something about how comfort zones are meant to be broken.

I used to think home was on Timberlake Drive, but when my dad died, I was forced to realize that "home" was actually my dad. I'd thought a home had to be a place on the map, a place with a longitude and latitude. But instead, I learned that my home had its own heartbeat. Now, the only place I can find my home is in my imagination – in my dreams, in old pictures, and especially in the memories that will forever stay engraved in my brain. The "street address" for my home is in my heart. You can't find home on Google maps. You can't ask for directions.

No one will ever replace my home. Nothing will ever compare to the bond a daughter has with her father. I hope to find other wonderful relations in my life, but none will ever become what I lost. I will not compromise just anything in my life to find a new home. Just as important, I will do anything so I don't completely lose the home I had, the father I loved. I refuse to let go.

Some may say that if I do this, I will never stop grieving. Others will call me foolish because, in reality, and on paper, on a death certificate, it's official. I lost my dad. No matter what I do, he is gone, for good. What I have to say to them is, "it would be foolish to let my dad's legacy die, to cave to the pressure and the emotional toll death takes you on. I will not let my home crumble, mold, and lose its sparkle. To do so is what I call foolish."

The difference between a home being a physical place and home being a person is that when home is a person instead of a place, you have control. You have the control to keep that your home for forever, and beyond. Nobody can foreclose on it. No tornado can rip it to fragments. No flood can engulf it. When your home is a person who lives in your memory, as well as in your life, that home never gets too small for your family, it doesn't become outdated or depreciate. When your home is a person, you build real-life connections. You learn life lessons and build the greatest relationship. This is the home you keep coming back to. This is the home that never disappoints.

People will tell you – just as well-meaning people told me – to move on. People will tell you it's time to forget. I don't have to, and neither do you. They don't understand that you can't move on, or you won't, or that you just don't want to.

Instead of doing what others tell you, do this: do what's right for you. Find ways that YOU know will make you happy, ways that will guide YOU somewhere magnificent. If you do these things, one day your physical home might feel like a real home again. However, it might not. I can't make any promises here. "Home sweet home" is a real thing. Home is where the heart is, or at the very least, home lives in your heart.

June 6, 2014 — *Feeling a lot of sense of anxiety as my first trip home approaches this week. But here I am about to go do the inevitable. I don't know what I am going to do when dad isn't at the airport to pick me up. Just trying to take this overwhelming feeling one step at a time.*

ALEXA GLAZER

HEARTBREAK HOTEL

As human beings, we are all afraid of feeling our feelings. Afraid of "catching the feels." Definitely scared of heartbreak. We fear getting emotional in front of anyone. We even fear getting emotional in front of ourselves. Alone. On our own time. In our own way.

So we all try very, very hard – most of the times too hard – to hold back that oh, so vulnerable feeling of letting people fully in. Of going beyond that point of no return.

When we reach that point where we need to cry until we have no water left in our bodies. When we want to release our anger by throwing cake against the wall or punching someone straight in the throat, and I've done both (whoops). When we have the urge to laugh until you want to pee your pants, or when we do pee our pants – I have also have done this, but don't go judging me now (that's just not nice).

Heaven forbid you feel one of these things at the wrong time. Chances are, you will, you have and you will continue to do so. It'll be like those unforgettable BareNaked Ladies lyrics:

"I'm   the   kind   of   guy   who   laughs   at   a   funeral
Can't   understand   what   I   mean?
Well,   you   soon   will
I   have   a   tendency   to   wear   my   mind   on   my   sleeve
I have a history of taking off my shirt"

One Week lyrics © Warner/Chappell Music, Inc

At least these BareNaked wonders own it. So admit it –
that's the first step, right? – we all are emotional beings. The first
step in knowing you have a problem is admitting that you have a
problem. I'll start us off and you follow.

"Hi my names Alexa, and I hate feeling my feelings. I think I
have an ugly cry, a squeaky laugh – or at times, a silent one. I
may or may not have peed my pants laughing once or twice,
and probably could have refrained from punching that one
person in the throat that one teenaged time of mine, but... I am
human.

"I think it is at least somewhat okay to do those things we
don't want to do – the things we may now wish we hadn't
done – in all those unexpected times in our lives. That's
when all unexpected feelings happen. I could say "forgive me
for my feelings," but instead I think I'll say that asking for
forgiveness for being me would be bullshit.

"I will not apologize for being me. I will not apologize for
letting my emotions take over in times of heartbreak, or when
I am feeling a little more courageous than normal. I will not

apologize when I don't need to. Cheers to catching "the feels" at all the right and wrong moments life has to offer me."

Now it's your turn. Go ahead, I'll wait. Admit to all the bullshit things you've done in your life, then either forgive yourself if you need to or just affirm that you don't need to forgive yourself for being human.

Let's be honest. We all think the feelings we get are signs of weakness (at times, me too). Challenge yourself to disagree with that statement, and know that I'm also trying to do the same thing. Look at yourself in the mirror tomorrow morning and say "I am strong." Maybe even flex in the mirror. Listen to Rachel Platten's "Fight Song" and jam out.

Kidding aside, you don't have to do that unless you really want to. Sometimes I think it is necessary. There's nothing like a little pump-up to start your morning off right, to say to myself, "Girly, you are a badass. You have quads of steel, an impeccable view of life, and you deserve a piece of chocolate today. Keep kicking ass and taking names."

With all this nonsense said, that heartbreak stuff is the real deal, folks. This whole feeling, especially the feelings we don't actually want to feel, it hurts at times. This "being human" idea – sometimes, it really frickin' sucks. At its best, it can be unforgiving and unpleasant. The thing about your heart – after it breaks – is that it never goes back to the way it was before. It's like fine china. When it breaks, you can glue it back together, but the cracks will still be there the next time you go to look at it. The beauty will still be there, too, even though now it is damaged goods – now with a little taste of character.

Your heart, it does the same thing. It breaks. You fix it. Well, you try and fix it. You try and pick up all the pieces that fell onto the floor, but chances are you missed one. As you were frantically crying out your emotions, trying to feel normal, move on, and be you again, you failed to pick up a piece.

The first time your heart broke you lost a piece forever – one that you couldn't find – then the second time you heart broke, you missed another piece, and then the third time the cracks don't match up, and you're left with a heart that's still capable of love and kindness, but it also has some battle wounds, scar tissue that won't go away.

These heart-wounds are fierce. They create the type of scars that – when you look at them – they tell an entire story. Trust me, there are plenty of stories behind a broken heart. Every story is different. During the aftermath of heartbreak, I've noticed that when you are happy, you tend to forget what a broken heart feels like – and thank goodness for that. Those memories of the pain come and go. You get sad at times because those memories are always there, but you don't feel those memories (when you recall them) the way the actual pain felt like. Then that next moment of utter shakiness happens. A new heartbreak may occur. Now you remember those old feelings. The exhaustion of heartbreak. The hurt. Well shit, that's life. Buckle up. Or as Phil Glazer would say, "grow a pair."

In point of fact, you forget how physical heartbreak is. The crying – the overwhelming ache in the pit in your stomach that doesn't allow you to eat, let alone to even have an appetite. You forget the tossing and turning, those sleepless nights filled with nightmares and sweats. You forget that you have zero control over your thoughts. Zero. You forget that you have no motivation to get out of bed, to have fun, or to do anything productive with your day.

You forget the numbing you get when the pain subsides for a second. This isn't a "good" numb. It's an empty numbness that defeats you, puts you on your ass and makes your limbs fall asleep while your eyes, your mind, and your heart rate can't.

My first major heartbreak was losing my dad. That is one I will never move on from. I will never forget every detail of that heartbreak. This heartbreak hurt the most because I didn't have a choice. I didn't get to say goodbye, not that I think that doing so would make enduring the loss any easier.

The first time a boy broke my heart I was destroyed because trust was broken. It caused me to question a big part of my childhood and young adult life. This is because we were literally growing up together. We were young. We were naïve. We were in puppy love. As time went on, though, I became my own woman again. I learned I could – in fact, I would – love again, and be loved in return.

The second time a boy broke my heart, I knew better. I knew wouldn't chase him, no matter how badly I wanted to on days when despair ruled my soul. On those days that were extra hard, I promised myself I would not beg. I am not a dog. On those days, I would just live life, let the pain subside, move on as time passed, remember the good times, and have fun being a little selfish.

When you are young, you say I love you because I need you. When you grow up, you realize I need you because I love you.
It is not important to find your other half. It is important to be a whole, then find someone or something who enhances it – someone who adds to the picture but does not complete the picture. Time gives you experience and experience teaches that you can love things, but not need them because the only thing you really need is you. "I want you, but I don't need you."

Heartbreaks do not have to be love-infused – they don't have to involve an intimate relationship or losing a family member. I have felt heartbroken at times from:

Finishing my ice cream too fast

Shattering a cell phone screen – or four of them

Having to put my first dog to sleep

Being bullied into thinking I wasn't worth it

Not doing well on a test I studied my ass off for

Losing a national championship

Getting into fights with friends

Anything is up for grabs when it comes to your heart and your feelings. Let it happen because there is no point in fighting heartbreaks. They always win.

So I think the best thing to do in these times of "weakness" is to find different outlets to release that gut-wrenching emotional energy. That's all emotions are, energy that builds up in our body that need to be released. Let me tell ya what though ... do whatever your little heart desires if it will help to get this energy out of you and into the world.

Safely of course, please don't go purging now.

Listen to really loud music, so loud you almost blow out your eardrums. Dance your booty off, so much you start to sweat a little. Hike up really high mountains, so high you get to the top and it looks like the world could go on forever. Run until your lungs are empty, or until your legs can't take another step. Take a nap in a really comfortable bed, one in which you wake up four hours later. Play a sport you're really bad at, so you can laugh at yourself. Say something a little crazy, somewhat cocky, always entertaining and a bit sassy in the mirror to start off your morning on the right foot.

Basically, when it's time to blow off that energy-that-is-emotions, do anything and everything to its full extent to release that energy. I bet that when you're done, you'll feel at least an ounce of a bit better.

July 10, 2017 — *I keep reminiscing all of the good times. All of my favorite memories and it makes me miss you. I'm not sure how I feel or what I want quite honestly all I know is that your on my mind and on my heart still more frequently than I would like.*

November 3, 2017—*One day someone is going to love me as much as Mike loves Eleven in Stranger Things.*

When you ask someone about love, they tell you about heartbreak. – Brene Brown

You finally know what love feels like when you've lost it. When your heart breaks. When you feel unloved by what or who you love the most, you now know what your love limits are. When you are isolated and feel alone and someone finally brings you in as their own, when they befriend you, when they make you family, this is when you know what belongingness is. How it feels to be wanted and needed. It's the opposite feeling.

THE GRIND

"You have to learn the rules of the game and play better than   anyone else." - Albert Einstein.

In Alexa terms, to go through **the grind** is to thrive under all conditions. To see the bigger picture. To do things when they are not easy. To confront unexpected issues or changes. To do what is necessary even when you are too tired and don't feel like doing anything. To buckle down in those moments, when you do not want to do them – but you do them anyway because you see the light at the end of the tunnel. It's to form an adrenaline rush so strong your passions run wild because you feel it deeper than your bones.

The grind shouldn't scare you. It should pump you up. Now that I understand "the grind," whenever I hear the word "grind" I get all fired up. It gives me the chills and gets me ready to dig into my deepest of depths. Ready to soar. Ready to make all of my goals and dreams a reality. If you want something badly enough, the grind doesn't matter. That's because the grind is all about having your discipline dictate your success. Chase your vision through those tough mental, physical, and emotional moments.

Turning pro is free but not without a cost.
In order to be the best, you have to do the things that are going to make you the best. The decision to do it, that's free. Those are your passions speaking out. The cost is not hard cold cash. It's the sacrifices you go through in the process. The things you're willing to give up because you   want   that   end   result.

Here's an example of the grind: your parents get married before they are twenty years old and are saddled with raising two little girls before they're twenty-five. My dad found himself working seven days a week, my mom was working five days a week. On top of that, they dropped us off every night at one sports practice after another while coaching softball teams, spending weekends away at their daughter's dance competitions ... parenthood became my dad's grind, and lord did he live for it.

This attitude toward the grind has been engrained in me my entire life. I've learned that confronting the grind means having the courage to be vulnerable, to do things when they are not easy or convenient. Most recently it has been working on me ... being selfish ... pushing myself and my goals to the top of the priority list. Time waits for no one, so if you want to build an empire and conquer the world, you need to confront that grind with every opportunity you have.

I've had the pleasure to not only watch my parents grind but to watch plenty of others grind as well. To grind through their passions. Every situation. Every boundary broken. To watch collegiate team's grind through two-a-day practices preparing for nationals. Watching a friend grow his business into an empire. Watching friends study for finals, baseball players and friends train to report back to spring training and friends toughing it through boot camp.

We use the grind in everything. It's not just a physical grind to get you to the top. It's not just a grind to reach you to your career goals, body goals, and screaming life aspirations. Sometimes the grind is all mental. It's getting through your most stressful days, getting through grief, anxiety, and sadness. Part of the grind is pushing past your mental stability and aiming higher or looking at your lowest mental instabilities. It's pushing when you're insecurities are calling your name. When you know there is light on the other side of the door but the current room you are in is pitch black, you're scared shitless and the door is locked and the key is nowhere to be found.

The process of losing my dad, the grief portion of my loss was very much so the grind. It was going back to a new semester when my mind was anywhere else than my school work, classes, and the books but having to get tutors and get my work done regardless. It was going back to dance team practice and busting my ass even harder in the gym, in the routines, at games, because I felt like I had to prove to people I was the same dancer I was before. It was going back to relationships and friendships pretending to be happy and throw on a fake smile because I didn't want people to know how broken inside I was. That's the grind. Sometimes it's pretending. Sometimes it's faking it till you make it or better yet, become it. All the time though, it's thriving. Thriving because you know that's what is in your best interest even when it is just fricken' hard as can be.

June 27, 2017—If you want something bad enough you'll make it happen. I'm making it happen.

WHATCHU KNOW ABOUT THAT POST-GRAD, QUARTER LIFE CRISIS LIFE?

You've heard about the "mid-life" crisis, when men buy sports-cars and women discover Botox? Did you know there is also what I call a "Post-grad quarter-life crisis?" Believe it!

I went through ... scratch that ... I am still going through that whole post-graduate quarter-life crisis. I call this my "what the hell do I do with my life now?" life-phase. The "oh my God I wanted to grow up and live in a "real life" world for so long and now I am here and have no idea what to do next moment" life-phase. Shit. The quarter-life crisis isn't nearly as fun as it sounds.

There are some benefits. For instance, not going to school and not having to study day-in and day-out, that has been nice. And will continue to be nice until I go back and get my masters. But right now, I'm thinking that grad school is for another time.

However, one thing that's not so nice ... that awkward silence ... that "Uhhhhh ..." answer I give when I'm asked, "what you are doing with your life now that you have a college degree?" Confronted with that question, I have had my moments of sheer panic, my moments of tears streaming down my face, and my "I don't care I am 'living' so who needs a savings account?" moments.

Let's rewind this a little bit. Back to eight years ago. Back to post-high school graduation. Back to the year following high school, the year I started school at a Tri-C, a local Cleveland-area community college. I was living at home, teaching dance at the dance studio where I grew up, serving tables at my Aunt and Uncle's Italian restaurant in downtown Cleveland, and working at my mom's work. You could find me working for extra cash whenever I had the extra time. I was saving every penny I made, working myself into the ground, building up my nest-egg while finding out what I wanted my next step to be. All of my friends were away at school, so these things I did I just did to occupy my time. Work and work and more work.

Trying to make up my mind, I went back and forth between planning to go to THE Ohio State University, that or UNLV, the University of Nevada Las Vegas. Eventually, I decided, at 20 years of age, that my next step would be to move across the country. To move 2,300 miles away from home. To move where no family lived, where I would eventually spend all of the money I saved, just to change my entire lifestyle. To move where there was a fancy and famous street – the Strip – complete with flashy lights, strippers, and gambling.

At the start, I lived with my now-ex-boyfriend who decided to make the move with me. I bought my own groceries, paid my own rent, and never asked my parents for money. They helped me out with school tuition, my car, and my cell phone. But living money and "fun money," that was all me. Whenever things got difficult, I didn't run back home. That thought never even crossed my mind. It was never an option. Instead, when I was stressed, I did what Coach Phil had told me to do. I strapped on a pair, put on my big girl pants, and learned sometimes the hard way how to be an adult.

In my years living across the country from home, I became a national champion, a Division One athlete, a hermit, a friend, an ex-girlfriend, an academically-"dishonest" student, a party girl, a waitress and hostess, a life coach, an entrepreneur, and … well, the list continues.

I was never all of these at once, and, thank God, I will never be some of those things again. Some of these personas came to me at the lowest points in my life, while I embraced others at the highest points in my life. I am no one-trick pony. That's for sure.

While being a college student, I've taken many classes, which also helped pave the journey from being an undergrad to becoming a student of this new-to-me post-grad, quarter-life crisis student life. Aside from taking biology, accounting, marketing, finance and management classes, I've taken the most difficult and some of the best classes in my college career – you know, the classes where you actually learn something. Those are the ones from which you put in the most and take away the most. The ones that, when you finally finish them, you actually feel like you accomplished something –the ones where you actually care about what happens in the end. Those are the classes that consume all of your energy. The ones that have the most homework. The ones that creep up on you. Stress you out. The ones over which you procrastinate.

Some of these classes you never want to step into again. You don't care if you ever see the material or look at that professor again. Others, you like. You'd be okay having to take that class over. The material was worth every penny and every moment spent on the class was valuable.

In the end, whether the outcome was good or bad, you cared, and you genuinely wanted to succeed. At the end of those classes, you wanted to thank the professors for their guidance and you wanted to pat yourself on the back for coming out alive.

These are the classes I am talking about ... and the major is Life. For instance ...

How to become a National Champion 321 (Fall 2013): Wake up early. Like "before the sun comes up" early. Like even when you worked the night before or studied for an exam and you've gotten just two hours of sleep early. Like you wake yourself up at 4 am so you can get to the gym before 5 am early. Still, you also go to school because the coaches tell you

"you're a student first." Then you go to practice, a lot of practices. Practices filled with lots of running – with ankle weights.

My sport was competitive dancing, and here's what I learned.

You kick your own ass in and out of the dance room. You do toe touch after toe touch, headspring after head spring – you do those until you get a bald spot on your head. Any and every chance you get, you ice your injured and sore body. But the effort pays off. You're motivated, proud, and believe in yourself, your teammates, and coaches. You never quit. When things get tough, you work harder. Then, when it's time for the competition, you perform a flawless routine, then cross your fingers, hoping and praying that the judges like you as much as you like you. In the end, your hard work pays off. You win. You get the trophy, the medals, and that national championship ring.

Being a Student-Athlete But Not Actually a Student-Athlete 400: For most athletics, you have four years of eligibility, but since, it's dance, you have five. Being on the dance team, you get mixed feedback of what you are.

You're a student-athlete. You're not a student-athlete. You're not NCAA sanctioned, but you still have to do study hall. You have access to the training room, but once there, you are a burden because you just "dance," and everybody knows that dance isn't a real sport. You practice too much, and we don't practice enough. Forget any (non-existent) athletic funding. Instead, let's pay $2,000 out of our own pockets to cover the costs of participating in competition, then let's fundraise the rest. Let's have fun going to events every week.Let's sell 80+ T-shirts a season, along with calendars and posters that if we don't sell we actually have to pay for.

You have the supporters and the haters. The ones that see a competition routine as an athletic and difficult task and the ones that only see you as booty shakers and hair whippers. I'll admit, it's a little bit of both, but it's still an athletic competition.

All in all, you take it for what it is worth. Whether you want to call us a sport or not, competitive varsity dancers are very athletic beings. For that we believe we should be respected as athletes and not just girls wearing Modlash 33, with Viva Glam lipstick, waving around pompoms.

Competing in a Bodybuilding Competition for Amateurs

331: Body-building competition is like nothing else. Bodybuilding puts demands on you that make competitive dance workouts look easy. Here's what you do:

Work out a lot. Eat really healthy. Walk to and from the gym (and pretty much everywhere else). Watch everyone else eat homemade cookies and candy on Easter. Be grateful for a "cheat meal." Use spray tan so much that you look like another ethnicity. Buy a $200-plus "suit" that is smaller than your undergarments, and don't forget the clear stripper shoes. You have to have the clear stripper shoes. Learn how to deal with muscle cramps, and with water depletion – aka serious dehydration – because if you do bodybuilding right, you're bound to have some good ones. Don't just place – heaven forbid you did all that for just a trophy or sword.

Packing For Your Dad's Funeral 127: Have your best friend do it. She feels for you but has the time, energy, and mental stability to pack for such a horrid trip.

Grieving 101: This class doesn't deserve a grade. You don't pass or fail. This is especially true when people tell you you're failing, that you're not progressing, that you need more help, and that you need to figure out your shit, then you actually do get your shit together.

However, in this class, instead of pass or fail, unless you kill yourself out of grief, you get an "S" for satisfactory. You manage. You get by. You challenge yourself. Every damn day, you challenge yourself. You show up because that's all you can do. You take the punches, one by one, however, they are thrown. You get on with your life, bruised and bloody but unbeaten.

The Theory of Heartbreak 100: Be naive. Give second chances. Third and even forth chances, too. Trust so that this trust can be broken, because it will. Have a big heart, big enough to survive being broken. Be comfortable. Too comfortable. Listen to no one but your own silly mind. Ignore everything anyone has to say.

Shatter a Cell Phone or Two 123: Throw it against the ground. As hard as you can. As mad as you are. Throw it and stomp on it and when you pick it up you will see the screen that once was a smooth and flawless piece of glass is now a war zone for your fingers.

Anatomy of the Injured 1200: Earn your spot on the dance team with an already injured back. Make that stress fracture, the one you already had, into a real a fracture. Herniate your disc, then add another stress fracture. Sprain your ankle once or twice. Bruise your heels to the point that you can't walk on them. Get a cortisone shot, even knowing it will only work for a day.

Oh, and how could I forget? Get an infection in your knee, so your knee looks like a softball, so you are on three types of drugs and crutches, so you are icing it every 30 minutes and, finally, so you wind up praying you don't start hallucinating from all the painkillers you have taken. When all else fails, get back surgery at age 25. A fusion, so that two of your vertebrate become one. So that you make metal detectors go off from the plates and screws in your spine. Basically, you become bionic back or Iron Woman with four screws and two rods in your spine.

September 11, 2017 I'm officially a 25 year old living in a 95 year olds body...

__December 7, 2017__ So today I did a thing... I went under the knife and finally got back surgery after 12 years of pain and a few months of numbness in my legs and feet. Livin' the dream looks a little different for me today but I am ready for the recovery ahead of me and can't wait to get back to dancin' it out in the kitchen. Back surgery, my names Alexa and you got nothing on me, I'm a world conqueror, hear me roar

So You Think You Can Dance I, II and III: Fly to Los Angeles, California with your dad when you are 18 because your dance studio raised money for you to buy a plane ticket. Get there and get cut right away, in the first round. Make an awesome friend. Have, forever after, the memory of standing in line with the one man who is both the world's best dad and your biggest supporter.

Then, when you are 19, your dad once again packs his bags for you. He drives ten hours to Atlanta, Georgia. Stands in line again for you, this time to get cut in the second round. This time you have the memory of your dad standing in the cold with you and wiping your tears of disappointment while walking out of the theater.

Then, you take a year or so off. The next time you go, dad won't be there, not because he doesn't want to be but because he can't be. Instead, he's there in spirit, watching from the best seats in the house, heaven. So this time you drive to Los Angeles with a great friend, Kasey and her family. You remember standing in this exact line, at this exact place, back when you were 18 years old, standing there with your dad by your side.

This time things are different. The dancing is better, the passion is deeper, and the hope is stronger. You make it past the first round, the second round; and, when you have the chance to dance in front of the TV judges, you get a standing O. People are in tears. You feel like you are in a dream. You understand what it means, *Livin' the Dream.*

You fall to your knees, with tears in your eyes, because you have never felt that way when dancing, not in your entire life. You jump on your friend, you give on-camera interviews, and most important, you feel your dad smiling from ear to ear, proud as ever.

You move straight to the next round, which is weeks later, also in California. You eventually get cut again but you can't help but be proud of the journey, the memories, and the experience this show has given you. This has been one of the best days of my life by far.

The Principles of Falling In Love Fast and Hard 901: You had me at your "walk out." The Shining Star kind of walk out. Outside of that California gas station. Or maybe it was the Carmex you left in my car. No, it was the singing, it had to be the singing, the four hours of non-stop singing. Whatever it was, this class, it makes you laugh, a lot. It tickles you and rubs your cheeks. It makes you feel safe. It puts so much happiness in your life.

It makes your heart smile day in and day out. In this course, you find someone you want to spend time with. Someone to share dreams with. Someone who will teach you how to hit imaginary dingers and toast Ketel One with no chaser.

How to Blow Your Transmission 000: Don't get an oil change. For a really long time. Let your car soak in every ounce of oil it has and once it's empty ... try driving it. Take your boyfriend to get his car fixed and on the way, when your car will only accelerate to 15 mph, your car will come to a rolling stop.
It'll start one more time, just as a tease of course. Then, it'll stop again. This time it will **never** turn on again. This is when you know you've blown your transmission. You'll have to pay $7,500 to get it fixed or have a mother like mine who, a month later, drove across country to bring me a new car.

Cheating 247: I like to call this class, "how to push your college graduation back a semester." In my case, I cheated on a "take-home exam." Only I would get caught cheating on a take-home exam, but fair is fair and I did cheat. So what happens? You cheat on your mid-term, your teacher doesn't grade it for weeks and weeks later. So ... you keep going to class ...

Every. Single. Week.

Until, one day, he emails you, informing you that you have a meeting with him in his office. This meeting is to tell you that you have failed the class. I forgot to tell you ... this meeting was held the second to last week of the semester. "Thank you so much, professor,, for letting me continue to grace you with my presence in a two and a half hour class until 9:45 pm on my Tuesday nights all semester long. It was a pleasure." Moral of the story, don't cheat. Even on a take-home exam.

Moving for Dummies 500: Move five times, to five different places, and do it in three and a half years. That's three apartments, one casita, and one house. Live with an ex, with a coach, and then learn to live blindly with peers and people who can (who might) become friends. Get a U-Haul that your car can't pull, ask to borrow trucks and cars, pay $70 a month for a storage unit, borrow beds and pay for the help in (fast?) food and Starbucks.

Bucket Lists for Adrenaline Junkies 101: Skydive. Jump out of a perfectly good a plane, with a man strapped on your back, in hopes that his parachute will open. Videotape the dive. That way you can see that your face indeed looks like a dog's face when he sticks its head out of the car window. Go with good friends so you can share this unforgettable experience with them.

Bucket Lists for Adrenaline Junkies 102: Jump Off Bridges Into a River. Count down with your at-the-time boyfriend so that you jump together, and then when three comes ... you jump alone. Into cold water, where you lose your breath and find that the current is a little faster than you anticipated.

Bucket Lists for Adrenaline Junkies 103: Cliff Jump. On your 12-mile kayak adventure, find a cliff and jump off of it. Jump with people who are facing their fears. Scream, yell and jump off the cliff into the, yes, once-again freezing cold water.

Bucket Lists for Adrenaline Junkies 104: Bungee Jump. When you want to feel that stomach drop feeling, jump off a bridge. Backwards. Over a river, with mountains on both sides, and beautiful green trees everywhere. Make friends with the good-looking, weak knee accent speaking, extremely nice Canadian men working the bungee jump. Did I mention the accents? The type of accents that make your knees weak? Yes, make friends with them so that you're laughing as you jump off a bridge. So you get to strap them in and watch them do backflips off the bridge. So that they let you jump a second time.

Road Trips for the Spontaneous 247: Live in the moment and see places you have never seen before.

Getting Dumped For The Hopeless Romantic 308: For once in your life, learn to be selfish. Know that your heart will mend one day – but not today. Once during a break-up, I said: "I love you but I am not in love with you. I want you but I don't need you. I have been through worse."

Or ...

"I want to hate you but I can't hate you because I still love you and I don't want to love you."

Those were the parting shots from two different break ups. Two different situations. Two different feelings. Your breakups will be different than mine – but when they hit, just know you will be okay. Not today, but someday, and probably sooner than you fear, though never sooner than you hope.

How To Be Your Very Own Boss Babe 401: This is where I learned: To make my dreams a reality. To create list after list. To be more organized. To embrace time management. To never compare myself to others. To always believe in my passions. I love when people challenge me, when they laugh at my ideas, and when they tell me I won't or I can't. They are oh so wrong, and this book is proof of that.

Baseballs and Ballparks 030: When you want to go to every major league baseball field, hit ten of them in one season. Go home and see an Indians game. Drive to Arizona and watch the Diamondbacks. When you're on a Pacific northwest road-trip and, while in San Fran, decide you might as well go watch the Giants and the Mariners in Seattle. Take a day trip a watch the Angels. Fly four hours home and then spend 58 hours in the car driving to watch the Mets, Yankees, Phillies, Braves, and Rangers and enjoy a hot dog and a cold beer in your hand.

Self-Publish a Book For Those Who Have Never Written Anything in Their Lives 414: Many others – those who have always dreamed of writing a book but who "never found the time" – might be mad at me right now because, while I never really dreamed of writing a book, yet here I am, writing a book (of course, since you're reading it, I've already written it – so maybe right now I'm writing a spin-off or sequel).

But you can learn from this: when your heart wants to do something you never dreamed of doing, do it anyway. Just try. Until you do, you'll never know the greatness that will come from doing the impossible. Go write down some of your thoughts. Until you do, you'll never know if you'll be able to (or even want to) write a book one day, but until you get started, you'll never know for sure.

Life Lessons 365: These classes have molded me into one kick-ass woman. They have: Plunged me to rock bottom and sent me soaring as high as the moon. Given me a look at what life is really like. Put me in touch with some of the worst and best people I have encountered in my life … so far. Heard some of the nicest and some of the meanest thoughts. Been told I am an inspiration, a hard worker, and a leader. Told I am disrespectful, disloyal, and rude.

The point is, as you road-trip through life, you have to learn how to take things with a grain of salt (and sometimes with a 40-pound bag of rock salt). You have to know yourself, and I mean really know yourself. How to pick yourself up and take yourself down. How to trust that what you are doing and why you are doing it. No matter what you do, it helps if you have (and follow) a reason and a path.

I don't know everything the real world has to offer me, not yet, not even close. But I now have a much better (some might say a too-much-better) understanding of the things that life can throw at you. Cheers to the last seven years.

To my college education coming to an end. To my Business Management major and my Entrepreneurship and Dance minors. To my first real job. To the many tears and many smiles. Cheers to one of my biggest accomplishments to date and for the many more to come. **"Goodbye college, Hello real world."**

After these classes I have taken, after the lessons, I have learned, what I am still learning is that what I am doing so far is A.O.K. I have been taking this period, with its many crises and heartbreaks, to do a bit of re-evaluating. Re-evaluating myself. My goals. My dreams. My bucket list. My closet space. My shoe collection.

Along the way, I have essentially been de-cluttering my life. I have taken time away from the clutter of day-to-day things to see if pure passion would bring me back to them, or if they were merely stages in my life that I was now ready to move away from.

With that said, I have taken a little break from **writing** to begin gaining new knowledge by **reading**. Reading anything and everything I can get my hands on. Self-help books, murder mysteries, perspective stories, autobiographies, motivational books, and pretty much any books that I couldn't put down. In learning about life, I'm looking for edge of your seat books. Reading so much has made me want to write more, and to have my story and this book finished so one day people like you can enjoy it the way I enjoy others.

Adventuring 321. I think this has become my favorite part of life. I have been trying to see and do as much as I can, while I can. Whether that is road-tripping and spending hours in the car screaming out lyrics like I am starring in a music video or having to hold my pee for over an hour because I am sitting in the window seat next to two sleeping people.

I started my bucket-list idea of taking a picture in front of every state sign (if only I thought about this when I drove across the country from Ohio to Nevada ...) This adventuring has expanded my collection of *Livin' the Dream* pictures and has given me a chance to expand to a baseball edition so the big man upstairs can watch all the baseball I get to watch.

Work Work Work Work Work 365: (as sung my Rhianna) Only as I stated earlier ... I am not using my Business Degree and not exactly sure when I will (though this book and what follows definitely follow my Entrepreneurship minor). So what the heck am I doing? Or trying to do? So many choices – let's see:

I worked at an Italian restaurant, a Ramen restaurant, and a Russian vodka bar. I worked at the pool. I was trying to get as many dance gigs as I could. Finally, I even worked with a non-profit with some fellow UNLV Alum and athletes, trying to teach high schoolers how to be awesome and make the right decisions in life. But what now? Now, following that entrepreneurship dream, I am working on creating an empire. Creating a legacy from someone else's legacy.

Am I saying I am never going to panic again? Or that I am going nowhere in life and I am nothing but a bump on a log? Nope. Sure, I'll probably cry about it tomorrow. Then get over it and get back to work. Until then, I am going to remember that what I am doing is normal. What I am doing is the path that I am supposed to be on. In time, I will know what I want to be when I grow up, or at least when continue to grow up. Hopefully, I'll figure that out sooner rather than later, but hey **you can't rush greatness.**

PHIL GLAZER RULES: DISCIPLINE

Working hard was something that was never questioned – or allowed to be questioned for that matter. It was expected. I was taught that disciplined hard work was the pathway to success in life. Growing up, I learned what it was like to have discipline – and why discipline was so important. At the age of three, I started dance lessons. This may seem like no big deal, but those first lessons turned into dancing thirty plus hours a week, taking classes in every dance style, losing social time, and standing in front of a mirror day in and day out perfecting my craft.

Then, beginning at age thirteen, I worked for my mom when they were busy; I did this to start making some extra money. This was basically me doing the bitch work, but we all have to start somewhere. At the age of sixteen, I got my first real job. By "real" job I mean being a hostess at a Brown Derby Roadhouse. I got this job, not because I wanted to, but because I was told I had to. Because with even the little free time I had, I was told I wasn't allowed to be a spoiled brat. From that day on I rarely asked my parents for money. Don't get me wrong, they helped me pay for a lot of things, like my first car, my school, and my cell phone. But never did I ask for money to go see a movie or buy a new pair of shoes.

Quite early on in my life, I was taught what discipline was. We were a sports family and became involved in just about everything. Softball, soccer, dance, basketball, cheer, student council, D.A.R.E. You name it, my sister and I did it. It didn't matter if one day we didn't feel like going to practice, we went. Unless we were on our death bed, we went to everything we signed up for because we were taught that when you sign up for something you give it your all.

Not only did we go to practice, we practiced at home. Not only did we go to work when we were scheduled, but to this day I have never called out or didn't show up for a scheduled work shift. That may seem rough (especially for this generation – hey, our kids today are a *bit* more spoiled) but it's what my sister and I did. We grinded and grinded again.

With what I was taught so early on I was able to move across the country at 20 years of age with $30,000 of my own money. My own money, money that I'd made with my own two hands, along with my time, and a fair measure of blood, sweat, and tears.

My hard work, my dedication and the discipline that was instilled in me got me to where I am today. This same discipline is going to get me wherever I go tomorrow. It's not always easy but easy is dumb, and this life is worth the toughness that discipline imposes.

Remembering Phil

"When I think of Coach Phil, the first word that comes to my mind is "Discipline." Now, when most of us hear the word discipline, it might bring negative emotions. But that is the exact opposite of how I feel about Coach Phil and Discipline.

Coach Phil stressed to us as a baseball team and as teenage boys the importance of being prepared and of being in control. In baseball, the lesson was to be prepared for the next ball, the next play, the next out, the run. In order to succeed in the game, we had to be disciplined. In life, the lesson was to be prepared for the next test, the next chapter, the next disappointment, the next hurdle, and the next celebration. In order to succeed in life, we had to be disciplined.

Coach Phil cared about the Dirtbag boys. So when we fell short of being a disciplined team, we ran! And we ran and we ran and we ran some more. We ran as a team. You see, it didn't matter if you were the fastest runner because we all ran until the last Dirtbag finished. We were a team, one of us no more important to the team than the next.

We played the game of baseball. We won games; we lost games. We played the game, all the while becoming disciplined young men. Because Coach Phil did more than coach the game of baseball, he coached us in the game of life, too. He loved us, and he cared about us. He gave us an awesome gift. Discipline.

At the end of my Dirtbag career, there was no doubt I was a better baseball player. I was also a better man. Because of Coach Phil, I know I am a better college student, a better athlete, a better son, and a better friend. Thank you, Coach Phil, for living the dream and for coaching me to live it, too." – ***Chris Lane***

*"He was such a great person-stayed true to he was and kind to everyone he met. Even in highschool he was as kind as could be and that infectious smile and attitude won him many friends and admiration from both guys and girls. His hard work and dedication carried him far in his life and although too short on this world for all of us, his memory is very vivid." – **Kimberly Rutherford**

PHIL GLAZER RULES: USE TWO HANDS

"Use two hands" is a baseball term. Players are taught to catch the ball with two hands so:

A.) The ball doesn't fall out of your glove; and,

B.) Because your hand is already in your glove, you can throw the ball faster, enabling you to make another play; and.

C.) So you don't get a mouth full of blood like yours truly because you think you are just way too cool to use two hands.

Lesson learned.

When one of my dad's players dared to drop a fly ball because he or she didn't use two hands ... brace yourself, ladies and gentlemen. Prepare to run. Then run some more. Then prepare to catch one hell of a lot of fly balls, and keep catching more fly balls, over and over again until you never again forget the proper way to catch a fly ball.

When I think about the term "two hands" now, I can see how my dad used this lesson in real life. "Two hands" became shorthand for: "Do things right. Do things right the first time, the second time, all the time. Don't take shortcuts because, in the end, taking shortcuts will only hurt you ... as well as the things you are trying to accomplish.

Go all in, or you might as well go all out.

"Two hands" means using synergy. After all, why use one when you can use two? Using two hands creates a better outcome with less work. When you catch that fly ball with two hands, you will have a better reaction time when it comes to throwing the ball.

If you use two hands in life, you are more likely to get things done; faster, better, and more nearly correctly. "Two hands" is a way of saving all of your teeth and the rest of your face, as well as creating a better foundation for your next step, whether that step involves throwing a ball or reaching your next big goal.

Of course, there is an exception to every rule. In baseball, for instance, it's not always best to use two hands. Now, this is kind of painful for me to admit because I am stubborn and have always lived by this rule thanks to my dad. So I thought I would look into the exceptions that might just prove the rule.

There are several reasons why certain players – including many big leaguers – don't use two hands. Among these, here two possible reasons are:

1.) The good reason: If you are not standing right in front of the ball (when it's not hit directly at you, which is a lot of the time), you might not want to try to use two hands. Hey, this is baseball – not archery. The batter is not trying to hit some target. The batter is just trying to hit the damn ball as hard and as far as humanly possible. If he or she is doing any aiming at all, he's trying to hit it away from the center fielder. Therefore, the only target he's aiming for is anywhere over the fence, or at least midway between two outfielders. In this case, if you're the center fielder, "two hands" might not apply because you need to dive to reach for the ball before it becomes a stand-up double.

2.) The bad reason. The outfielder just thinks he is way too good – or way too cool – for using two hands. Instead of doing it right, he wants to put on a show. Face it, he's right about one point. It looks "cooler" to catch the ball with one hand. So the fielder wants to give the fans what they want – he wants to show them some baseball swag.

Using just one hand is all fun and games until some hot-dog drops a ball. Then the only show he's putting on is for the other team – and it becomes a particularly big show when a run is scored because of this unforced error. This is what happens when a player drops a routine outfield fly ball to a blow ninth-inning lead and lose a game when a fielder "misses" (i.e., drops) a two-out pop-up. This can even happen in the playoffs when your team (I won't mention "Cleveland Indians" here) is trying to make the World Series. Ouch.

Now how cool do you look?

OK, so use two hands. Great advice if you're a center fielder. But what does this mean in real life? Be smart. Play smart. Save your hot-dogging for a bun.

So, when you are put in a situation that isn't cut and dried – when you can't use two hands – figure out the best alternative. Do what will give you the best solution and do it with conviction. That's another way of "using two hands."

Remembering Phil

"He would get so mad at me for not using two hands when playing softball ... so mad that he even got me a special glove that forced me to use two hands. I remember getting yelled at like the boys for not using two hands It truly was just because he knew me. He understood how I functioned. Yes, as I got older, I didn't laugh and I understood. But also when I got older he didn't have to yell, he rarely yelled. He never stopped teaching me. From 10-to-19. He never gave up, he always said there is more to learn and always somewhere to be to do something. Always expect the unexpected. He was referring to errors in softball. But I have always taken what I have learned from him outside of the field and I will always do that." **–Lauren Piechowiak**

PHIL GLAZER RULES: LET ME GET OUT MY FINANCIAL CALCULATOR

This is one of those rules that has a story behind it. Or many stories. My dad used to make this comment to my mom and me. In reality, we didn't know there was such thing as a "financial calculator," we just thought he was trying to be a little fancy and make it seem like he really knew what he was talking about. He always brought this up when we talked about money issues – you know, budgeting, buying a new car, evaluating different payment plans, getting new credit cards, etc. When it came to money, my dad was one of the smartest men, which luckily rubbed off on me. I am a penny pincher and have all my separate envelope funds with things like "Christmas," "Birthdays," or "Roadtrips" written all over them. When money goes in, it doesn't come out unless it is to fulfill whatever I have written on the outside.

The "let me get out my financial calculator" comment was really just his final touch when we were making big decisions that concerned money and finances. The best part about this was in college when I took accounting and finance ... and realized I had to get out my financial calculator. This is when dad's saying came full circle when I realized that there actually is such thing as a financial calculator. Therefore, his lesson:

When you know you have the answer to something, use it. When you are able to figure out something complex more simply, do it. When there is a way to come across the answer in helping you make a final decision, don't waste it.

PHIL GLAZER RULES: SUPER DIAMONDS

Here we go another baseball term. My dad did this lovely activity with his boys, which he called super diamonds. Super diamonds happened at the end of a game.

Super diamonds were: What held these boys to a standard. What made them puke at times. What made them gasp for air. What put a competitive spirit in them because they knew they weren't allowed to come in last. What made them sore. What made them question their love for baseball. What made them sweat, or cry. What taught them how to strap on a pair. A super diamond meant that at the end of the game, you ran and ran and ran.

You ran: To learn a lesson. To set a standard. To get in shape, and stay in shape.

This is how it worked: When somebody on the team made a mental error, you ran for it. When your team lost, you ran for it. When somebody wasn't where he wanted to be or was supposed to be, you ran for it. When somebody missed a sign, didn't remember the basic fundamentals, threw a bat, talked back, showed up late, missed practiced, yelled at a teammate, or didn't catch the ball with two hands, you bet your ass you and your team ran for it.

This was all about holding yourself, your teammates, even your coaching staff, accountable. At first, parents complained that "hey, coach, that's not fair – our little Johnny isn't the one who screwed up, so why does he have to run?" Players complained that "hey, coach, I'm not the one who screwed up, so why do I have to run." And they kept complaining … until the change happen. Until people stopped making errors. Until the super diamond numbers got smaller. Until lessons were learned. That's when the complaining stopped. That's when the throwing up stopped. That's when these boys became men. That's when the parents started to trust in my dad and his coaching skills. That's when they realized that, because of his coaching skills, their kids were being transformed from boys into men. Transformed not just into great baseball players, but into great human beings.

Remembering Phil

"With the MLB draft coming up, you have been on my mind coach. I think about you often and everything you taught me as a young kid about aspects of the game I never thought of. You were a great coach and better person. We all miss you. – JP Sorma

THAT GUT FEELING

You know that feeling you get deep in your gut when you just know something is off? The feeling I talked about earlier in "The Phone Call from Hell." When your blood pressure gets higher, your heart beats more times a minute, your mind wanders, and your palms get all sweaty? The feeling that the universe is quite aligning the way it is supposed to. For me, this feeling revolves around anticipation. The *I feel uncomfortable in this moment and want nothing more than to shut down* feeling. Anxiety.

Now for me, the holidays hit me like a ton of bricks. For our family, this means Thanksgiving, my dad's birthday, Christmas and New Year's, followed by my parents' anniversary. The holidays are supposed to be a time for joy, family, and memories ... but for me, the holidays are filled with lots of negatives: some anxiety, some tears – sometimes lots of tears.

What do you do when you're constantly trying to do the right thing, but the right thing isn't what you want to do? I'm

151

talking about the rebuilding. I'm talking about accepting life's changes. About taking anticipation for what it's worth. About rebuilding a life, especially when you realize you'd always thought you'd never have to rebuild that life.

Anticipation. I get that feeling in moments of fear and nervousness, moments when I'm sad. But I also get that feeling anticipation in happy moments. It took me a while to realize that I could have such bad-feeling anticipation and anxiety for happy days. Those are days that I'd thought you're supposed to be celebrating accomplishments, reveling in life.

I didn't know it was even possible to have anxiety over happiness. To be so turned upside down because of this anxious feeling in my bones that anticipation could get in the way of actually feeling happy. Let me tell you, it most definitely is possible. I learned this the hard way because, believe me, I'm the queen of getting this overwhelmingly anxious feeling.

Count on me to over-analyze, over-think, and over-reminisce every moment. Count on me to suck the joy out of happiness, and to wallow in the pain of sorrow or loss. These lessons about anxiety and over-analyzing didn't come easy!

How can reminiscing about good memories create such sadness at times? This is how. With any memory comes the realization that you can never relive it. It's impossible. No matter how hard you try, *you can never duplicate a perfect moment.* Luckily, you can never duplicate a bad one either. Here's why:

Settings are different.

Feelings aren't the same.

Everything is situational.

The people are different.

You are different.

However, the memory will always remain. The thoughts remain. Some of the feelings remain. Sadly, some people have fewer happy memories and more sad or bad ones, which can be terribly unfortunate. I've been there so often that I've learned to cope – or to at least try to. Now, especially when I'm feeling down, I do my best to relive those happy memories. Although I want to say this helps me, when it comes to dealing with the anticipation and anxiety, even revisiting great memories doesn't quite fix the anxiety.

For example, the memories I carry with me about my dad are clear as day and as contagious as his smile. However, those memories, that's all I have left. *Memories don't give you a future, only a past.*

Those memories may help you in the present, but they may also hurt you because, instead of living your life, you're busy reminiscing about something you no longer have. Happy or sad, memories are memories. They shape us. They are the reason for our characters, feelings and overall perspective on life.

But how does anticipation relate to memories and our futures? How do we deal with memories of people or experiences that now just belong in our minds? Especially when it comes to lost loved-ones, people for who we only have memories, that's scary. The realization is that all you have left are memories makes you feel alone. As Dr. Suess said, "sometimes you will never know the value of a moment until it becomes a memory."

I don't know about you, but for me, the feeling of being alone gives me and – I'm guessing here, but I think it gives any human being – a measure of anxiety. If you're like me, this anxiety makes you start to search for something that's not there, to anticipate the next "sign" that will show up in your next dream. Unfortunately, days, weeks, months and maybe even years go by without getting what you're looking for. The point is to keep living. Not looking. Not searching.

When you look for answers you only receive questions ... and when you try to answer questions, quite frankly you only run into more questions.

What are we supposed to do with this feeling, this uncomfortable and unsettling feeling? I realize this is counter-intuitive, but to deal with that anticipation, you have to do the opposite of what you want to do. Which is this: the anticipation of those memories make you want to become a hermit, to crawl into a dark hole, to become a vegetable, to isolate yourself from the world. That's how people intuitively deal with harsh, painful, unsettling feelings. Here's why:

With anticipation comes wishing. Wishing things were different. Wishing you stopped feeling pain. Wishing your tear ducts would dry up and a tear would never fall down your cheek again. However, the truth is, honestly, if the loss is bad enough, you never really want that hurt to go away.

Yes, you want to feel better.

Yes, you want to stop crying.

Yes, you want things to feel right again.

But the reality is both simple and frustrating. Whenever you feel as if it's time to move on, you feel guilty. You feel like you're betraying the person you lost. You feel like you're disappointing the one who you promised you would never disappoint. Disappointing the one who you told you'd keep their legacy alive no matter how hard that may be, and no matter or long they were gone for – that each day, you would cherish their life and miss them more intensely than before, more intensely than you'd ever dreamed was possible.

But then ... you realize that you no longer hurt the way you did when you first learned about the loss, and when you realize that, you feel guilty. You feel guilty when you realize you just full-on celebrated a moment of bliss, moments of hard work and endearment, moments of happiness, and during that celebratory moment, you didn't let that memory bring you down. The way you're "supposed" to feel in the wake of an insupportable loss.

Dealing with loss, I anticipate the days that I knew my dad would want to be a part of ... Father's Day. Birthdays. Wedding anniversaries, and even death anniversaries

There are also days I selfishly wanted him to be a part of, days such as ... My college graduation. My wedding day (whenever that may be). The first time I spoke on a stage and started changing the world. The day my trademark got published. The day my book – this book, the one you're reading – finally became an actual book.

We anticipate these life milestones because we know that, when an experience happens, especially when we lose someone or something, things change. We can't help anticipating those "change moments," even though – despite the anticipation – we never feel quite ready. We are unsure of the traditions that are no longer there to experience as they "should" be experienced, the family members who become more distant. Those changes give us the kind of anxiety that typically prevents us from enjoying those new moments, to create and embrace those new traditions, or to create happy moments that can also live on in our memories.

We have to learn to leave the guilt aside, to trust that we are still here and still need to live an ongoing life. We have to learn to set aside that guilt which makes you think you can't be happy when that change does occur. The guilt that tends to rule your feelings. The guilt that doesn't allow you to turn your mind off to the negative thoughts, feelings, and actions.

We all feel those things, but not all of us know how to recognize them in the moment, nor do we instinctively know how to deal with the pain, the emptiness, the anxiety. In those moments of anxiety, at those times when anticipation sets in deep to my core, I try to keep myself occupied. I try – and do – whatever is best for my soul, whatever is going to get me out of the rut.

Sometimes I cry to release the sadness. Other times I laugh as I remember the happiness.

I can't tell you exactly what to do because it's different every time and for every individual. All I can do is challenge you to accept the fact that change is going to happen. That change is a part of life. That whatever you lost or gave up is always going to be a part of you – it will never officially leave you – but if you work at it, you can learn to cope with that loss. You will (eventually) allow yourself to feel, to push the anticipation aside and conquer it – to learn that the sacrifice is ultimately worth the reward.

When that gut feeling occurs, when you want to hurl and throw things in a tantrum, don't give in to those negative, hurting and hurtful feelings. Remain positive. Remain hopeful. Remain afloat. Most important, know that these feeling will pass in time. This may seem like a contradiction to my views on "things happen for a reason," but trust me, both are true.

Listen to your gut, but don't let your gut rule you. When this gut feeling happens, when you want to cry, don't cry because of something that is an increasingly distant memory, but instead, smile because you were "lucky" enough to have those things that are now just memories actually happen. In the end, that gut feeling is a good thing – it means that you collected moments to remember, moments too precious to become things you will one day throw away.

Be positive in negative situations.
Opposites attract right? In negative situations you need to offer the moment something it cannot find within itself. Negative situations tend to give you the most growth when you look at the positives that can come from taking the high road. Adding two negatives only puts you deeper away from positivity. Change your mindset, change your outcome.

December 1, 2014 – Today I remember the times you told me to be strong, the times you made me laugh, the times you told me to catch with two hands and dive for the ball, the times you wore a toga for me on a stage and danced in front of a huge crowd, the times you told me to strap on a pair or soap it up, for driving me or flying me across the country to follow my dreams, for never missing a performance and being a dance dad, for showing me how a woman should be treated, for believing me and telling me how proud I make you, for tying my hair in pony tails that were way too tight, killing spiders, watching reality tv shows, listen to me babble about nonsense, for loving with an open heart, and being the best dad anyone could ever ask for. My time with you was too short but I treasure every moment.

December 1, 2014 – *Happy 50th birthday to the man who brightened all of my days. I know you are playing or coaching some honest to goodness ball up in heaven today and that alone makes me smile. I miss you more and more each day and hold on tightly to everything I can of you.*

June 15, 2014 – *Happy Father's Day to the man that made me the woman I am today, the man that has brightened so many lives, and the man I miss more than anything in this world. I wish you were here to spend this day with, instead we will honor the perfect dad that you were.*

January 27, 2015 – *One year ago today I lost the man that taught me everything I know. The guy that told me to strap on a pair and reminded me that I'm livin' the dream every day. Most importantly this dad of mine gave me what I now realize to be one of the greatest lessons, to be Glazer strong. Today I will celebrate you and the life that should have continued, I will remember the laughs, cries, talks and dances we shared, and I'll play some ball with you. I love you to the moon and back.*

December 1, 2015 – *Happy birthday to my angel in the outfield. Missing you in this life, not just today but every day.*

January 27, 2016 – *the things I would do to have one more conversation with you. Missing you extra today Bamm Bamm.*

June 18, 2017– *I know you can see me, but I really wish I could see you today. Do me a favor and show up in my dreams tonight so we can play catch and dance the night away.*

BE SELFISH, *DO YOU.*

"Freedom is being you without anyone's permission" – unknown

Sometimes being selfish is a good thing. It means you're devoting your life to you. Of course, you could always take a negative spin on that concept and go off the deep end, but taking care of yourself isn't such a bad thing. Sure, it's possible to take this notion to an extreme, and some people do choose to take that route, and in the process, they make self-care a bad thing. But there is a special kind of selfishness that is a good thing. Being selfish about your own personal well-being is what I'm talking about, being selfish about your own happiness, goals, and self-love. This means things like regularly exercising, following a proper diet, pursuing your dreams and fulfilling your purpose in this life. None of those is a bad thing.

In certain cases, the best thing you can do for yourself is remove the clutter. Understand that sometimes this is the key to making moves in the right direction. Sometimes this clutter causes you to be stagnant. No hard feelings please, just understand that this is a natural course of life. The natural course of removing clutter.

Removing the people – and things, too – in your life who aren't necessarily hurting you, but who are certainly not helping you, that is a good kind of selfish. To fulfill your own purpose in this life, it is important to surround yourself with like-minded people, people who aren't *trying* to make you a better person but who actually *are* making you a better person. This also means doing things that fill your soul with joy, so much joy you want to dance it out in the middle of the grocery store with them or sing carpool karaoke in the front seat of your car.

With that said, my current Alexa life theme song is ***"Don't Kill My Vibe"*** by Sigrid. Self-explanatory enough? I want no one in my life who doesn't serve a purpose in my overall goals in life. Maybe that's mean, or a bit harsh, or maybe you're just being a little too sensitive. What I have learned in this ***don't kill my vibe*** mentality is that nine times out of ten, when we expect things out of people, we tend to get disappointed. Womp, womp, womp.

But when that happens, the only person you can hold accountable for any sort of expectations is yourself ... therefore, be selfish. ***Do you*** (instead of waiting for others to ***do you*** for you), because you matter, too.

Your goals matter.

Your life matters.

You frickin' matter, sweetheart.

Being selfish – at least in this way – means you are saying "Yes!" to your purpose in life. "Yes!" to anything (and possibly everything) that is going to help you in the short run, and maybe in the long run, too. It's about saying "Yes!" to making more time for yourself so that you can truly excel in achieving all of your wildest dreams. I learned some of this concept from Shonda Rhimes, in her own book, "*Year of Yes.*" Damn, this concept is great. Saying "Yes!" to everything. Saying "Yes!" to you. Saying "Yes!" for one whole year, regardless of the discomfort or mental instability it may cause for the short run. So ...

Be spontaneous. Work out and be healthy. Adventure. Get lost in a good book. Dance it out. Whatever it is that you need to do to spike up your heart rate, or maybe even to slow it down, that's what you need to be doing. Whatever it is that makes you smile for no reason, go do, at least do it once. Even when it's scary, even when it seems like it's the wrong time, go do it. I truly believe timing is just based on a mindset to allow things to happen when they are supposed to happen. Good timing, bad timing, who knows? Just go for it.

But most important, whatever you think your purpose in life is, do it. That's why we've talked about being selfish. You have a purpose in life, and only you can fulfill that purpose. Do whatever it takes to try and fulfill that purpose. You can have a sense of power over your life – you have the means and the will-power to do so, even if it means you've got to be a little selfish. So be truly young, wild, and free, no matter what your age. Maybe that's only being young at heart, but still, go do it. Life is too short to worry about everyone else but yourself.

All. The. Time.

I know there are many concerns with this selfish idea, and some of them seem legitimate – at least until you realize what "being selfish" about achieving your life's goals and purpose really means. That attitude comes because we don't like the word. "Selfish" has a bad connotation. A negative chill. Other concerns with "selfish" come from being comfortable in the relationships you are in, from not wanting to rock the boat, from not wanting to hurt people – or to be hurt – from not wanting to disappoint (or be disappointing to) someone, or something.

I get it. I totally get it. That was me. That was my entire life. It was my life right up until about a year ago (as I am writing this) when I got dumped. Yes dumped. At the time, I said "poor me," but now I say "yay me," because instead of worrying about what others think, I am now focused on excelling at my purpose of dream-seeking, of conquering the damned world. Being selfish doesn't mean burning bridges, not by any means. In fact, don't burn bridges – you might get singed.

However, since I know that life isn't going to hand you your dreams on a silver platter, I have now become a strong believer in doing what is best for you, so that you can, in turn, have the inner strength to do what is best for the others in your life. Sometimes the decisions we have to make aren't those that we want to make – or even face – but they are those that, any given time, we need to make.

With that said, it's okay to still feel your feelings. At times, those feelings can be hard to swallow. Having been there and done that, I can actually assure you that feeling those feelings will probably be painful, stressful, frustrating and – did I say it? – painful. However, one step at a time, you will start to feel better. Give it time – you'll find other necessities in your life. Those fairy tale ending, dream job, *livin' the dream* kinds of necessities. Those will be the necessities that remain in your life forever. In the end, sometimes being selfish, isn't so selfish. Hmmmmmm, how's that work? That's "Contradiction Alexa" speaking once again. I know, I know. Think back to when I said other contrary things, such as:

How sometimes the decisions we make – or the decisions others make – aren't what we want, but they are what we need … we just didn't know it. How maybe letting people and things go is the right thing because they or you weren't benefiting from the relationship anymore.

Those seem contradictory, but that doesn't make them any less true. Sometimes the greatest truths also seem like the greatest contradictions.

Being selfish isn't always selfish.

Selfishness is the key to self-love. If the end goal in mind is to create a better environment for you then rock on. You first, others second. No one can love or care for you if you don't truly love or care for yourself first.

Which means it's time for you to start getting selfish about what's best for you, and for your life.

Starting now, your time is up. You've been put on notice. It's time to act. So go wrap yourself up in wanting to be selfish, at least in terms of saying "Yes!" to everything, trying new things, and going out finding yourself. That could be a real challenge, but you might just find that you weren't lost after all. Instead, you just weren't looking for you in the right place.

It may sound corny, but goodbyes aren't always forever. I think there is a thing called fate, which is made up from those "everything happens for a reason" moments, even if we don't know – and may never know – what that reason is. Timing isn't always right; or is it? But even when it is right, it may not feel right. Why? Because, whatever-it-is, it usually happens right when it's supposed to, even when we don't typically feel like that's what's happening. Or what should be happening. Not here. Not now.

As human beings, especially the kind of introspective "I want to be better" kinds of human beings you are if you're reading this book, we tend to over-analyze our thinking, whether we're thinking with our brains, our hearts, or our gut. So, in the moment, in *this* moment, be selfish, ***do you***. If you're still not sure, that's okay – do it anyway. You have my permission. Not that you need my permission or anything.

What I can't do is tell you the right answer, the right way of keeping or removing certain clutter from your life. I certainly can't tell you the right and wrong way to be selfish. Where do you draw the line? Honestly, I don't really know, because it's your line, not mine. I'd say as long as you're still kind to others and to yourself, you're winning the selfish game. But as soon as that kindness wavers you need to check yourself. Check yo self, don't wreck yo self. Yeah, you heard me. Maybe instead of drawing the line, just try touching the line. Straddling the line. Just getting to the line.

I also can't tell you when to listen to your heart, or to your brain, or to your gut. I don't know the right answer to that either. You'll have to listen to your heart, or to your brain, or to your gut to figure that one out. The only answer I know is that no matter which part of you you're listening to at any given moment, you've got to say "Yes!" to you. Say "Yes!" to putting you first in a time of need, confusion, or frustration, to being present, being selfish, being proud of who and what you are doing with your life … and being proud of why you are doing it. I can't stress this enough – if something you're doing doesn't make you proud to be you, maybe it's time to rethink your decision.

While you're on your selfish journey, if anyone is killing your vibe ... don't allow them to. Stay strong. Be you, *do you*, love you.

I'M GOING TO LIVE UNTIL THE DAY I DIE

I have said this before and I will say it again ... too many people live their lives as if they are already dead. Stuck in the bland moments of life, they're numb to the adrenaline rush that life offers each of us every single day. Lost in the idea that everyone and everything is out to get them, they go through the motions as if life is nothing but a series of misconceptions, tragedies, and bad luck. Now let's be honest. At times, life is filled with misconceptions, tragedies, and bad luck. In part, those Debbie Downer experiences are dependent on whether or not you believe in luck, good or bad. Frankly, I'm not quite sure if I do. But luck or not, when we dwell on those thoughts, we let them sink us. Wallowing in frustration, we let society mold us into living ordinary lives, instead of taking command of ourselves and living extraordinary lives.

As Prince once said, "my dearly beloved ..." Too many times in life we judge our own self-worth and come up short. We judge whether or not we can live the life that we've always imagined and dreamed of, then, having judged ourselves harshly, choose to settle for less. I'm sorry, but that's just lame. But here's how it happens:

We get caught up in the boring motions of adult life, and in doing so we let real life slip right past us, waving it goodbye in the process. We wake up, but we're still tired, and we assume that's normal. We go to our nine to five job but aren't happy – not with our jobs, not with the lives those jobs buy for us. We go home and barely talk with our significant others, even though they are the most important people in our lives.

Worst of all, we run this sad episode we call life on repeat, living repeated reruns instead of embracing new adventures. Why? Is it because that's what we think society tells us to do? Really?

I'm not going to pull any punches here. I call this approach to life bullshit. Instead of wallowing in mediocrity, go live. Don't just exist. That's lame. Get after it. Get yourself out of the ruts you've dug for yourself. Write yourself a bucket list, then act on it. Make that bucket list your life. And here's a tip: don't waste your time on bucket list items that you'll "do" once you retire. Instead, focus on things you can do this coming weekend or next summer, or – go ahead and get crazy – later this afternoon.

Do it now! Why not? Frankly, I don't want to hear it.

Why? Because, having tried out all those excuses myself, I don't exactly have sympathy for those that say these things aren't possible. Not with those who pity their own lives, nor with those who make others feel bad for whatever their current situation may be.

If you hate your job, quit. Come up with a Plan B, focus on it, and make it happen.

If you don't think you are making enough money, work harder, ask for a raise. What's the worst that can happen? The worst they'll say is "no, do more." If you're still okay with your shitty job and the little money you make, but despite having "settled," you're still complaining ... set higher standards for yourself. Expect more. Be better. Stop with the complaining.

If you want to travel but you say you don't have the money, budget better, go on shorter trips, don't stay at a resort. Camp out if you have to. But hit the road.

If you're relationship sucks, fix it. Relationships are work too. If fixing it doesn't work, get out. Not everyone is meant to be with each other and that's okay, but instead of settling, find a love that you love being in.

If you are stuck stalking someone else's life that you think is better than yours, then ask yourself "how do they do it." Or better yet ... ask them how they do it better. Wow, weird concept. Ask and sometimes you really do receive.

Now, I know that last little paragraph could come off a bit harsh. I'm sorry. Kind of. Or maybe not. Because I want you to succeed. I want you to live. I want you to do everything in life that your heart desires.

With that said … sometimes, if you can't do it yourself, you need someone to be a little bit of a hard ass on you. If I hurt your feelings, go grab a tissue, wipe away those tears, and let's get back to the positive portion of this section. Or, in the words of Phil Glazer, "grow a pair."

Life is short. We see that crushing brevity more and more each and every day. Even as you contemplate your three-score-and-ten, be realistic. Despite your hopes, you actually do know that you can never anticipate when your last breath will be taken. You'll never know when you'll have missed your last chance to fly to Europe or go on a safari in Africa. Not until it's too late.

You can't even know when you'll take your last bite from your favorite meal at your favorite restaurant. It might close, you might be forced to move, or … well, you know the other option. This just happened to my favorite restaurant back home. I am now grieving the loss of what a fire did to my favorite corned beef sandwiches and deli cut French fries. So instead of trying to figure out when that day might be … or even if you're content to be surprised when it comes, either way, just live. Live today. Live every day.

But as you live, imagine the life you would choose to live if you knew you only had another week, or maybe a month, or just one more year. I imagine if you knew, you'd make the damn best of it. The truth is, that could be your case without even knowing it.

With that said, the importance of having and working your own bucket list is quite simple. Physically writing down your thoughts about the things you'd like to do, at least once before you die is important. It gives you the accountability to actually become the go-getter your mind and your soul wants you to be. Writing down things you can do now – instead of waiting for "after the kids grow up and move out" or "after I retire" – that defeats the whole purpose. Unless your kids have already moved out, or unless you have already retired – and in that case, what are you waiting for?

Your bucket list should be about things you'd love to do right now. Fly a plane – or jump out of one. Hike the Appalachian Trail or climb Mount Kilimanjaro. Those are things from my bucket list, some of them already crossed off.

But that's me, and this is about you. What do you want to do? Make a list, then start working the list. As you move through your list, crossing off one thing after another, you will start to see progress. You'll see accomplishments being made. You'll realize your once-just-dreamed-of fulfillment is the real deal. You'll have something to look forward to, something to work towards. You'll discover an inner motivation to make the best of each day. So buy into this bucket list idea now, or consign your life to be forever boring.

Please don't choose to be boring. You're better than that. If you aren't, you wouldn't be reading this book. However, also keep in mind that just as dreams and goals change, so do bucket list items. Don't be afraid to change your list – to cross off something you no longer want to do or to add on new items that get you excited. Go get a piece of paper. Grab a pen. Start writing. Go, Go! Right now.

And remember this. If you don't cross everything off your list, that's A.O.K., too. This bucket list idea isn't meant to rigidly control your life. Instead, it's all about shaping a direction your life will take. With an active bucket list you actually use, you'll wake up tomorrow to discover that you're *livin' the dream*. And that's important. Things change. If you don't already know how you'll need to learn how to accept that change. But don't use change as an excuse for "I can't" thinking. Anything that's humanly possible is possible for you – but only if you make up your damn mind to, as Nike proclaims, "just do it."

I remember, in 8th-grade class with my best gal pal, Nicole Vanderwyst, writing a 100-item bucket list. We wrote this list with so freakin' much enthusiasm – we also did it during our computer class. Whoops. Sure, looking back, some of the things we wrote down were a bit out of the box, things like walking through a car wash, growing a peach tree in our front yard, eating an entire pizza by ourselves – and the most important – staying best friends forever. Despite our lack of experience, we still thought all 100 items on our list were possible … Even today, I wouldn't mind doing any of those things, and I still don't think anything on that list is impossible.

When it comes to your bucket list, dream big or don't dream at all. Write down those out of the box, crazy items, then do them. Imagine the rush ... and how much cooler you will feel about yourself ... when telling the story about the time you actually walked through the car wash yourself, instead of driving through in your car.

When the social media platform MySpace was "in" – this was before Facebook became so dominant – your profile was EVERYTHING and more. That was when it mattered who was in your Top 8, how many likes you had on each picture, how many friends you had (even though half of them aren't actually your friends).

Lots of people had other uses for their profile, but I used mine as a form of a vision board. As I look back, I remember putting two pictures in my "about me" section: one of New York City and one of Las Vegas. I put these destinations on my page, telling the world that that one day I would call one of these two places home, maybe even (eventually) both of them. When I proclaimed this to the world, I had never been to either of them – but something about each city appealed to me. Maybe it's that they are both entertainment capitals of America. Maybe it's that I wanted to dance for a living, or maybe that I wanted to be in a city with bright lights, or maybe it was just that I wanted to move away from home.

Now, ten years later, I look back and say, "shit Alexa, you really do live in Las Vegas, and it's all because of your MySpace posting." Am I kidding, even just a little bit? Sure, but it's still awesome to see I made some item from my MySpace vision board a reality. Imagine, something as small as a MySpace "about me" page helped me change my life. To me, that proves that some goals don't change, even when you stop thinking about them.

That's the beauty of writing things down, saving them on your computer, posting them on social media platforms. Those acts become physical proof that you can look back on and see if you've accomplished them. That can also prove to be an awesome timeline.

I like to think I am an adventurer, a dreamer, and – to coin a phrase – a wanderluster. Making a bucket list gives me a sense of vision, along with an idea of the direction I want my life to go in. This can – no, this will – work for you, too. Let your own personal bucket list be an eye-opening experience – as you write it down, as you update it and change your goals, remember that energy flows where attention goes. If you've seen the movie or read the book *The Secret,* you know the importance of the vision board, as well as the phrase "energy goes where attention flows." It's all about visualization of what you want your life to look like and proves that things like vision boards, bucket lists, and positive thinking really works.

Before I die, I want to ...

1. Take a picture in front of every state's "You are now entering …" sign. 20 down, 30 to go. Ohio, Indiana, Mississippi, Utah, Arizona, Idaho, New Mexico, Oregon, Nevada, California, Delaware, Wyoming, Michigan, South Carolina, Maryland, Washington, Alabama, Louisiana, New Jersey, Texas, check!

2. Attend a game at every major league baseball field so my angel in the outfield can watch some games with me. 11 down, 19 to go. Indians, Diamondbacks, Mets, Yankees, Phillies, Rangers, Braves, Giants, Mariners, Rays, Angels, check!

3. Go on a real-life safari in Africa and volunteer working with kids and building homes

4. ~~Attend a RiSE Lantern Festival.~~ This was hands down the best experience of my life so far.

5. Be listed in Forbes' "30 under 30;" some people laugh at me when I tell them this one, I say "watch me."

6. ~~Publish a book~~ (the one you're holding in your hands right now) – now that you've read this far, you can cross this one off for me.

7. Do a TED talk, or many.

8. Be on Ellen. Not because I want people to know the name Alexa Glazer, but because I want ~~people to know~~ how to live the dream.

9. ~~Start a movement,~~ check! Keep the movement moving though … I need your help. Pretty please.

10. ~~Skydive.~~ I get a high out of jumping out of perfectly good airplanes, just for fun.

11. ~~Bungee Jump.~~ Been there, done that, did it again, and want to do it again and again.

12. Conquer the world. By conquering the world I mean changing the world for the better.

13. Travel to Europe. Immerse myself in a new culture, eat the food, be a local, get lost.

14. Start a family and raise a bunch of little dream seekers. How cute will they be?

15. Own a mini cooper. Then a jeep. Then a Porsche.

16. Be my own boss. As I write this, I am currently working on making this my reality. Boss babe Alexa at your service ... or more like you at mine.

17. Ride an elephant in Thailand, or anywhere else where you can ride an elephant. I'm not trying to be picky.

18. Have one of my books become a New York Times Best Seller, because if I am going to publish a book – this book and more to come – then why wouldn't this be my goal? But I'll start with this book becoming an Amazon Best-Seller and work my way up.

These are just a few pieces of my never-ending bucket list. Some items represent bigger aspirations than others, some may be harder to accomplish, others are more dangerous, but they all can be done. More important, by the time I'm through, they all WILL be done!

You can do the same – create a challenging and exciting bucket list, then get started on fulfilling it. Feel free to borrow any of my items that appeal to you, but by all means, make the list yours. Don't be complacent. Don't live an *Average Joe* kind of life. **Be the go-getter, a bucket list-writing, victory-dancing, dream-catching fool you're little kid-self always wanted you to be.** Don't let the little kid in you be disappointed in the adult you've become. **Speak what you seek until you see what you've said.**

Before you die... what do you want to do?

Why the things we fear most often stop being fears when you accomplish them. "I want to go to space but my biggest fear is the unknown."
We want to do things that scare us. Why? The adrenaline, for sure. But also, to feel accomplished.

PHIL GLAZER RULES: DO THINGS WITH PASSION ··· OR DON'T DO THEM AT ALL

I was taught to go all in or go all out. This is a lesson you need to internalize. Passion motivates you to get things done. To actually go all in, or go all out. Passion takes you to another level. The best part about doing things with passion – or not doing them at all – is that passion is what sets your soul on fire. It's what frees your mind. Even better, your passion inspires others to work just as hard – if not harder – to find and live out their own passions.

Our "why" – our purpose for life – it typically guides us on our journey, but our passion is what drives us. Without having a passion that ignites you, your life will be stagnant. Your work will be unfulfilling. Because your actions won't have a backbone, you will never reach your greatest potential. The things you live for will have no heartbeat. Dead of a heartbeat, dead of life.

Many people tell me they don't know where their passions lie. Yet there's a simple way to go looking for it. If you can't stop thinking about something, if you know you'll grind and do anything for it ... that, my friend, is where your passion can be found. Passion isn't necessarily about money or fame. It's about whatever fills your heart up with the most joy in life. Through personal experience, I've discovered that passion makes you giddy.

It makes your heart burst with love and it fills you with warmth. It's a feeling kind of like your first love. When you can't stop talking about it, when you smile from ear to ear talking about it, when it frightens you a little bit, when it makes your heart skip a beat, when someone brings it up and you instantly perk up, this is your passion.

Remembering Phil

"Do things with passion. As a Coach, Phil was very passionate about the importance of right and wrong. I

remember a situation when I was probably 12 years old and playing catcher. A girl knocked me over because she didn't slide into home. Coach Phil was immediately arguing with the umpire because that girl was breaking a rule and could have caused an injury. As a player, I always knew Coach Phil was in my corner in every situation. His passion in general was contagious. Coach Phil was the first one to be excited and encouraging. He was the type of guy you want in your corner: a person who is ready to fight next to you when things are unjust and the person ready to celebrate your victories when you've been working hard." – **Patti Mariano Kopasakis**

ALEXA GLAZER

HUMILITY

Lastly, to live successfully, to overcome all of life's big and small challenges or just to have a great life, you have to be **humble**. Humility gives you the ability to always aim higher, to not just be good but to be great. Humility makes you magnetic to others and brings you closer to people who make your heart feel all warm and fuzzy inside. Being humble gives you the hustle to go about *Livin' the Dream* ... Being humble is about achieving goals in silence. It's about focusing on making yourself better – but it's not thinking that you are better. It's about knowing that beautiful things don't ask for attention they just sit there in all of their beauty, quietly and intently.

My dad's humility was a constant understatement. He never focused on his success. Instead, he focused on the success of others. He constantly praised others for their hard work and dedication, though only when that praise was warranted. He taught me to stay humble, but to hustle hard.

For me, humility has come in the form of gut checks. These are what I call the *gut checks of life*. These gut checks focus me on understanding that no one is safe from heartbreak, hurt, or reality. When you are able to accept these moments, to lose any ounce of entitlement you feel you have – or are owed by the world and by others who share your world – you gradually become more humble. You have to be.

The big process of humility for me in my dad's death was not asking for sympathy. This to me shows humility because no matter how bad I didn't want this to happen to me, death is a natural part of life that we can't escape. If I continued sitting each day asking for attention and said poor me because my dad died I wouldn't really be living. I would have been doing myself and my dad an injustice. I know this may not seem humble but not seeking attention is humility.

Therefore, it can be attached to so many traumatic moments in your life. Being humble is not playing victim to those traumatic moments but letting them shape you and to help others who may be going through something similar. I like to think that more people are willing to empathize with you if you aren't begging or asking for sympathy and attention anyway. If you are humble about your situation people will naturally gravitate to you to help when need be. That idea is huge in my eyes. Staying humble and grounded because you now have become an expert in whatever you lost or gave up and you can now lend a hand to so many others.

The heartbreak thing is quite important in the idea of being humble. Many times we are so hurt and torn apart from a break up that we want to talk trash, pretend we didn't have any true feelings, that it wasn't as important to us as it actually was, and let's try hurting the other person by pretending they are a stranger you've never met before. Guilty. Sometimes this is necessary other times you have to get off that pedestal and kill others with kindness. Let the process of heartbreak take its natural course.

Recently, my humbling experiences have been in the form of the book you are currently holding in your hands. This has been four years in the making and here we are with a published book. Talk about a "someone pinch me" moment. My movement called *Livin' the dream ... THE MOVEMENT,* and how people are actually making it move. People actually like following my life, my story and are actually inspired by it all. Say what? Lastly, watching lightbulbs go off in people's minds and hearts when I speak. This is so cool you guys. This is what it is all about for me.

My life revolves are these things, my book, my movement and speaking have become my entire life. I eat, sleep and breathe *livin' the dream* thoughts and actions. With that said, I tend to forget that not everyone knows all the details of my dreams. They don't know the details of my story like I do. They don't know the details of what sets my soul on fire. Therefore, being able to talk to people, to geek out about my accomplishments, tell them my passions, and watch people feel something is beyond humbling. I am watching my *livin' the dream* army grow daily and I can't get enough of the support and love.

Being humble, hustling hard, it helps you to realize that not you, and not one person, deserves a moment galloping on their high horse. Learn to humble yourself and the rest will fall into place. I promise you. People do not like cocky. People like confidence. What people really like is other people who are humble. Who are going places but have an open mind and open heart.

YOU ARE CORDIALLY INVITED TO MY PITY-PARTY

"THERE ARE PEOPLE WHO WOULD LOVE YOUR BAD DAYS" -- UNKNOWN

Where: My bed or couch of course
When: Anytime of the day really
I am always up to complain
Right now, I would really like someone to **not talk** ⋯
but just listen to me
Even at the best of time ⋯
I really like being the center of attention
So, please ⋯
No feedback during the pity party ⋯
This includes unsolicited advice.
Just show up and listen
Attire: Pajamas
If you show up and look better than me ⋯
I will have to kick you out
Food and Alcohol: Ice cream, wine, Ketel One
If you're on a diet and are planning on not binging with
me, well then don't bother coming ⋯
RSVP: No RSVP Required. Just show up!

Sometimes, when life happens, when the struggles hit, when the complaining sinks in, we want nothing more than for this pity party of ours to continue. Either that, or we just can't figure out a way to get out of that party. We either enjoy the party and want to repeat it over and over again because it's all about us ... or it's a realization and you want to get the hell out of the environment. Kind of like when you're the only sober friend at the bar and realize what a shit-show everyone and everything else is.

We want the attention on us because, at the moment, that attention seems like something positive – it sure feels better than all that negative shit that's going on.

Face it – there are times when each of us wants some sympathy without having to ask for it. We don't necessarily want people to feel bad, but we do want them to be on our team while we feel bad. We just need a cheerleader. Or eight.

Hey, I get it – I've been there. We all have. It's almost fun, for a moment, but at some point, you have to say "Sister, get your shit together and stop feeling so bad for yourself. It's not really all that bad, and the worst of it's bound to pass, sooner rather than later." Or, as Coach Phil said, "just grow a pair."

Typically, the reasons we have pity parties are because:

We are feeling a bit stressed

We failed a test

We got fired from work

Our pet fish died

We're fat (or, more likely, we feel like we're fat), or ...

We have that famous period bloat

We've got no money and the bills keep coming

Other reasons include: "my dad just died" or "I just got dumped." Those come to mind because those have been my most recent pity-party moments. Basically, life has lost its gravitational pull – everything seems to be turning sideways.

When you invite people to your pity party, or when you get invited to someone else's pity party, you should probably bring things like a box of tissues, chocolates, or an uplifting movie. Anything to make them laugh. Maybe this means having a couple jokes on hand as well.

Also, know this. If someone comes to your pity party, you are morally obligated to go to theirs, even if you don't want to, even if you've got a date or have to study. After all, fair's fair.

I am going to put you up for a challenge. Do not cave into the temptation to wallow in pity at the pity party – and if you think you're the one who needs it, fight extra hard to avoid giving into the temptation. Try really, really hard. The pity party only sets you back. It is impossible to take steps in the right direction when you're feeling like a grumpy Mr. Potato-head, which (I promise) is what you'll feel in the aftermath of your own pity party. So ... fake it till you make it. Sometimes, faking it is all that is a necessity. Instead ... practice some self-love. Do things just for you. Things such as:

Things that are going to make you better, or at least feel better.

Things that get your mind off the negative.

Things that bring you to a better place in life.

As you consider this, here are some thought-provoking ideas about ways to live a pity-party free life, a healthy and happy life. Remember, this is according to me, written with only the most beautifully sarcastic but brutally honest thoughts and truths – you may experience things differently, but don't count on it.

1. **Drink water ... your body needs it.** Sure, you're going to have to pee ... a lot. But there are worse things in life than spending a few more minutes in the restroom. Having lived for half a decade in the driest city in the US (we get, on a good year, 4.5 inches of rain, and in this town, if you don't drink a lot, you will pay another price for it ... but this even applies in high-humidity Miami, or Cleveland, or even Seattle, where people don't tan, they rust.)

2. **Sleep ... no matter how beautiful you think you are, believe me, you need your beauty rest.** Ever think about why you're so damned crabby? Or why you have those ridiculous bags under your eyes? Or why you scare the bejesus out of yourself when you looked in the mirror for the first time this morning? Get some rest, sleepy beauty.

3. **Laugh often ... it can't hurt, and it may even help you get washboard abs.** Let's be honest. Laughing is fun. So much frickin' fun! If you don't like a good laugh, well then I don't know what to say to you, Mister Grumpy Pants. A belly laugh will do your endorphins and your adrenaline levels more good than you

might believe. You may even get those happy tears streaming down your face and that's when you really know the laugh is real.

4. **Eat breakfast … it's the most important meal of the day and – done right – it's wonderfully delicious.** Do you want to be skinnier? Skipping meals isn't going to do it for ya soul sister (or brother). You're only slowing down that metabolism of yours. Speeding up your metabolism is how you lose weight, but you need energy to spark the process. Whether you prefer a Mango Smoothie or traditional bacon-and-eggs (with buttered toast, a glass of OJ and maybe a side of pancakes!), this really is going to get your day started right. Try not to do those sugary cereals and cinnamon rolls day in and day out.

5. **Work on self-reflection … if you don't, who will, and I'm here to tell you, this is your life.** "Alexa," you ask, "are you telling me I have to meditate?" No, of course not, but now that you mention that, it wouldn't hurt you to try. Instead of mumbling OM, just analyze yourself … integrating your mind, body, and soul are quite important to your life. Try it, then get back to me once you know who you really are. I promise you'll love the difference, and I really am interested in meeting the new more relaxed you.

6. **Stay on top of your goals … then go out and reach them.** Why set yourself a batch of goals if you aren't going to do them, if not today, then at least one day soon? You want it, so go get it. Remember, a dream remains only a wish until you take action to make it happen. Don't waste your own time wishing, that's just nonsense.

7. **Be more mindful.** Be aware of your surroundings. Look past the obvious.

8. **Be grateful ... appreciate the small things.** You already have food and shelter and a great book in your hands. Let's just start with that. Remember, no matter how bummed you feel right now, other people don't have food, shelter ... or this book! Enough said.

9. **Stress less ... it's only an unneeded worry.** I bet if I told you stress could cause over-eating or under-eating, acne, lack of motivation, anxiety, sleepless nights, and blah blah blah, you would maybe try to stress less. Although some of you – admit it – would start stressing out about eating disorders and acne. Well, guess what? Stress can cause over-eating or under-eating, acne, lack of motivation, anxiety, sleepless nights, and blah blah blah. So stress less folks. How?

Eat regularly, and at specific times. Every damned day. Do some exercise, even if it's just jumping to conclusions or running your mouth (no, not really). Be nice to people you don't know (that waiter, or the guy who held the door for you at the 7/11). Do something nice-but-unexpected for someone you know. Random acts of kindness are the jam and go such a long way. Dress (every day) like you're trying to impress someone. This doesn't mean a full face of make-up and some stilettos, but maybe just shower and you'll feel much better. Get your hair done, or your nails, or do something else that pampers you. A massage could definitely do some good too. Write or call (text is OK if they're OK with texts) someone who hasn't heard from you in a while.

10. Stimulate your brain ... it constantly needs to be educated. Find people to challenge you. People who you don't see on a daily basis. People who aren't your absolute bestest friends in the entire world. People who make you think outside the box and vice versa. Your brain needs to be challenged.

11. Be comfortable with being uncomfortable. Shit, this one sucks. Why did I have to write this one down? (stupid, stupid) ... But like it or not (and I think we can agree that it's "not"), it's still the truth, so we have to figure it out someday. Today's a good day to start. Leave that comfort zone of yours at least in some aspect of life, at least once each day.

12. Exercise ... hey, you're not as old as you think (or even if you are). I think I am old, I really do. But let's be honest, I'm not. My body still functions pretty well. My guess, yours does too. So what if you feel a little sore, even a lot sore. Or tired, like reeeallllly tired.

Still, do something to get your body moving. If you can't do anything else, go for a walk. I have a friend who, for health reasons, has to walk three miles per day. It's not always convenient to go outside – let alone to a gym – so he walks 80 cycles around a course he's laid out that includes the kitchen and dining room, the family room and living room (hey, it's a big house). He gets what he needs, regardless of the weather. So don't tell me you can't go around in circles without leaving your home or place of work. I give you no sympathy for this one.

13. **Edit your life ... remove the garbage.** Whether that garbage is people, attitudes or unfashionable clothing, say GOODBYE to it. You don't have time for everyone, and your closet doesn't have room for all your old must-haves.

14. **Judge less ... go against stereotypes.** Your eyes you just rolled at that girl in the mall for taking a selfie, or maybe there's that shrug you just directed at that guy at the gym posing in the mirror ... or even that kid you made fun of for having a zit or two on his face ...

Why? What's the damn point? You do you. Focus on that. Remember, someday, you'll do something that will have others rolling their eyes, and won't you just love feeling superior to those annoying jerks. Humble yourself and ditch your judgey attitude.

15. **Don't procrastinate ... you'll accomplish more of what you actually want to do.** Want less stress in your future? Then stop putting off every single task until the very last possible minute. I've done it, I do it, and it sucks, so let's just stop it. Right now. Let's make a pact to make a to-do list and actually accomplish it.

16. **Stop complaining ... because it's not changing anything.** This is the pity-party y'all. You really think that complaining about how little money you make is going to make leaves turn into hard cold cash? Or that your Venmo account is

going to mysteriously have 1,000 extra dollars in it? Wrongo! Grind till you die.

17. Take steps of action … or nothing will ever get done. You lazy piece of ass, get up off the couch, stop watching Netflix while eating a pint of ice cream (I say this even though it very well explains me on occasions). Whatever it may be ... stop it and be proactive. Make shit happen.

18. Let go … and let be. Stop taking all those painful or awkward moments in life so seriously. Don't get embarrassed, feel lame, or be a constant worry-wart. Dance in your underwear, for goodness sake – Tom Cruise did it in Risky Business, and so can you. Sing even louder in the shower so all of your room-mates can hear you. Just live. It's more fun to take life not so seriously.

19. Don't compare yourself to others … you are you for a reason. Remember that perfection doesn't exist. "What?!? Alexa, you've got to be kidding, right?" Wrong. No matter how pretty, skinny, smart, funny, and just extraordinary, that girl you're stalking on Instagram seems to be, she still has issues. Trust me, she does. So do you. Be okay with being perfectly imperfect. It's a start.

20. Never stop dreaming … because that is just no fun. You know how, when you are sleeping and you dream the most vivid dream? The dream that your boyfriend broke up with you, the one that – when you wake up – has you instantly checking your phone for that dreaded dump-text. Or the dream about someone who is no longer with us, and you wake up with tears in your eyes. Maybe the one where you are falling off a mountain and your stomach literally drops.

If dreams in our sleep can feel this real, then there is no reason for our actual waking dreams to not become real. Dream big or you might as well not dream at all. Dreams aren't just meant for sleeping, they are meant for every-day life.

Now, before you get all hot-and-bothered, this list isn't meant to be some "Alexa bible" to a perfect life. I don't believe a perfect life exists in this universe. Or even just by today's standards of perfect. In fact, I got this list from my own doings and not-so doings. The person complaining about money ...me. The girl stalking pretty girls ... guilty. The one dreaming vividly real dreams ... that'd be me. Rolling her eyes at the selfie queen ... also me. Don't make those mistakes (or the other ones I didn't dare mention). Instead, live your life in a way where pity parties are not needed, wanted or desired.

What I am saying is that this list can be used as a guide to better our life. In time. Slowly but surely. Working on these things day by day and becoming a better more purposeful you. That's a win right there, ladies and gentlemen.

What are you waiting for?!

Throw out those invitations and go better your life.

You got this.

What goes up must come down.

Just as it is with gravitational pull, life is a series of ups and downs. When you have an up, naturally you will eventually have a down. When you are okay with life's ups-and-downs, when and ready for it since you know it is a scientific fact that there is a comedown, you become more alert.

ALEXA GLAZER

198

WISHING, WONDERING, HOPING.

On a daily basis, our brains are rattled by life. Wherever we are, we find ourselves stuck: in class, at work, at home or in a multitude of other situations. We have to wonder: what are we doing? As we go through the motions of living, all too often we wind up simply wishing, wondering and hoping. Wishing, wondering and hoping that things will remain the same as they once were – or that they will become different than they are now, or maybe different than they've ever been. It's that "the grass is always greener on the other side" mentality. Yes, maybe the grass really is greener, but it also needs mowing.

Most of the time, when we step into our chaotic brains, we do so only to realize that we are stuck outside of our current reality, on the outside looking in. This realization tends to force us in back away from risk and into our comfort zone. It makes us think that we are able to procrastinate in life and stay in this state of ease. It's entirely too easy, as time goes on, to start getting comfortable with being uncomfortable; however, doing this is much easier said than done. So instead of leaving this state of mind, we continue to wish, wonder, and hope.

We stay put.

In our mind.

On our own.

Without taking any actions.

Be comfortable with being uncomfortable.

Be comfortable with getting out of your comfort zone. Typically, we fear change and discomfort, even though we know that is what makes us grow the most. Leave your bubble – there is more to life than feeling all warm and cozy

---

Instead of thinking about the opportunities and challenges today presents, we are consumed by thinking about our bright futures, or about our shitty pasts, neither of which gets anything done – at least not anything productive.

Now, I personally don't think this is the worst thing you and I can do. Sometimes it does make sense to wish, to wonder, and to hope. But I also think, as with anything in life, we need to seek a balance here. This does not mean that our future, or our past, or our present should ever be outweighed by either of the other two. They are all three of them important. However, in order to learn about – and plan for – our future, we must be able to find value in thinking about our past. Our past made us who we are *today* – and that same past will be a major factor in who we become *tomorrow.*

OK, so, my own brain is frequently rattled by this "live in the moment" mentality, which seems to have become the goal everyone strives for. Yes, "today" is important, but the idea of living just for today is, at best, incomplete. I know the premise of this book is simple: we really do need to live today, because – despite our hopes and expectations – we aren't actually promised tomorrow. None of us are.

Taking that a step further, we've already lived yesterday. So, if we're not promised tomorrow, and we've already finished yesterday, what does that mean for us right now, today? How do we use what we know now – as well as what we hope for from our future – to shape a better and more "today-focused" lifestyle? How do we balance our thoughts, memories, and dreams in order to help us truly live for the current moments in life?

I speak about living in the now because no matter how much we might like to believe we've got a long future ahead of us, tomorrow isn't promised. Yet living just for today can't be all we do. I went to college, investing four years in my future, and did so in order to be able to find a career I love. I'm writing a book that – as I type this section – I hope to complete in four months and publish in eight months. I live each day of my career, and I write each day in my book, knowing that tomorrow – while it's likely for someone like me who drives safely, eats right, works out and is just 25 – is certainly not promised.

My point to this situation – and yes what I'm about to tell you is a big contradiction, but please hear me out – it is simple and straightforward. Everyone says, and seems to believe – including me (and I say this despite knowing in the most painful possible way that tomorrow really isn't promised) – things like:

Live in the moment. Don't let life pass you by. Worry less and live more. Stop over-analyzing. Quit thinking too far ahead. Stop reassessing major life decisions. Cease and desist looking too deep into every word or phrase. All of these are just different ways of telling yourself to live for today. However, while I've heard all these, and I've even said each of these to myself and to others. Instead, just do it. Do it all.

But "just do it" means more than just living for today. It means "analyze your past" – just don't over-analyze yourself. It means "think about your future," but that doesn't mean you should lose yourself in dream-weaving. It means dealing with the past and the future – both are important – but most important, don't forget living *right now*. Be present in your life.

This may seem simple, but trust me, too many people live their lives far from present. That means they are not living – at least they're not living their lives the way they should be lived, the way their lives deserves to be lived.

My theory on living your life both for and in the here and now is simple. In order to grow, first of all, you need to think about your past. You need to reflect on important life-lessons. You need to reminisce, recalling and reliving memories, good and bad. All of them. The memories that made you the happiest, ones that still make you cry tears of joy, and the ones that had you crying because your belly laughs were uncontrollable. But you also need to revisit those painful memories, the ones that made you want to scream in terror or cry from gut-wrenching sadness.

You have to think about the moments you made in your life, the ones you made without thinking or planning. You also need to reflect on memories that have filled you with guilt, envy or jealousy. Without making and keeping these lessons from your past an important part of your life, there is no such thing as a future – you'll just continue recycling the past.

As you contemplate your future, if you don't embrace the life-lessons from your past, life will keep throwing the same challenges our way until we finally figure out what we're supposed to learn. Only then can we move forward.

I am a strong believer in the idea that your own experience is the best and most useful kind of personal advice. Even if – and sometimes especially if – your experience was a bad one, the lessons you learn from that experience becomes a new, valuable way to problem solve. You don't have to re-live the same problem again in order to come up with solutions that really do work. Relying on your past experience, when a problem does resurface, your outcome will be better because you've been there and done that and figured it all out.

Just the opposite kind of benefit comes from our future. Of course, you can't remember your future, but you do have to think about it, and – despite the importance of living for today – you still have to plan for it. Without a set of goals, supported by the plans that will bring those goals to life, there is no motivation behind what we are doing, day in and day out. As I like to say when contemplating a future without goals or plans, "I don't know where I'm going and have no idea when I'll get there, but I'm making good time and getting great mileage."

Without a goal – and a plan to achieve it – there is no finish line, not even the nearest mile marker. In order to feel like your life is worth living, you have to see a light at the end of the tunnel – and it better not be an oncoming train. With that said, before we can plan ahead, we need things to look forward to. These are the small victories that become markers on our path to success. Without these small victories, we'll feel stagnant, numb and unmoving.

What we tend to forget, as we either recall the past or look forward to the future, is that the present, the "right now." This can be frustrating. Even as we reach out to grasp it, the damned present's already over. It just happened – there, in the blink of an eye – but now it's already part of your past.

The present seems to happen in seconds ... then, just like that (visualize a finger-snap), the present is gone. As each moment of the present disappears forever, what we're left with are more memories of an ever-larger past to look back at, as well as an ever-shorter future to look forward to.

That present moment when you read that last paragraph just became a vanished present, just one more memorable thought. That realization about the present may seem like one big contradiction, but it's also the truth.

As Dickens pointed out in *A Christmas Carol*, we need all three elements – past, present, and future – in order to understand and fulfill our lives. ***Our past creates our present, and our present dictates our future.*** Life is one big circle, which continues for as long as we have – then, once we're gone, it continues for everyone else. Forever. It never stops. And, as Buzz Lightyear says, this circle of life extends *"to infinity and beyond."*

As you think about the past, the present and the future, don't let people – not even me, your friendly and helpful tour-guide to the rest of your life – tell you what you can and can't do. Don't let people tell you how to live – or how not to live – your life. Don't allow unsolicited advice that so many people seem to want to give you distort how you choose to live your life.

However, instead of getting angry, try to forgive those "helpful" people, who sometimes forget they aren't living YOUR life. They don't seem to realize that their advice directly affects you, not them. They're not aware that free advice is worth every penny you'll ever pay for it. Despite the well-intentioned "help" received from those who want to run other peoples' lives (in general) and your life in particular, the need for each of us to make our own life-choices is why we each have our very own pasts, presents, futures – as well as the ability to make decisions about how the first two will shape the third.

While this may sound like a contraction – another one yes – before you write off this contraction, keep this in mind. While you have to chart your own course, you should also be sure to ask for help whenever you feel like you need it. You don't have to follow the advice you ask for, but getting input from others can be very helpful in your decision process. Just remember that each of us has our own canvas. We are, each and every one of us, different. We each tell a different story, shaped by our unique filters on life. That's the beauty of being individuals.

There is no externally-dictated right or wrong way to live *your* life. It's your life – make the most of it. I actually challenge you to go do so, even as I remind you again to listen only to that advice which rings true within you. Even mine.

Living life well is a matter of wisely using the time you have. Since you're not promised tomorrow, living life well means making the most of today, every day. Obviously, I'm all for living life to its fullest, for taking hold of every moment – and I advocate this for a very good reason. So, while I encourage each of us to live our own lives to the fullest, every day, I also recognize that it's hard to do this even once, let alone every day of every week of every month of every year.

It is also true that we all need to take the occasional day off from life. While me and my book here are all about living life to the fullest, I'd be kidding myself – and we'd be kidding each other, too – if we both didn't acknowledge that you and I can't live every damned day to the fullest, without at least acknowledging that, on some days, "the fullest" is more a glass-half-empty than a glass-half-full. This is no secret – I was there. Giddily-happy one day and rug-sucking insecurely miserable the next.

Admitting this may seem a bit scatterbrained, or even – horrors – yet another contradiction, but the truth is, just like you, my life is going in many different directions, sometimes all at once in a single day. But regardless of where my life's going, what's important is what I am feeling at this moment. That shapes what's going to happen in the next moment, as well as in all the future next moments. Yet after way more than a few conversations with my people, I'm learned it's okay to be where I am in life. Right now. And every future right now, too – you know, the right nows I'm not promised, but hope nonetheless to live to see anyway.

Looking back over the past four years, the more I thought about my life, the more eager I became for something more. I eventually decided it would be more gratifying to thrive, to have something to make me find and embrace all of the confidence in the world than it would be to be paralyzed by fear, or wrung out by the burdens life throws my way. By the same token, though, I admit that I wasn't eager to jump into something that I wasn't completely passionate about "just because" it's what I thought I should be doing after college. I certainly knew I didn't want to live a checklist kind of life:

Graduate – check!

Get a job in the field I studied in college – check!

Find a man – check!

Marry the man I found – check!

Have a family with four blonde-and-blue kids – check!

Instead of doing what everyone tells me I should be doing, I decided I want to move to the beat to my own damn drum. Sometimes I even want to beat the hell out of my own damn drum! And right now, I like the sound of that. Actually, it sounds pretty damn fulfilling.

With all those seconds and minutes and hours on my hands every day, the thinking going on inside my head has me focusing on the concept of time. At least in part, that's what this book is really about. Time, and what we do with it. What people think happens when you've got too much of it. As if.

After my dad died, and after every other major, painful setback in my life, I found that people – everyone from my closest family and friends to casual strangers – always seem to say things get easier with time. Four years later, having lived through some life-altering shocks, I don't necessarily agree with that statement. Sometimes yes, other times, no. On the bright side, the more time you have, the longer you have to think, research and work. But on the other side, the more time you have, the longer you have to sit on your thumb, to procrastinate, and to explore the art and science of being lazy.

Time is not the only resource you need before you can hope to make everything in life to get easier, but it's got to be one. You can't fight through life with time as the only resource there at your fingertips. For example, time doesn't tell you what your career path should be, who you ought to date – or marry – or even what the next stage in your life is. Time doesn't make you stop missing people, either. Time doesn't build success. Time doesn't cultivate love. I can take this riff on time and run in so many directions, but I think you get the point.

This matter of time comes to mind because, on days when I have more time on my hands than usual, I find the days become more a matter of trying to fill all that time with healthy, positive, beneficial, uplifting things. Days with too much time also gives me – and you – a lot of alone time. Time to be an introvert, or, in the case of missing people, time to make missing them even harder. Oddly, that's okay. Time on your hands when you're missing someone precious to you makes you better understand and value those who still matter, as well as to understand how some people matter a little less.

With success, time on your hands can also make you lazy. Sometimes this means that laziness can create success. It just means that you are trying to be more efficient. Time doesn't just give you opportunity. It gives you moments. Moments to live through and remember. Moments to build an empire out of a person and a life for yourself. Moments to hold on to.

The key to success is laziness.

Why? Efficiency. The reason successful people are successful is because they were, at some point, too lazy to do things the same old way. Lazy in the sense that they wanted to find faster and more efficient ways of doing things. Better products. Better services. The man who invented the tractor knew what it was like to follow a mule around a cornfield.

On the off-chance that one day someone will tell you that "over time, things will get easier," don't take that without a grain of salt. It's true that time helps feelings diminish some of the sharp edges that come with painful feelings and memories. And, over time, it will become easier for you to finally discover that you're okay with just being you. Sometimes it's even okay to be a bit selfish. Other times it feels right being selfless. Each day brings something new. However, these feelings will happen not because time passes, but because, over time, you've worked to make these things happen. In those moments when you're told about the magical healing powers of time, you should think about this:

Time may not make things easier for me, but what time does offer me is still rewarding. Time offers me the chance to be forever grateful. It offers me moments to cherish – moments to grow and become a stronger, more independent person – more the "me" I want to become.

In those times when you need to be alone, remember that you're not alone – and not meant to be alone – at least not in the long run. No matter that the people you miss are away, or that they are gone. Alone-time can be cherished and used, but time is also meant to be shared with people as well. People we love. People we would miss were we without them. People who are here. People – and things – who make our hearts happy.

Time is the ultimate "use it or lose it" element in our lives. Don't let time pass you by. Don't wait for success to happen … in time. Don't wait to feel better … in time. Don't wait for anything. Chase the things that matter, but only chase those things that really matter.

Time is precious. No matter how you use it, find a way to make the time given to you worth using. When time goes by slowly, embrace it. When time goes by way too fast, remember it. Time will come and time will go. It's up to each of us to use it in ways that are most valuable to us. *So wish, wonder, and hope. Look back and look forward. Remember your past, live in your present and plan for your future.*

Live in the moment. Embrace it. Focus on the now..
Don't forget about your past ⋯ and never stop planning your future. Learn from your past. Live in the moment. Yearn for your future. It's important to embrace each moment as it happens. Make the present moment last a little longer by taking the time to remember how lucky you are to have that moment.

MY ALL-TIME FAVORITE QUESTIONS

Here we go again …

"What would your dad say?"

This has to be my all-time favorite question. Worse, in the way that opposite poles on a magnet attract, I think this is also others' all-time favorite question to ask me.

However, what I mean *really* by "all-time favorite question" is that this is the worst, most painful, least possible-to-answer question I have ever been asked. Then asked again, and again, and again. It's one of those "beaten into the ground" questions. It's the question where, when asked, all you can do is stare at the person asking it, then execute a slight, precision eye roll – not big enough for them to actually notice (but you still feel better for it), then finish it off with one of those awkward little smirks at the end. My sarcasm is very real here. When someone asks you your own most-hated question and depending on how the question hits you, follow my example and either go with full-bore sarcasm that lets them know what you think, or downplay it to the point where you know it's there, but they don't.

Why is it that people feel free to ask the worst possible question, but never ask the really good ones? And, beyond this one, what are my other all-time favorite questions? Typically, my real all-time fav questions would be more along the lines of, "Do you want to go get some ice cream?" Or maybe "Do you want to go get margaritas and eat three bowls of chips and salsa?" My favorite questions are ones that I can answer, honestly and without sarcasm, "Yes, please! Now, that is more like it."

Instead, the questioning conversation goes something like:

"Well, honey … What would your dad say if you did that?" (which could be innocent, but which suggests that, whatever dad said, it wouldn't be positive)

Or …

"I bet your dad would be so proud of you" (which could also be innocent, but odds are that it's sarcastic, hurtful and not really even a question, but you get the idea).

Or …

"Do you think your dad would like him?" (another could-be-innocent question, but one that really implies that, of course, dad wouldn't like him)

Or …

"Is that something your dad would do?" (no way this could be innocent – obviously, they don't think so)

Or ...

"What does your dad do for a living?" (it's got to be innocent, but for people in my situation, there's no way of dodging that one, is there?)

Or ...

"Who is going to walk you down the aisle?" (which could be an honest question, but to ask that they've got to know my situation, so frankly, it's just snarky, as well as intrusive and None Of Their Damned Business)

Quite honestly, that list goes on and on and on ... For reasons known to some higher power, but not to me, people seem to eat up these questions. Now, I know that many people asking them come from a good place. Some of them don't know my situation, so I really can't blame them at all ... in fact, I generally don't actually blame them. And despite the pain, some of the questions are valid. But hey, I admit it, I can just be a little sensitive sometimes. Can't we all?

But, it's the people who do know my story, the ones who actually know the answers to all those questions (but who ask them anyway), those are the ones who really chap my ass. And what is the answer to all those questions? It's simple:

"WE. WILL. NEVER. KNOW. BUT THANKS FOR REMINDING ME. NOW, CAN WE *PLEASE*, PRETTY PLEASE MOVE ON?"

If I could answer these questions out loud the way my mind answers them inside my head, those answers would sound a little something like what you're about to read below. Again, I know that, in most cases, people aren't really (not really) intentionally trying to stab me where it really hurts. To pour salt into a freshly opened wound, then rub it, vigorously. To hit that bruise that's already been hit, over, and over and over again.

But, like I said, I can be sensitive – I imagine other people in similar situations are sensitive, too. In fact, I'm going out on a limb here to say people in similar situations have some of these same "here's how I'd like to answer that question" thoughts going on in their heads, too. If you actually say them out loud, you'll have fewer "friends," but the ones you do have will be real friends, and more polite, too. To anybody who does give these answers out loud, I give you props. I would love to see some insensitive someone's reaction to you; however, I stick to keeping those beautiful come-backs in my head. And now, in the book, you're holding.

Actually, as illustrated, there are two ways of asking most of these questions – one that's an honest (if misguided) inquiry, and one that's intentionally sarcastic and shaming. So of course, for these questions, there are also two kinds of answers. One I'll share with you. The other, for the (ahem) person who's trying use a painful question to put me down, involves a crude Anglo-Saxon phrase, usually accompanied by a raised finger.

So, here we go:

"What would your dad say if you did that?"

If either of us knew, you wouldn't be asking me that. So can you just try and help instead of pointing out that the one person I really want to ask, the one person I know would have the answer is the one person I can't ask?

"I bet your dad would be so proud of you."

If you're being honest about this, I bet he would be, too, but I would rather hear that from him. Thank you though, really (sarcasm optional).

"Do you think your dad would like him?"

Honestly ... do I think? Maybe? No. I don't know. He met one boyfriend of mine, a high school sweetheart, so he wasn't exactly asking intense questions back then. If this new guy treats me well, then yes, I think dad would like him. Why do you ask? Do you think maybe dad wouldn't (or shouldn't) like him?

"What does your dad do for a living?"

He watches us. Somewhere between heaven and earth. But you know, I don't think they have jobs up there, do you? And certainly, he's way beyond needing to do anything for "a living ..."

"Who's going to walk you down the aisle when you get married?"

Not him. Maybe I'll walk down the aisle by myself. Maybe my uncle? Maybe I'll pick a random stranger and give them that amazing job? Are you volunteering?

"Did you get like a huge amount of money when he died?"

You're kidding, right? Shut up. No, not just shut up. Go away. I don't want to see your face anymore.

When I'm stuck in the shits, when I have done something that others may not approve of, or maybe when I haven't done anything wrong at all but people just want to chime in anyway, those are the kinds of questions people like to ask. Especially in moments when I need guidance, help with life decisions, when I'm sad, upset, or maybe when I'm having a prideful moment, or when I'm embracing a huge celebration, these are the kinds of questions I'm asked. And as soon as you are in a similarly-painful life-situation, these are the kinds of questions you're going to be asked, too. Count on it.

Each of those kinds of questions is one of those, "please, oh God please, please don't let that question come out of your mouth" questions. For me, these intrusively-painful questions rank right up there with the "I know exactly how you're feeling" statements. Which, of course, nobody really does, because everybody feels their own pain in unique, hidden ways. Even people who write books about their pain.

Bottom line, these are the kinds of questions, when I sense they're about to be asked (and why can't the persons I'm talking to just then be as psychic as I am at those moments), that I have the same reaction to each time:

Just. Please. Don't. Do. It.

Because ... Now, not only am I in a tough place, but I'm about to be asked the one question I will never have an answer to.

To anyone tempted to ask one of these kinds of questions of you (or me), know this: you're only causing more problems for the person you're talking to – presumably to a person you like, or maybe even love. You're making a sensitive situation even more difficult. More emotional. More time-consuming. Just more …

For example, when anyone asks me the question "what would your dad say?" it's a show-stopper. My mind is immediately consumed with so many questions. More questions you can probably imagine. And not just more questions. More possible answers. I am overwhelmed by the anxiety of disappointment and the sadness that comes along with any of those questions. So let's be honest: as much as I wish heaven had a hotline or a 1-800 number … it doesn't. Someone should work on that. A hotline, instant messaging, a mailing address, anything. Dad, God, Buddha, Santa Claus, are you listening?

October 20, 2017—*Sure sucks when the one person you want to call you can't. Heaven needs a hotline.*

Another showstopper is a moment like this. I was working at that ramen restaurant, talking to my customer who was oh so friendly and we were really hitting it off, talking about life. I mentioned I was traveling home to Ohio that weekend, which happened to be Father's Day weekend. That's a tough holiday for my family and me. However, the guy didn't know my situation, so he excitedly asked "Oh! Are you going home to surprise your dad for Father's Day?!" My face probably turned pale white in that moment and I stumbled over my words a little – I was caught very off guard, to say the least. Finally, I responded with "Oh no ... just going home for the week."

To my surprise, this man didn't stop. He must have judged my expression and reaction pretty hard because the next question he asked was brutal ... "Is your dad alive?"

Woah. Wow. Talk about my heart stopping. Again puzzled at this intrusion into my private life by a stranger, this time I responded with "Actually no he isn't." But he didn't get it. He then asked how young dad was when he died, and then preceded to tell me, "oh well I know exactly how Father's Day feels to you – I lost my dad, too."

Boom and boom. "Is your dad alive?" and "I know exactly how you're feeling!" just came out of his mouth. Ouch and ouch. Now, this man didn't originally know my story, but when he found out, he totally missed – or misread – the body language and other social cues that screamed out for him to stop talking about it. That was such a fun, unforgettable moment for me.

Another quick story. This one also occurred around Father's Day of the same year. I was also working at one of the pools in Las Vegas. I once again got to talking to my customers about life, and once again, one of them asked if I was going home for Father's Day ... this time I just said "Yes." I had learned my lesson from the night before. But my answer didn't work – instead, this response opened new doors.

After I said yes, this man, a total stranger, proceeded to tell me how young-minded his father was, how he was living life to the fullest, how he was still crossing things off my bucket list, how he was sick but had recovered and was better than he had ever been. He talked and talked about how grateful he was that his dad was alive; he even mentioned that his dad was seventy years old. Well … in the meantime, while I stood there blank-faced, I was crying behind my sunglasses, trying to hide the tears that were rolling down my cheeks and pretending it was just sweat.

Two very different scenarios. Both had initially good intentions, yet both left me feeling very hurt, shaken and uneasy, but for two very different reasons. Both I will never forget. Together, they taught me that anything you say can lead to someone feeling it's time to share a memory, or striking a chord you didn't know you hit.

Until then, until we have all the answers – or at least a hotline to heaven – here's a bit of advice. Advice that you know, you can take or leave. But especially if you already know the answers to any these questions because you know a backstory … try and not ask. Try very hard. However, if you don't know my backstory and the question just slips out of your mouth … it's not your fault, but don't – DO NOT – compound the problem. Instead, just run with the punches and do your best to recover. If you ask an innocent question, only to have someone give you a snarl of an answer in return, an answer that makes you uncomfortable … try to put yourself in their shoes for a moment. Imagine how awkward they feel. Then, drop it and move on to something safe, like the weather, or sports, or ... basically, anything that isn't at least potentially personal.

Instead, maybe don't ask those questions at all. Instead, just support people and cheer them on with statements like:

"You got this."

"Whatever you decide will work out."

"Follow your gut."

"Trust your instincts."

And especially, "I've got your back."

PHIL GLAZER RULES: "I DON'T WANT TO SEE YOUR FACE ANYMORE."

This rule isn't rudely intended. It's a comment that tells you that you and the person who said that just need a break. It's what you say when you don't want to start an actual argument. When you know this issue is no big deal – there are worse things that could have happened – but for the moment, you're still upset. When there is no need for confrontation, but one might just happen unless you just cool off and walk away. When you don't look at their face anymore ... not until you can look at it with a smile again.

Remembering Phil

"I could laugh for days about this line. Nikki struck out looking and couldn't find her glove in the dugout to run out to the field and your dad screamed "get out

there. I don't want to see your face anymore." We were maybe 13? Of course, Nikki was just scared and grabbed her glove and ran out there." – **Lauren Piechowiak**

WATCH AND LEARN

I don't know about you, but growing up, I heard the statement "watch and learn" from many people. Generally, as an answer when I asked, "how do I do this?" When I was young and wanted to be like my sister, "watch and learn." When I was learning how to do a "pop up slide" in softball, "watch and learn." When I was trying my damned hardest to do a real pull up, "watch and learn."

Now, I hear this when one of my girlfriends wants to go hit on a guy at the bar "watch and learn," or when a friend was trying to convince a teacher to give her a better grade in the class, or even when I'm working out because I have a very competitive group of friends. Basically, we learn-by-watching, by observing people as a way to "see how it's done." So we watch and we learn.

Recently, I've found a new reason for using this "watch and learn" concept. For me, it's reached another level because I am now trying to learn life lessons from this concept and not just

225

little lifestyle tips. I've discovered that when you go through real struggles and make real sacrifices in your life, those actions bring you to a state of watch-and-learn observation.

At least, this is what it did for me. When these times occur, I find that I now observe more and ask less – these are the times when I have learned important life lessons by how others interact – by how they handle certain situations. This is what I want to pass along to you, so watch and learn.

When you use your eyes rather than your mouth, you tend to learn a lot. But here's a warning: sometimes this can unintentionally bring about jealousy and envy. I know this because that is what "watch and learn" has done that for me. Or to me. However, there are other times when it can give me perspective, which comes when I realize my life isn't as bad as I'd made it out to be. Again, watch and learn.

As I grow and mature as an individual, I now find myself watching-and-learning day in and day out, especially when what I'm observing involves any sort of father-daughter or father-son interaction. When I'm confronted with one of those occasions, I get jealous. I admit it. I want what they have. A father. Yes, I know that I have a father – though I no longer have a physical version of "father" – but the knowledge that I still have the memory of dad does little to damp-down the flare-up of jealousy.

Now, of course, this observation state doesn't only happen when I'm confronted with one of those father-daughter situations. I am also a new, young, and still slightly naïve entrepreneur, which means I observe other new and young and maybe still slightly naïve entrepreneurs, looking for lessons. When I see them in action, I wonder how they have grown so fast and have become so successful and I haven't. So ... I "watch and learn," hoping to find hints as to why they are as successful as they are. The same kind of feeling goes with fitness (why are they more fit than I am?), bloggers (why do they write more consistently than I do?), friends who are married or in relationships (where's mine?), and the list goes on and on.

Unfortunately, sometimes the jealousy goes on and on, too. OK, jealousy happens, but it's not something any of us wants in our lives. So what do we do when we are jealous?

We pretend not to pay attention when in reality we are watching every move of the person who makes us feel jealous. We watch intently, all the while trying to justify that hawk-like observation because, somehow, we aren't really missing what we're actually missing with painful intensity. We watch to see if, in some way, we can replicate what we see others doing, even if it may not be the reality we're actually in. Sometimes we get sad, anxious, and envious.

Having your dad in your life for just your first 21 years feels like a tease. He and my mom had always been there to teach me my key values, my morals and discipline and, damn, do I think they did a hell of a job doing just that. Now the time is here though. The time has come for me to really apply all that I have learned over all those years – to become the grown-up dad and mom had always hoped I'd become. But now, half of that parent bond is missing. Not having dad, number one, put a lot of pressure on my mom, and, number two, it puts a lot of pressure on me to try and just not ask too many questions, but instead to trust that what I learned in those first twenty years, when coupled with the observing I am doing now, really is working.

We don't have all the answers, my mom doesn't, and, truth is, my dad didn't either. This is where the tease begins because our minds think that our parents did (or do) have all the answers. Once one or both of them are gone, we feel like we are missing out on something – and definitely someone. Frustrating as it sounds, the feeling of that tease never really goes away. Life leaves us wanting what we don't have, and never will.

There have been plenty of moments that have stopped me in my tracks. Each one of those made me snap into this observation mode – and for me, it's a kind of "people watching" mode, but on steroids. This feeling might arise while you're watching your best friend (my best friend) walk down the aisle with her dad on her wedding day, then dance with her dad all night long. You can't help feeling guilty, but you wouldn't be human if you also can't help feeling envious, too. She got those moments, ones that I would give up anything to have one day. Reality is harsh: for me, it'll never happen. So I watch to see what it's like, and I learn once again the harsh lesson that this person will never be me. Instead, we will honor my dad in some other sort of way. He will be with me on those big days, just not in the form I want him to be. Knowing you will never get to walk down the aisle, or have that special dance with your own dad is a hard feeling to swallow. Unfortunately, life doesn't give you a choice. You play the cards you're dealt.

Everyone has suffered some kind of loss, and everyone has their own issues. No matter how we might wish it were otherwise, those days come out of left field. For me, it's sitting in the stands at a baseball game on father's day, watching others "play catch with your dad on the field day." Then feeling envious that I will never play catch with my dad again. It's seeing someone's phone vibrate, then light up with "Dad" on the screen, knowing that I will never see that name on my phone again. It's seeing someone hug their dad knowing I had my last hug four years ago. Those are the "dad moments," as I like to call them, and they happen quite often. Those are the stop in your track moments I was talking about.

You may still have your dad and mom, and if so, you are blessed. Yet you've lost something near and dear to you, something that others have, and when you see them having what you've lost, you're going to feel pain, envy, jealousy. Trust me on this.

Now, I'm not the only one to have "dad moments", as I like to call them, though their loss might be something other than their dad. I observe other people, too, and I see them suffering – and I see them enjoying the simple things I'll never again experience. I people-watch everyone, and when I do, at least at times, I get a little envious of other people's lives. Traveling is a good example.

I love traveling, but I can't do nearly enough of it. Watching friends or travel-bloggers literally living out of a suitcase while doing the most extravagant things, I admit it, I get jealous.

Or seeing that "couple goals" on Instagram, even though the couple I'm observing probably isn't as happy as they look on social media, I sometimes get jealous. At other times, however, when I see what couples are up to, I am gratefully happy I am single and only have to worry about myself.

Looking at people with six-pack abs, perfect hair, you know, the ones who dress cute all the time, even when they aren't trying to, this can be enough to make me jealous. More often than not, when we watch others to learn, we also get in our own heads. We think we've failed at something, or we worry that we didn't live up to an expectation. When we observe, we often become harder on ourselves, if only because we think we are doing something wrong. We can harshly judge others because we think these things were either handed to them or that their lives have been too easy – they haven't had to live through the things we've been through.

That's what observing doesn't give you … a backstory. Their story. The huge missing puzzle piece that would show us why they are the way they are.

I remember one moment in particular. I was serving tables at a local restaurant and had a few regulars who lived in the building upstairs. In particular, I'm remembering a family of four. A mom, a dad, and two little daughters, just like my sweet family.

One day the dad came in with his two little girls. When they ordered the drinks, I offered "Chardonnay for your wife?" He replied with "No not today, this is a daddy-daughter date!" It was something so simple, but it struck a deeply painful chord in me. It was a moment of sadness, an "I miss that soooo much" moment, thankfully followed by a moment of, "at least I was lucky enough to have a dad that did this exact same thing, and truly enjoyed every moment of it just like my customer here."

For instance, in the fourth grade, we had a father-daughter dance at my school. Everyone dressed up. All of us little girls got to wear a little make-up, pretty dresses, and our dads bought us flowers. The dads dressed up in suits, and we got them a little boutonniere to wear on their chests. My dad was sick as a dog that year and was absolutely miserable the entire night. However, while I know this now, I never knew it back then. Being the man he was, dad sucked it up, put his suit on, slapped on a happy face and danced with me all night long. Truth is, he didn't really have to suck it up. He wouldn't have missed our father-daughter dance for the world. Although he felt like death, it wasn't death, and he knew the difference.

Those are the moments he wanted to cherish and wanted me to cherish, and he would do anything to make sure that happened – which it did. This man, my customer was doing just that with his daughters.

I'm not going to lie. I sat and watched that table for the rest of their little date. I was jealous and slightly envious, and frankly, that's okay. Mine was a normal reaction, mine were the emotions you feel when you lose something you don't want to lose. But while I was hurting for myself, I was still able to be happy for those little girls, and for their dad.

The truth is simple and painful: sometimes it's hard, in the moment, to see what's going on inside you. It's hard to watch what you once had ... or what you could have had. It's even harder to avoid being envious and jealous – we feel those emotions for a reason. When I see what's going on in me, what I try to do is shut out those harsh, negative emotions, replacing them with those wonderful memories I do have. Replacing bad feelings with the good times, good times that are real, good times that really happened.

In my case, I can't change my situation. I can't reincarnate my dad, I can't give him a second chance at life. So I watch. A lot. I learn through my vision. I watch body language and listen for knowledge. I do this to learn because I am at a slight learning curve to life deficit without him. Observing is a way that can lead to me becoming jealous and slightly stubborn, but it can also be a powerful tool for personal growth, and that's the goal behind this all.

Use watch-and-learn it to your advantage. Become a visual soul, and let those lessons be learned. Use those otherwise painful situations and people as resources to help you grow.

PHIL GLAZER RULES: LEARN FROM THOSE WHO HAVE EXPERIENCED MORE

Learning means taking in any advice that you can. My dad always answered questions. Not just from us but from anyone. If his experience could help someone he absolutely would share that experience with whoever asked. I have learned that you can't be afraid to ask questions. I've also learned that most people – when you are asking them about something they experience or something that has become an expert in – love to help. They feed off of it because it allows them to show that they have succeeded in what they are doing or have done, and it allows them to do so without bragging.

Learning from others is all about perfecting your craft, and there are so many ways of doing so. If I want to be a great dancer, I can't just dance all day, every day. I need to perfect every aspect of dance. That means watching others dance, watching videos, watching me. It's about asking questions whenever I am unsure. It's about reading books, on motivation, on other dances, on techniques. It's about working out. It's about eating well. It's about perfecting your craft by making your mind, body, and soul all join in together.

To become an expert at your craft, including the craft of life. Understand it. Learn from it. Change what needs to be changed. Doing all of this with courage. Do this and you won't spend any moments filled with regret, guilt, fear, or anger.

WHEN IT HAPPENS AGAIN

The scary thing about writing this book is knowing that I am going to have to go through all that I've lived through again one day. Tomorrow? Next week? In a year?

I don't know and frankly, I don't want to know. I'll cross my fingers, toes, and eyes, hoping that this doesn't happen to me again, not for years and years down the road. But I know I can do the wishing and praying thing, over and over and every day … until it inevitably happens again … because all that wishing and hoping and praying doesn't mean that next time things will work out in my favor. Nor will those efforts even give me any peace of mind. In fact, no matter how many wishes and hopes and prayers I try, they give me no peace of mind.

Hell, the whole reason for this book is because life did **not** work out in my favor the first time. I lost my dad, and that was horrible beyond words. But I still have another parent to lose. I have been heartbroken – not just once, or twice – but many times.

I've been heartbroken from an unwelcome variety of different circumstances, and am not looking forward to the next time that happens again. No matter how much I don't look forward to them, I know heartbreak will surely happen again. I have watched grandparents, roommates, and friends get sick – the kind of sick that makes you lose your hair, the kind of sick that makes doctors pump poison through your veins. Although they are all healthy right now, I know that someone else who's close to me will get sick ... and that the next someone else might not end up healthy at the end of their fight.

The thing is, despite the pain death brings, there is no shame in dying. There is no shame in getting sick. There is no shame in the fear we have when these things occur, or even when we anticipate them eventually occurring. The only shame is letting that death, that sicknesses, that fear control us. To let it ruin our spirits. To set our souls on lockdown. That's where the shame lies.

I'd like to think that going through these struggles once makes you more ready for the next time. I really would. But, having lived through them more than once, I don't believe that this is how it works. Instead, I believe everything in life is situational – that everyone and everything has a unique story. That for each one of those unique stories, everyone is allowed – in fact, everyone is required – to feel how they need to feel while the shit hits the fan. Everyone handles life's moments a little differently, and as we grow from experience, we even handle the same "kind" of situation differently. Every time. With that said, I believe that these struggles will never actually get any easier. Why? Because life isn't easy. It's not supposed to be easy. It never will be easy. Enough said.

I know that is a brutally honest statement. That "life isn't easy, and it's not supposed to be easy" gives us the chills, and clenches us in the pits of our stomachs. It makes us want to roll our eyes, just a little. When we say out loud that life isn't supposed to be easy, when we try to accept those words, we have to cringe, at least a little because, secretly, we want it to be easy.

If you feel that way, don't worry, you're not alone. There are times to this day when I wish it was frickin' easy too, folks. At times, I wish I could snap my fingers and have someone feeding me grapes and waving me down with palms – you know, the easy type of life. Then … I think back to reality. What has "easy" ever gotten me? Nothing. Nada. Zip.

The good things don't come easy. The good things – the best things – come from the hardest moments, from those working your ass off moments. Good things come from the definitely not easy, not-someone-feeding-me-grapes-on-the-beach moments.

I have some experience with struggle, death, and heartbreak, but I am still going to grieve, miss, cry, and be angry the next time something painful like that happens. Again. Realizations like this make my stomach churn, make my palms sweaty – they make my mind roam to places I don't like going. Knowing that the bullshit never actually stops is cold comfort indeed. Life keeps on producing that bullshit regardless of whether we think we are ready for it or not. I say that I am scared when I write this because I am, but life demands that we all need to be brave.

September 13, 2017—When you're able to honestly say that you're grateful for life's bull shit you know you're maturing and ready for the next pile of shit.

The truth is all of those struggles, all of those bad days, all the heartbreak, the butterflies – and even the good days – they will all happen again. Not in exactly the same way, but close enough. And they will happen when you least expect them, too, just like they did every other time they hit. I have learned while going through life, that Morton Salt is right. Chances are that when it rains, it pours.

When things are going good, really good, almost too good, that's when you need to prepare yourself for the worst. But don't let that fear or anticipation – or the next round of heartbreak – defeat you. It just means that it's once again time to embrace the moments. All of the moments. The good, the bad and the ugly moments. It's time to continue to be brave, friend.

No matter how many times you go through something, each new time gives you a new chance to triumph once again. A new chance to learn something new. A new chance to add another victory to your life. When something bad happens, your mind will expand. Your wisdom will brighten and – although it may not feel like it at the time – your life will continue on. If you can find the beauty in those moments, you will become one of life's warriors, triumphing over the pain that life gives you. That life will continue to give you. So be ready to show these moments who is boss. You're the boss. Then you'll own those moments. You'll win, even when you feel like losing when you feel like you're drowning. You'll win.

The only thing I can say to you – and to me – is good luck to us. Good luck when things get ugly. Good luck when your heart breaks, when you suddenly remember that heartbreak isn't just a turn of phrase. It actually hurts. A lot. Good luck when dumbfoundedness comes back into your life, when you feel a little bamboozled. Good luck when you thought you would be prepared for this day, but actually, you're not prepared at all – because who can ever truly be prepared for a day like that? So "good luck and break a leg, kid."

Remember this: you made it once and – despite how you feel – you will make it again. Today is a victory regardless of how tough it may have been to get here, to this exact moment in your life. You are a champion because you've been through it and guess what? You are still here, here to read this book, here to go about your day no matter how painful it may be. You're still a champion, no matter how you're feeling right this minute.

Be proud. Because, although I don't know you, I want you to know that I am proud of you, because you're a survivor, and you'll come through this triumphant. Hold your chin up. But hold it up because you want to, not because someone else is told you to. Not even me. Give yourself a round of applause. Because, shit, you deserve it. Eat some chocolate. It'll make you feel a hell of a lot better. Hold up a trophy. I mean, why not? Pat yourself on the back, because you're kicking ass and taking names. Pound your chest with your fists and scream a little – showing that confidence will release an animal inside of you that you didn't know existed.

Recognize that you've been through the unbearable and that you've "beared it." Maybe barely, but you did bear it. So you will again. And again. And, probably, again. You'll win the day, and on that day, you'll smile and say (under your breath), "I'm okay." When you're able to honestly say that you're grateful for life's bullshit, you'll know you're finally maturing, finally ready for the next pile of shit. Then, "when it happens again" happens you, despite your past experience, you really won't be ready, you won't be happy – but you will live. And live through it. Again.

On the day that this happens, again. I'm allowing you to say this: "I know today kind of sucks, it's a shitty day. That thing, it happened – I knew it would happen – but I didn't want to believe it would actually happen. But it did, and I will get through it." Say that, even though you may not believe it. Then say it again, and again, until you do believe it because it is true.

I am telling you that, on this day, to not necessarily have a good day – because you won't, because you can't – but instead, just have a day. Don't beat yourself up. Let yourself feel for a moment. Stay alive. Keep winning. It'll get better soon. One day. Until then, today, just have a day.

Secure and safe isn't always secure and safe.

I would say that many people move and travel to the United States because it is "safe and secure." It has opportunity. It has freedom. Safe? How many mass shootings and attacks have we now had? Secure? What is the unemployment rate? How many people need jobs? How many children go to bed hungry? Are you promised insurance or social security? Not so safe and secure, huh? This isn't new in America. Ben Franklin said, "those who would give up essential Liberty, to purchase a little temporary Safety, deserve neither Liberty nor Safety."

RIDE OR DIES

"Stay away from negative people, they have a problem for every solution." - Albert Einstein

"Ride or Die" was originally a biker term; now it means that, for any given problem, someone is only really close to you if they will Ride any problems out with you, or Die trying. This section is about those family and friends who chose to be my real friends, to ride or die with me through the most painful moments of my life. It's also about those who decided to watch from the sidelines, rather than to ride. Or die.

A Ride or Die person is someone who is willing to ride out anything with you, for you, and beside you. They will ride alongside you, or they will die trying to do so. A ride-or-die needs to be a mutual relationship. The ride-or-die friends who stand by you, without flinching, these are your ride or dies, and you need to be ready to ride or die with them, too. They won't flinch through your tough times, and when the tough times hit them, you won't flinch either. A true ride or die exists, when the shit hits the fan, you are each other's "go-to person." You will be by each other's side through the thick and the thin. And worse.

***

First things first, and as those two lead-in paragraphs should make clear, this section was extremely hard for me to write. I had to think about it, draft it, write it, re-write it, then re-write it again a few million more times. At times, this section gave me anxiety, it made me emotional. It even gave me some of my sassiest moments. As I wrote it, I was worried about people's feelings – then suddenly, I stubbornly only worried about my own feelings, especially the ones that had been hurt by people, especially people I'd trusted my entire life. So I went back and forth between wanting to put this in the book – no matter how painful or who it hurt.

In the end, this section of the book is an essential part of my process – my writing process, and my personal process. This "stuff" that happened in this section is still happening. I said up-front that I would be completely open and honest with y'all – if you've read this far, we're now friends – and with my friends, I stick to my word. Ride or die, I do my best to hold up my end of that bargain. In this case, this means me being open, honest, and vulnerable, even while addressing some of the most difficult issues I've lived through – and live with still. That means I am holding up my end of our friendship-pact bargain

In this section, I'm not going to apologize for what actually happened in my life. When "stuff" like this happens to you, follow my example here. When life tries to destroy you, you shouldn't apologize for how you deal with it. Your real friends will understand, and everybody else doesn't count. Don't focus on the "shoulds" or expectations imposed on you by family members and friends. Instead, just focus on what and who gives you the support you need in a crisis, and the happiness that you need in the rest of your life.

I am going to say right now to some of my family members, you may not want to read what's in these next few pages. What follows is an open and honest summary of what you have done in my life, for my life – and, in some cases – to my life. If you feel you've got nothing to be ashamed of, by all means, continue reading on. If you do, but if you nonetheless hang in here, then maybe you'll learn a thing or two. But despite what I just said, this isn't a section I wrote so that I could point fingers at anyone. No, this is my honest attempt to describe what is an essential part of everyone's process – or it should be – at some point in his or her lives. I have written this just to show my readers, who are by now my friends, that "stuff" happens whether we like it or not. It's how you deal with that "stuff" which makes all the difference.

Certain events surrounding my dad's death and its aftermath brought out some people's true colors. I learned that some family members can become toxic. Toxic to us, and to others. I learned that toxic people use gossip to fuel their fire, and that gossip-fueled fires just keep getting bigger and bigger, hotter and hotter.

However, despite the pain they can cause, not all toxic people have bad intentions. Some of them can still be caring and loving people. Typically, the caring and loving they exhibit in their lives is selfishly intended. These people exist because their wants and needs have to be the focus of their lives. If they can achieve this center-of-attention by being outwardly loving and caring, so be it. However, they aren't willing to compromise – that's something they expect others to do. Basically, these people aren't inherently bad people, but they aren't good people, either, especially not for those of us suffering through loss or crisis. Once you figure out who they are and what they really want, you'll realize that you will live a better life without them rather than with them.

Think about this. Life is hard enough without toxic people in your life. It's hard enough just dealing with good people, let alone with people who live, not to build you up, but to tear you down. No matter how much you care about these toxic people, you'll be better off – in this case – if you care more about yourself, especially when you're in a crisis.

Furthermore, you've got to understand that sometimes, there is a point of no return. Toxic people will do something you might eventually forgive, but you never will actually forget. So, as hard as it may be, know that it is okay to remove yourself from a situation – in essence, to remove toxic people from your life, no matter how "close" they are on the family tree. You've got to do this in order to make a better environment for yourself. In this case, you've got to become your own "ride or die" friend and ride into the rest of your life strong enough to say no to toxic family members and (so-called) friends.

***

When life decides to shake things up, when significant life-altering changes occur, your life dynamics typically change, too. Relationships change. People change. Families change. At these times, you tend to gravitate towards the people you think should be there for you.

The ones that are supposed to stand unflinchingly.

The ones who you think should carry some loyalty to you.

The ones you always thought were your ride or dies.

The problem with all those statements is the fact that I said "should." Unfortunately, this is another one of those "shoulds" that goes along with what seems like natural, reasonable expectations. Except that having a "should" is always a bad idea, because it creates the potential for a life-altering disaster. Not intending to offer yet another contradiction, you shouldn't have "shoulds" for other people. No matter how much you know they "should" be there for you, being human, they tend to disappoint you. Usually at the worst time. Womp, womp, womp.

It doesn't matter if these "should" relationships are ten years deep or even if they are life-long bonds of kin and friendship. It doesn't matter if you carry the same bloodline or the same name, or even shared the same womb. Even your most cherished ride or dies don't always and forever stay your ride or dies, even when (or especially when) you and they both know they "should." However, lifetime links aren't necessary – sometimes your ride or die turns out to be the person you just met yesterday. A new friend transforms overnight into a person you feel you've known your entire life. A newly-inducted family member who doesn't flinch through shaky times.

Having lived through my worst of times, I've learned that one of two things can happen during these awful new "change" phases in your life. You either become closer to, or you move further apart from the people you always believed were your ride or dies. Make that "so-called" ride or dies. Growing up, I quickly learned Phil Glazer's Rule Number One: family comes first. Family is everything. Family is where loyalty, love and kindness lie. Unfortunately, as I learned the hard way, when my dad died, family loyalty wasn't exactly a two-way street. My family, the people I thought were supposed to be – who "should" be – my ride or dies, some of them failed me all the time, and all of them failed me at least once. At times, we all failed each other. In saying this, I am not trying to cast blame on anyone.

It was during this failure when I really learned that family does come first – it must come first. However, and this is probably Phil Glazer's Rule Number Two: "family" doesn't need to be biological. I actually heard – and learned – this from a huge male figure in my life. My mentor. He became family to me, and in doing so he became a huge influence on me. This began almost the moment I first moved to Las Vegas. He was one of the men I have talked about a lot in this book, and for good reason. He's the one who preached that family "are the ones who stand by you without flinching." This is what my mentor does, and has done, for me. When my dad died, this man was there for me far more than were those who, by ties of blood, were actually members of my "family".

That's when I learned this lesson was right – family is not defined as people who share your bloodline. Real family members are people you choose to share the most intimate parts of your life with you and to be a solid wall when times get really tough. Real family members are charter-members of your own ride-or-die club. The members of my non-biological family give me comfort, because regardless of the ride or dies who should have been there but instead chose to flee – or worse, to turn on you – with the volunteer family members who made the choice to be there for you and with you, you're never family-less. It's your choice, but now you know that at least you don't have to be family-less.
***

Over time after my dad died, family members on his side, the Glazer side of the family started to move further apart from me, Nikki and my mom, and when it hurt too much, we returned the favor. At first, this shift in loyalties caught me off guard. It upset me. While I've come to terms with it, this situation has continued to frustrate me. I know that if dad were still here, he wouldn't let this happen and that my late grandfather would also be very disappointed. They'd be the voice of reason, the ones who'd try to heal the breach and bring us all closer. I promise you that if anyone else in our extended family lost a piece of their own immediate family, dad would never let this kind of distancing happen.

Of course, this painful rift didn't happen to anyone else. It happened to us – me, mom and Nikki. If he was here to protect his girls, we can't be sure what my dad's action really would be. But we have a strong sense that, in fact, he wouldn't allow people to feel un-included the way we do now.

This pulling-apart has been both stressful and eye-opening. It has given me a new perspective on what family actually means and – in my case – who my family really is. Feelings have been hurt, not once, not twice, but more times than we can count. Family parties have been awkward. Conversations have become boring, superficial and painful. Phone calls are getting far and few between. Which brings me back to what I said earlier about the difference between forgive and forget. Someday I may choose to forgive the price, my mom, Nikki and I have paid when some of dad's family challenged us, but I can't imagine forgetting what they've done.

***

I find it's strange that when world-wide tragedies happen, the world comes together. I talk about this a lot. That in those times of the most horrific of crises:

Love overcomes hate.

Love overcomes the evil.

Love overcomes even those with the darkest minds and the most stubborn of hearts.

In our humanity, we hurt for people we don't even know; we reach out across town or across the country – or even across the world – to empathize for and with one another.

On October 1, 2017, Las Vegas, my home, experienced modern America's deadliest mass shooting. A man with a lot of guns fired into a crowd of 22,000 people. He killed 58 people. He injured 546 people. I live ten minutes from where this occurred on the strip. Just an hour before it occurred I was on the strip at a hockey game. Minutes after the shooting I drove to the strip to pick up a good friend and roommate who was at the festival.

Seemingly within minutes, the entire Vegas community came together. Someone coined the term "Vegas Strong," and behind the banner #VegasStrong, we all came together.

However, while the world reached out to Vegas in shared horror and concern, two people on my dad's side of the family reached out to make sure I was okay. Two. You know who you are and I thank you for that. When a shooting took place right outside my door, two of my dad's immediate family members reached out to make sure I was okay. Friends reached out, some new some old. But just two Glazer's.

Others later claimed that they "waited" for me to post my status on social media. Why? How much trouble is it to send a text? Others later claimed that it didn't even occur to them to call, text, or reach out. Here I was in the place where this mass shooting happened, inundated with concern from people who called and texted and emailed, people – some of whom I haven't seen or talked to in ages. They were here for me. But where was my family?

In the aftermath of the shooting, I've asked myself, if people come together in the wake of a tragedy or disaster thousands of miles away, why has my family, especially my dad's family, the Glazer family, cast me out? What caused this part of my family to separate in the months and years after that awful death in our family? What was it about losing one of our own that tore us asunder. Was it the fact that we lost the glue that held the Glazers together?

The initial and obvious answer is that no one and no family is perfect. Another answer is that there is no guidebook, no "Ten rules for what to do when a family member is involved in a mass-casualty disaster" they can turn to.

No matter how personal the pain, I have to admit they did not fail on their own.   When people share an intimate tragedy, such as the death of a beloved family member, each survivor has his or her own issues-of-loss to deal with. Some have lost a father. Others have lost a husband, a son, a brother, a nephew, or a cousin. Some lost their best (family) friend, while others suddenly realize it's now too late to heal a breach that never should have been allowed to fester.

It's not possible to foresee what will happen when hardships or painful losses occur. You can't know in advance:

How each person will react.

Whose feelings will be hurt.

How each of us will grieve, or that we each grieve so differently.

It's unfortunate, the way things sometimes work out, but realizing the truth can also provide a sense of relief. Our differing reactions to loss proves who's there for you when you need them the most, and who's going to rush out for an unscheduled two-week all-expense vacation to LaLa Land as soon as they hear the news. Experience, no matter how painful, proves who has selfish motives or self-focused feelings. It proves who you want to surround yourself with. Who is really family, regardless of shared blood or family trees.

I thought family was supposed to be at the top of your list of your ride or dies. That regardless of the less-than-positive things which can and do happen in a relationship with a "supposed to be ride-or-die," the fights, the disagreements, the arguments that you've had, the hurt feelings you cause or receive, if the shit hits the fan, you'll forget all this and pull together. Like family. That you'll always (eventually) heal those wounds and together, you'll come out on top. Those are the rules. You're *supposed* to always mend, to heal, to come back together. To be a happy family again.

Unfortunately, that's the Hollywood fairytale ending talking again. That's what happens in all those Jennifer Aniston/Sandra

253

Bullock/Drew Barrymore feel-good movies. That may still be some people's perception of reality – it might even be your perception of life – but it's not mine, not any longer.

The people I now call family are my real ride or dies, friends. These are the people in my life I'd stop (or start) anything, pick up or drop off anything and do anything for, to or with. The people whose lives I share with no boundaries, no barriers, no limitations. Who I'll be there for when the shit hits their fans.

However ... don't ever expect people to do the same. Hope they will. Pray they will. But don't expect they will. That's just a recipe for disaster and hurt feelings. Just because you're a ride-or-die for them doesn't mean they'll be a ride-or-die for you. And, when your crisis hits, you may just discover that somebody you thought of as no more than a casual friend was actually a ride-or-die who is there for you.

As kids, we were all taught the Golden Rule, that we're supposed to treat people the same way you want to be treated. But actually living by the Golden Rule, that's not what happens in the real world, but you have to grow up to discover this. When you mature, that gap between what you were taught and what you experience in life defines the why and the how of having expectations for other people.

You know what they "should" do – frequently, they know this "should," too. Still, too often, people you thought you could count on tend to not live up to your Golden Rule expectations.

When that happens, you're left behind, in the dust and ashes, disappointed and confused and hurting even worse.

It happens to the best of us because we believe in the best of them. At least I do. Innocent until proven guilty means giving people the benefit of the doubt. We believe in those people we once thought were forever friends, forever family, our own personal ride or dies. However, there are times when these people leave us empty. Somewhat numb. Somewhat disappointed. Somewhat hurting and bleeding. Sometimes they come up a little short, and – let's be honest – sometimes maybe we do. While I've been critical here about those who let me down at the worst moment in my life, I think that's the case in my situation too. I've let others down who were counting on me. Pointing fingers just makes a bad situation worse.

Instead, you have a decision you have to make.

How long do you try to make a painful situation work?

How long do you let people hurt you before you pull back and protect yourself?

How long do you let the stress build before you have to blow it (and them) off?

How long do you keep the weight on your shoulders before you either drop it or it crushes you?

Eventually, you have to make a choice. Once you do, your life-burden becomes a lot lighter. You start to float again. Your mind gets right. At first this feeling, it kind of makes you feel guilty, because hey, no matter how badly they let you down, they are your family. I did. I felt and (at times) still feel guilty because I want to want to walk away from what I once thought would be my forever family.

My family, we've had our challenges. Some issues we've finally resolved, some may never be resolved, and some are no longer worth the weight crushing our spines, hurting our hearts, and disappointing our minds. Time to just let those go.

We've been uninvited to family functions or questioned – "what are you doing here" – when we just showed up. Well, we were invited, weren't we? Or if not, hey, we're family – since when did we need an invitation?

We've had our own family members talk about us behind our backs. For example:

"She's moving to fast."

"She shouldn't be doing that."

"She clearly doesn't care." Oh, I am sorry, I understand …

"My mom, my sister and I were supposed to sulk without complaining for our entire lives? Got it."

"You want us to be alone, in punishment for some un-named sin? Got it."

"Wait, I forgot, is that what dad would have wanted? Or is this family tragedy all about you?"

"Let me get this straight: dad would have wanted us to never be happy again. okay, my bad. I'll get right to work on it."

Since dad died, we've had family members (mostly on his side of the family) bullying us and calling us names. Like

"Entitled," which means, "to believe oneself is deserving of special treatment or privileges." If, by this definition, my mom asking all of us to try and maintain a family, even though my dad is no longer with us, then you're telling us that's what you call entitled. Okay, family, we'll go with that. As some decided to act in this way others decided to step up their game. People like my Uncle Joe, who I've become closer with since my dad left us. He even decided to honor my dad at his wedding with his baseball mitt and create a *livin' the dream* mural on the wall in his living room.

These painful family pills are tough to swallow. To allow this kind of thing to keep happening, for years on end, is even worse. Finally, after absorbing these somewhat heartbreaking moments as the price you pay for "family," you begin to realize that nobody likes conflict, but sometimes you've got to work things out. Just because you don't want to start a confrontation (because who wants that), and just because you're willing to strap on a pair and sweep those hurtful comments under the rug, doing so eventually makes the damage worse. Ignoring a cheap shot once is an act of maturity. Twice, maybe three times, and you've got the patience of a saint. But to keep doing it will only damage not just the relationship, but what lives inside you.

This happens because all that sniping becomes a constant build up. The weight continues to get heavier. It grows weeds. It develops mold.

Real life example, how do you think mold forms? It's formed when something is left untouched for too long. Mold reproduces through tiny spores. Spores that are invisible to the naked eye. They float through the air and land on moist surfaces (like tears), then mold grows. Our family got moldy. The hurtful things weren't happening in front of us. They weren't visible to our naked eyes. They were, however, floating into us through the mouths and ears of others, through gossip and sniping. Finally, those spores of hate latched on to anyone willing to be filled into the latest moldy drama. Mold is one of the best one of the best and worst ways to describe these relationships.

When you lose someone precious in your life, both you and other people start pointing fingers, saying things like "What would/could/should be happening if this person was still here?

In the end, reacting from pain and loss, from fear and anger, we all wind up pointing fingers at one another. The problem is, by doing so, we have each made life harder for one another. When we lost my dad, we also lost people we thought would be in our lives forever. It's hard to come to grips with the fact that it's really okay – and maybe better than just okay – if they aren't in our lives any longer. But it really is, in fact, okay.

It's actually okay that they have to leave you now.

It's really okay if you have to walk away because you feel taken advantage of.

It's honestly okay if you feel like lines have been straddled, then crossed.

It is indeed okay if you feel that everyone else thinks they know what's best for you, instead of them believing that you know what's best for you.

None of those "okay" situations is easy to take, but that doesn't change the fact that life-changes breed more life-changes. More important, those new changes are not automatically changes for the worse. Some are changes for the better, even if it doesn't feel like that, not just yet.

You're better off with two or three people who are really ride or die friends for life, than you are with twenty or thirty family members who, by gossip and sniping, by arrogance and ignorance, turn a bad situation into something infinitely worse. When you have the choice, choose the ride or dies every time. You might feel sorry sometimes, but you won't be wrong.

September 27, 2016 – Some guy told me you need a dose in your life of people who can shed more light and wisdom on you than you can shed on yourself. People that challenge your mind. I guess I'll keep listening to him. -- life lessons by the man.

October 24, 2017—The reason you shouldn't have expectations for others is because they typically disappoint you. Peace out to those that serve no purpose.

PHIL GLAZER RULES: GLAZER STRONG

Being Glazer Strong is about being proud of your name, the name that you can put across the back of your jersey. The name you use to sign life-altering documents. The name that goes down in family histories and adorns family trees. Being Glazer Strong is about being proud of where you came from and where you are going in life. To be proud of and to support those who carry and hold onto that same name. Being Glazer Strong means kicking ass and taking names. It means being a believer in kindness. It means defending love over hate. It means having an open heart and an open mind.

Showing strength comes in many different forms. Strength is not just having a hard exterior. Strength means having a soft interior. True strength comes from within. It comes from experiences, memories, and wisdom. It comes from fear and failure. It comes from victories and becoming champions of life. It comes from having a pure heart – and a soul that is willing to grind. It's being sensitive when you need to, but being a savage at other times. It's having the perfect combination of softness to your morals and hardness to your values.

Growing up, I never wanted to get rid of this Glazer name of mine. Now more than ever, I don't want to. Glazer is a direct relation to my dad. It's what directly connects me to his legacy. Being a lady with well-defined plans for the future, I know that one day I have the option to take my future husband' name. That marriage will be a very exciting moment, but it will also be a very sad moment.

This name, Glazer, has defined me for my entire life. It has become a legacy name. It's made me who I am. It's given me several nicknames that have become special memories for me and has given me an excuse to eat as many doughnuts as I want. "Why?" you ask? With nicknames such as "donut," "glaze," or "glazed donut," you're allowed to do whatever you want when it comes to a dozen doughnuts.

Having no brothers means the Glazer family name will not get carried on. Yet no matter what my future holds, I know that the Glazer name will always be with me. If I truly want to keep it then I can – times are different. However, unlike my learnings from so many other Phil Glazer Rules, which I just absorbed growing up, this is one conversation I actually did have with my dad.

When I told him I was keeping Glazer forever, he replied with, "Uh no, you aren't. That's not traditional." Fair enough I guess? Not the answer I wanted, but at least I do know where he stands. That would be the day the last man in my life makes me his and the day the first man in my life has to give up his little girl. The one day I take my last love's name but also the day I take away my first love's name.

Bittersweet.

I believe that being Glazer Strong sticks with you for life. Regardless of what or who I become, regardless of the name on my bills or the name my credit cards say, my heart will always be a

Glazer, my blood will always be Glazer Strong. I believe that *you* can have this kind of strength – and you can do so without being a Glazer. You do it by being loyal, loving, and kind. If you have a big heart that you want to share, you are destined to be Glazer Strong.

Remembering Phil

*"Feet planted, shoulders back, chest out. Glazer strong, Glazer Proud.." – **Joe Glazer***

PHIL GLAZER RULES: FAMILY COMES FIRST

My dad was overjoyed whenever he talked about family. His proudest moments were the ones in which he was talking about us, "his girls." I will never forget when my dad would talk about going to his clients' houses to discuss their life insurance plans. When my dad had to fill out paperwork, instead of having a dull moment in the middle of the sales process, he would pop in one of my dance solo videos for them to watch. He would then do a little "dad bragging" about us. Talking about us definitely put a smile on his face, and their smile typically followed.

Family always came first. My parents both worked hard in their careers, but when it came to softball games, dance competitions, track meets, geography bees, or leaving Friday night bowling in a snowstorm because their 16-year-old daughter locked her keys in her car while she was at work (whoops, sorry Dad). Family always was his priority.

I am very fortunate with the family that I have been given and the relationships that I have with them. Of course, for me, it is easy to say that family is my number one and that I value the heck out of it.

As I have gotten older, I've learned that "family" does not have to be limited to biological family members. "Family" does not need to be part of my Glazer bloodline. It does not need my mother's maiden name or to be Polish and German (it does help if you like pierogis though).

Family means love and safety. Family means being prideful and grateful. Family includes the people who you have the best connection with, the ones who you can share your brightest and darkest moments with. The ones who you can tell exactly how it is even if (or especially if) it's not exactly what you know they want to hear.

It's the people who will be there for you night or day and who you'll do the same for. The people who show up at your apartment when you just found out your dad died. The people who take you to get a bottle of Ketel to help cheer you up, the ones who leave college to drive back to their hometown to be there for you, and so many others who know exactly where you are in my heart. Whoever those people are, biological or not, that's what we call family.

January 19, 2015 — It's not about strength in numbers it's about being Glazer Strong.

Remembering Phil

"My cousin Mariah's wedding was the first large family function that Mindy was a part of. At this time, we had been together for long enough for me to know that she was "the one". I think Dad knew this, too. With that said, we were unsure how comfortable everyone was with the two of us being together. We went to the wedding together, with her as my plus one. We sat next to each other at the ceremony, ate dinner together, and once the dancing started, we stood to the side together and watched everyone dance. Inevitably, there would be a couples dance, and we already discussed that it would be best we not do it. The couples song starts, and we stay put. Thirty seconds go by, and Dad walks over and reaches for Mindy's hand. (Possibly one of the most adorable things, ever.) They go out to the floor, and proceed to slow dance, smile, and laugh. Shortly after, my Uncle Dennis walks over to me to dance. (Again, super cute gesture, since he sees me standing by myself.) This only lasts a few seconds, because Dad taps Dennis's shoulder and asks HIM to dance, leaving Mindy and I as dance partners! At this point I realize that

he had likely schemed this whole thing in order to make us feel more comfortable together. This made my night, and continues to be one of my favorite memories of him. After the wedding, I ask Mindy what Dad and her talked about when they were dancing. He told her: "No matter what, you will always be part of the family." At that point of our relationship, his confidence and validation meant everything."—**Nikki Glazer Stoicoiu**

"It was all about family, all the time." – **Dan Stewart**

"Family always comes first. His love for your mom, for Nikki, and for you shined through every day. He could not have been more proud of all his girls." –**Jean DePalma**

"There was a period of my life, between my parents divorcing and when my mom re-married where I didn't have a strong male influence in my life. Phil filled that role for a long time whether he knew it or not. He taught me how to throw a baseball and helped me break in my first mitt. He helped me buy my first car and get my first real job, then another job. He taught me how to manage my money and fed me my first jalapeno pepper at age nine. He only dropped me on my head once as a child

when we were playing in the living room, so what more could you ask from an uncle, I looked up to him, I just wanted to be around him I emulated him, but the truth is I just wanted to impress him. His opinion is still very important to me and I will continue to try to live my life in a way he would approve of. – **Jacob Sutherland**

SMALL VICTORIES

When you wake up every day it's important to always look for the **small victories** in your day. That when you wake up and your crabby, or tired, maybe sad you can take a chance on your feelings and look at your day in a new perspective. These small, sometimes teeny tiny victories have the potential to create large opportunities. You have to understand that the biggest victory we carry is the fact that we have a life to live and that the best part of living is to actually go out and live. Too many people live like they are already dead, especially after losing something or someone precious to them. These are the people that just exist on this planet or even more so just exist somewhere unknown in their minds.

One of my biggest lessons from losing my dad – one compounded by two painfully-failed relationships (each of them, at their peak, was, in my heart and mind, "the one") is this: I plan on living until the day I die. Do you? Do you value your life? Do you embrace the littlest of victories, do you live for reaching out for the dorkiest of dreams enough to actually live through them? You may say so, but I kind of think I should be the judge of that.

The most important moments for my dad were: Having conversations about our days with us when we got home from school or work. Playing catch in the backyard. Having a family breakfast on Sunday mornings. These were the small victories in life he aimed to achieve each and every day.

Chances are you have your own small victories, though you may not realize them. These could include:

Receiving even the slightest compliment from someone whose opinion you value

Getting to work without having to fight traffic

Finding five dollars in your pants pocket

Getting a front row parking space at the mall

Getting ____ (fill in your own small victories that give you a feeling of success)

In my many everything happens for a reason moments in life I have found the smallest victories to help me reach the end of the night without wanting to rip out all the hair in my head. On days I missed my dad more and saw a baseball, victory. Or maybe it was a cardinal in a tree, victory. For sure if it was flickering lights, victory. Those were all moments that brought me closer to my dad, they were small but mighty. During breakups, nights that I didn't wake up at 4 am from a dream with them in it, victory. Mornings I didn't wake up thinking about them instantly with a pit in my stomach, victory. Days I had an appetite to eat, victory. After I had spinal surgery, putting my pants on by myself, victory. Making breakfast without help, victory. Typing my damn shoes, victory. When we grieve things we lost or had to give up, that idea of sacrifice in life, you have to find these small victories in order to win the day. To make it. Sometimes just to get by.

These kinds of moments are the small victories in your day – they truly change the course of your day, and if you let them, the course of your life. They are like Mighty Mouse, small but powerful. Small victories help guide your day – sometimes they can turn your entire day around, especially a bad day. If you're having one of those crappy *I slept like shit, I'm hungry, I need to shower, and I didn't have time for breakfast* days, start looking for small victories that turn them around.

Friday, January 12 at 6:59PM. *– A text message to my Mom during the 2018 college cheer nationals. "The girls got second place for their game day routine (they absolutely should have won, they hit and did amazing) but I've been talking to them about small victories this last week leading up to nationals and a few of the girls came up to me after awards and were like "we don't care* *about first ..." picked up their silver medals and said "small victories Alexa, small victories" with huge smiles on their faces. I'm making a difference Mom." This moment for me literally made my heart sing because people are actually taking what I have to say and running with it. This team hasn't stopped saying small victories since the moment we began speaking on them. Their lightbulbs went off and I am so grateful for teaching and learning moments like these. This moment was humbling yet so satisfying.*

OUR PERFECTLY IMPERFECT LIVES

"Never perfect -- always genuine" – Unknown

Sometimes we wish we could erase all the bad stuff from our lives. That we could see our lives with the only the good parts. You know, the parts of our lives that people see on our social media timeline. The "couple goals," the wanderlust adventures, the "I woke up like this" feelings, all perfectly edited, all presented for all to see in perfectly captured candid selfies. Basically, we want to live our perfect lives instead of having to live our actually quite imperfect lives.

Perfectly imperfect

Being perfectly imperfect is embracing life's personal downfalls. Embrace your flaws. Embrace your authenticity. Embrace the imperfections that aren't society's standard. Perfect you, for you.

Real life, the life that exists without the careful polishing we put into our social media timelines, is unedited.

It's raw

It's life with no makeup

It's wearing sweatpants instead of designer jeans

It's standing there before God and everybody with tears streaming down your face

It's arguments with boyfriends

It's mental instability

It's double chins

It's breakouts

Real life is ugly. Well, at least parts of it are. Those are the parts we don't want to show anyone. Living life, we want to bask in moments of bliss – and that, most definitely, is all we want to show other people. But that raises the question: since everybody is flawed, why are we so afraid to show the world all of us? The good, the bad and the ugly. The honest to goodness human in us.

Sometimes, especially when life isn't heading where we want it to go, we have to fake it till we make it. We have to tell ourselves – despite all the evidence to the contrary – that our little lives actually are perfect. However, when you fake it, you have to force yourself to believe what you're faking and to believe it pretty hard – all the way down to the core. Otherwise, you come off as confused and unconfident – or worse, self-delusional.

After a break up of mine, as a kind of therapy, I began traveling. A lot. Even as I traveled, I also started my *"Livin' the Dream"* movement (http://www.alexaglazer.com/the-movement/). I began spreading positivity to anyone and everyone who I could find. I wasn't necessarily feeling this positivity in my own life at the time, but just for this moment, that's a minor detail. As I traveled, as I shared positivity and promoted my *Livin' the Dream* movement, I posted videos, pictures, and blogs that showed – that proved – that I was living the life ... or, in more exciting and motivating terms, I was *Livin' the Dream.*

I was knocking things off my bucket list right and left, going to places I've never been and surrounding myself with the best of friends and family. I looked happier than I'd ever been in my entire life – and although at first, it wasn't the truest happiness – the more I lived it, the more it became that.

Wow! Alexa (I showed the world) is handling this whole breakup thing with such grace, maturity, and ease. She's coping with loss and what others might consider a disaster. She's glowing in the aftermath of that breakup – she's basking in it. Baaahahahah! I wish. Maturity? Yes. Ease and grace? Absolutely not. If only they knew what was going on inside of me, mentally, physically and emotionally, they'd see a different Alexa.

But I conformed to the ideal of what everyone else does when they are actually livin' the dream, and in doing so, I only showed the world the good stuff. Even if I had to make it up before I showed it. Many people said they envied my life. Some even admitted that they were jealous of all the fun things I was doing. But ... I have a confession to make ... I faked it. A lot.

At least I started out that way. My heart was hurting. It was broken. The only way for me to get out of that pit I found myself trapped in was to fight on. By "fighting on," I mean fighting with my own mind. Fighting with myself to get out of bed. Fighting with myself to eat something. Fighting with myself to not drown my sorrows in Ketel One vodka, or shot after tequila shot. Instead, I did the things I knew would make me happy … eventually … things like working my way through my bucket list. I did this at the time when my very imperfect life seemed perfect to everyone else – remarkably, it eventually became perfect to me, too. This is "fake it 'til you make it" – or better yet "til' you become it" – which is sometimes what it takes to get through life – to not erase the bad memories but to pretend life (so far) was just a rough draft. A draft that is allowed to be corrected, changed and added to.

Imagine, what would it be like if we could erase all the bad stuff? If we could actually forget the things that, in memory, still cause us so much pain? Sounds ideal, right? But without those bad life-experiences, what do you have to compare to the good things in life? Without the pain, what in your life gives you perspective? What helps mold you? Apparently, not a damn thing.

The moments we want to erase are actually essential to our growth – they are the moments we become warriors. They are the unforgettable moments that create small and big life victories. Erasing the bad stuff would be like ripping out bad chapters of a book. Sure, you can do it, but if you do, what you create won't be a clean break. You'll rip the pages. The binding may break. The book won't be finished. There will be missing pages to the story and it'll never come full circle.

Details are important, that's why they are details. "The Devil is in the details," but so are the angels. Details are small, but unless they're respected, they can be deadly – or they can be your salvation. The facts that you think don't need to be there, the moments you find unjustified, the triggers you want to unthink, they are the details. They are important. They are valid. They create a full story, one that needs and wants to be read. From beginning to end with no pages missing.

As you go fight on through your perfectly imperfect lives, remember that in this life, perfection doesn't exist. Sure, each of us aims to reach that glorified picture of life. So we go through life thinking that money buys happiness. We think being skinny is the key to love. We think that being hot and sexy and perpetually 25 is the key to good life.

But we're wrong. Money buys stuff, but stuff doesn't give happiness. People who "love us" for being skinny aren't worth loving back. Being hot and sexy and 25 is just a way-station in a journey of three score and ten (or more). In all reality, it's the quirky stuff, the imperfect stuff, the dork in you that brings you closer to perfection. It's the way you snort when you laugh, it's the fact that you get blueberries stuck in your teeth after drinking a smoothie, it's the way you bite your nails, chew your food a little too loud, or get breadcrumbs on your face without noticing. It's life.

People make fun of me because when these things happen to me ... all of these things ... I just laugh and tell people "it's character." They hear that and laugh at me once more before moving on. Honestly, though, I love these silly, somewhat embarrassing things about me. They are all part of what makes me, me. Alexa Glazer. They are what separates me from you, and from others. They make me a real person. In fact, I think they are what make me cool (you knew I was cool, right?).

Embrace your imperfections. Embrace your little character traits, the ones people laugh at you for. If we focus less on what perfection is – and less on what we're "supposed to be" – and instead focus more on just finding happiness in our everyday lives, we'll all live better lives. I will and you will – living lives with less pressure and less nonsense.

Do this and you'll feel lighter on your feet and move through life a little easier as if you're dancing on cloud nine. You will start enjoying life, even the way it is. Trust me on this.

It's all about perception. About whatever you perceive as perfect ... or as perfectly imperfect. Striving for perfection, sometimes that means embracing self-talk. Telling yourself that the imperfect parts of life are what give you greatness. In truth, those imperfect parts make you appreciate the authenticity life has to offer.

You can't ask others what you have to do in order to be authentic. Being authentic means you already know. Without WHY your authenticity will almost always be inauthentic. – Simon Sinek

Being authentic means being you wholeheartedly. You can't replicate it. You can't be someone you don't want to be. You can't succeed by trying to be someone you aren't. If you want to be authentic, stop asking questions. Stop asking how. You are the answer to those questions. It's that simple.

People often ask me how to be authentic. No insult intended, but I find that a silly question, especially considering the road to becoming authentic involves being you, doing you, and owning who you really are. It's not molding yourself into a shape you're not meant to be in. It's not doing what I say, or even what I think of as being authentic. Doing what others say is authentic – that's "fake authentic," not the real thing.

We've all done that – we've all at least tried molding ourselves into something new and unnatural (at least unnatural for us) – a time or two – or maybe even more than a time or two.

Okay, I confess. I have. Most of the time, whatever you think is authentic really isn't even close. Fake authentic is what you see on social media and in society. Fake authentic is the sum of all those superficial characteristics.

If everyone can do it, then what you're doing is not different. It's not authentic. It's definitely not perfectly imperfect.

When all of those "everything happens for a reason" moments happened in my life, I was suddenly shocked to find that my life's journey was the farthest thing from that perfect lifestyle I had always strived for. Now, having worked through those previous ones, after seeing what's real (and what's not), I wait for the next "everything happens for a reason" moment happens with eager anticipation. I'm not a masochist, someone who enjoys pain, but I know I need those times to really grow as a person, to become more of the Alexa I was always meant to be.

This time, I tell myself, I'm ready for it. I am guns-blazing ready. Those moments make me authentic. What I do after those moments makes me authentic. My perfectly imperfect little life is all I want and all I need. Still, those moments hurt, but it helps to remember that the pain is leading to something better.

For example, here's a little timeline embedded deeply within my perfectly imperfect little life. Four years ago I was livin' the dream. Seriously, until that point in my life, nothing that was really bad had ever happened to me. I was what people call "lucky." I was living in Las Vegas, still dating my high school sweetheart, and dancing on one of the best dance teams in the nation. The only things I was "stressed" about were school (grades), injuries and making a few bucks to pay my rent. Life four years ago was what people called "easy."

Therefore, I concluded, what I was living had to be what people call "livin' the dream ..."

Fast forward in time ... Today, I really am livin' the dream. In those four years, a whole truck-load of bad things have happened to me. I hit rock bottom, and not just once. I hit it again, bounced a few times, then hit it again, one more time. I now know what it's like to actually feel your emotions in every part of your being. In spite of the struggles, hardships – and those days I had to fight with myself to get out of bed – I'm now a different person. At least in certain situations, I have learned perspective. Because of those situations, I became a stronger person and a better human being. Right now, I live a life that people say isn't "easy," a life that people often call "unfair." But it's a life that is perfectly imperfect, not "fake authentic" – I know myself and who I am, and I like that person, despite her flaws and the crack-ups she's had to live with and live through.

I'm sure that for some who don't know the real me, it sounds like I am livin' the dream. I'm traveling a ton, I'm winning national championships, I'm jumping off bridges (with bungee cords – I'm crazy, but not *that* crazy) and jumping out of perfectly good airplanes. And I'm doing this for "fun." Basically, I'm knocking one thing after another off of my bucket list.

Then, to top it all off, I have friends and family, people who I love and adore, and who love me right back.

With that said ... I've had people say "well, of course, she's livin the dream... she's young, blonde, fit, and living on the beach." But they're wrong. In my opinion, this "take" on who I am comes from someone who knows nothing about me, someone who stereotypes others based on their superficial appearance, someone who is making excuses for their own less-than-perfect or even perfectly-imperfect current reality.

However, I am livin the dream – my own dream – not because of the things I have or the experiences I've had. Mind you, I have worked hard my entire life to be able to have and do those things ... and of course, those peak moment things have enhanced my life. They've filled me with much joy, but that's not why I'm writing this book, to brag on perfectly-imperfect Alexa. That's not the message I hope you'll take away from reading this book.

Let's go back to four years ago. Back to when I thought I was 'livin' the dream' because life was so frickin' easy. Back then, one day, my mentor sat me down. He asked me, "Alexa, what's the worst thing that's ever happened to you?" Instead of answering him, and probably because I was naïve, I graciously said nothing. Worse, deep down felt that life would stay that way, all sunshine and roses and good things all around. However, that sheltered life left me a bit ill-prepared for what was about to come crashing down on me. In my own defense, life had actually been good to me. Based on that experience, I honestly didn't know any better, because frankly, I hadn't faced any major tribulations. Not yet.

I know better now. I now know what it's like to have the worst thing that could ever happen to you ... actually, happen. Because it did.

Once I'd survived the worst thing I could imagine, I began to try and help others. I did this at least in part as a coping mechanism, as a way to release the pain that still boiled within me. As a way, candidly, to gain inspiration – yes, I know that sounds selfish, but it's also honest. I helped others as a way to talk to my dad – to send my thoughts out into the universe, hoping he'd be there on the other end of the line.

When you're really suffering, it's important to find a way to release the sometimes awful energy that builds up inside of you when sacrifice happens. When life demands that you either lose something or give up something precious to you, you've got to be able to cope. That's when the question comes up: "What do I do when that void needs to be filled?

This is where the perfectly imperfect life comes full circle. At least, this is where that life starts to make sense to me. That's when I use those perfect imperfections – things that society still thinks of, things that I used to think of as wrong – to help others. I use that pain and tribulation to tell my story. I use what I've survived to inspire, motivate and thrive under all conditions.

You can, too. All you have to do is get honest with yourself, then try to do it. You won't do it perfectly, but then again, you're not supposed to. It's OK to come in last if you did your best.

July 10, 2017—Even when life kicks you in the ass, it's still pretty amazing.

How do we build a stable future in a world of instability, when the only consistency is constant change?
The answer is, we don't. We do our best. We try harder. We stop fearing change and become comfortable with change. We live life on the edge, ready for the next unstable bridge we have to walk over.

COLOR OUTSIDE THE LINES
"Never perfect -- always genuine" – Unknown

Live life without coloring inside the lines. That's right, color outside the lines – that's where creativity lies. Try rebelling against the things society sets up as the norms you must follow. Dream about living a life surrounded by colors that don't exist … except in your dreams. Live life on your own terms. Go wild for a while.

You and I, we live in a society that constantly tests our sense of self-worth. We share a society that requires of you if you're …

A woman, you've got to be a size zero

A man, you've got to have bulging biceps

Married, you've got to have 2.3 perfect blond-and-blue children

A blonde, you must be dumb

Stuck wearing glasses, you're smart, maybe even a nerd

Loaded with money, you're happy

Struggling to pay your bills, your entire life is in shambles

That's life today. But since when – and why – did our self-worth become based upon big-time stereotypes that are imposed on us by small-minded people? Who put them in charge of determining our social and societal norms? Who elected them the arbiters of our lives?

In order to color outside the lines of life, you first have to learn to straddle those lines. To break out of the box you're in, you first have to break some rules. You have to be a rebel. Now I am not saying go break any criminal laws, not by any means, but I am saying you should let yourself live on the edge, even if just a little.

Rules are made for people who don't know what to do. If you know what to do, then the rules aren't made for you – at least not all of them. Some rules make sense – like "cross only on red" – but for most of those other rules, society imposes on us, not so much.

That's what I believe, and here's what I do with this belief: I read the rules before I break them. I acknowledge those rules are there generally for a reason, though that might not be *my* reason. Then I take a deep breath and come up with an action plan. However, once I've got that plan, I make no promises on what happens next.

The thing is … no matter how much we tell ourselves we've got all the answers, the truth is, no one really knows what to do. We weren't born into this world with an instruction manual guiding us on how to go about our days. So, when it comes to society's rules, it's not really about right and wrong. It's about living – or just existing.

You may think you're due your three-score-and-ten, but life makes no promises, especially when it comes to tomorrow. You're here today, so live a little people. I promise that if you always follow all the rules, you will also miss all the fun. Every time.

Who wants to do that? Not me. No thank you.

Life has taught me that rules are meant to be broken because, among other things, there are no guaranteed outcomes. You could follow all the rules and still get screwed by life – or you might break all of society's most cherished rules and have a grand old time. That is why, if you are going to write a set of rules, you also need to – at the same time – write a set of consequences for what happens to rule-breakers when those rules are challenged, let alone when they are broken.

Rules are made to be broken.

If a rule is not meant to be broken, why do we write a consequence for when the rule is, in fact, broken? This is when straddling the line comes into place. Straddling the line, then sometimes crossing it. If a rule isn't supposed to be broken, consequences should never be made ... but they are, so I say break rules and make life a little more interesting for yourself – then deal with the consequences.

What is the point of creating rules in the first place then, if you're not going to have consequences? The definition of a rule is "a regulation governing a particular activity." The most important rules are those imposed by people with ultimate power and authority, and breaking those rules have consequences. "Thou shalt not commit murder" has more serious consequences than "thou shalt not jaywalk when there's no traffic around" or "thou shalt not wear white after Labor Day." When it comes to breaking society's rules – which, as I noted a moment ago, isn't the same thing as breaking society's laws – those who want to live by coloring outside the lines choose to break those rules, just because we can. Just because we should.

Breaking those unwritten rules is how you learn. That's how you have fun. That's how you experience life that's at least somewhat on the wild side.

Creativity is the key to living a fulfilled life. It's key to living a life that is not ordinary, but extraordinary – a life that surprises you, day in and day out. To have the creativity to think outside the box and to problem solve when you're in a rut. "Creativity is the greatest rebellion in existence," Osho said, and it's the damned truth.

To be creative is to go wild. It's to be free, to live on your terms, in your mind and out in the universe. So maybe instead of thinking outside the box … we should think about what we can do with the box.

Pure logic gets you from **Point A** to **Point B**, but we don't just want to get to **Point B,** we want to go all the way. When you push logic to the side and use that imagination you have been blessed with, you are not just going to get to **Point B,** and not even just to **Point Z** – imagination will take you everywhere, "to infinity and beyond!"

Imagination will take you anywhere you want to go, and to places, you never even dreamed of. If you want to go to a place that has unicorns, one where the streets are made of rainbows and the buildings are made out of chocolate, then, by all means, go there. Use your imagination to get you there.

Remember when you were a little kid? Back when you routinely colored outside the lines? When you ignored the lines entirely and used the entire sheet of paper for your colorful creations? When you finished your creative masterpiece and mom displayed it on the refrigerator for all to see?

That was fun, but when did we stop doing that? And why did we stop?

We stopped when we tried perfecting creativity, which is perhaps the ultimate contradiction. Or we stopped when others told us we were breaking the rules – that the lines were there for a reason. That's when we started coloring inside the lines when we started conforming. That's when we started to follow the rules because that 's what we were supposed to do. That's when we started to be boring. Lame. Predictable.

Perfect your creativity

Creativity is experimenting, breaking rules, making mistakes and having fun. Creativity is authentic therefore, making it perfect is flawing it and creating its own identity.

Today, you're lame. I'm lame. We all are lame. Our reactions are predictable. And it's our own damn fault.

Now that I've finally put that heretical idea out there, let's fix it. Let's be kids again. Let's be creative. Let's do the things we actually want to do, even if – or perhaps, especially if – we think it could be a bad idea. Let's stop being so frickin' lame!

We have more knowledge now than we did back then. We know the difference between society's unwritten rules and society's unbreakable laws. So join me as I spend every day trying to learn from *little kid Alexa*, to use the brains and experience I have as *adult Alexa* to create the best damn version of Alexa possible.

You do it too!

Mix the creative part of that little kid living within you with the best of the adult you … color outside the lines for a change, because you want to, because you choose to, and … BAM … there you have it. There's the best version of you.

World domination can be in your grasp if you just be you, do you, and color outside the lines a little more.

May 16, 2017 — I think in life, when you can really understand and see that not everything in life is black and white, that not everything has a definite answer, that not everything can be reinforced, investigated and scientifically answered, your life becomes more of an ease. When you start to realize that contradictions are out there, that they exist and that that is just life, you start to become more opened minded, less stubborn and wiser. I'm someone who thinks that personal experience is the best advice solely because you got through it. Whether the outcome was positive or negative or how you wished it would have happened or not, you have insight and the capabilities to reflect and possibly help someone else in their current situation. You become ready for anything.

BELIEVE IN BELIEVING IN SOMETHING, ANYTHING.

I believe life is a series of contradictions.

I believe everything that we deal with in life is situational. What happens to one person will, in no shape or form, be identical to what happens to another. Never ever. No matter the number of similarities they have to one another, those situations will never be exactly the same. Therefore, everyone has a right to feel how they want and need to feel. You have a right to your own feelings and anyone who tells you otherwise can "f" off.

I believe that rules are made to be broken. This is why, as soon as a rule is written, it is followed by a written set of consequences.

I believe in forever love, even though I've never experienced it.

I believe that ice cream is always the answer.

I believe that my dad is always with me.

Finally, I believe that to get through life, you have to believe in something, anything. Those are just some of the things I believe in. They are not things I have always believed in, and in the face of future experience, they may not always remain things I believe in. Hey, I'm just being a realist on that one.

However, while this book is about life lessons, it isn't about believing in God, the Boogeyman, Buddha, a higher power, heaven and hell, Santa Clause, spirits, demons, or ghosts. There are other books that deal with those beliefs. This book is about believing in something, anything. It is also about accepting the harsh fact that not everyone is going to believe what you believe. Another harsh truth of reality is that your own beliefs may change in time. In fact, you may go back and forth on your beliefs, and that is all perfectly okay. Change is a natural course of action. Although it makes moments uncomfortable it's teaching you to adapt to adversity.

So why do I believe in these things? Why do I believe that you need to believe in believing? Believing in something gives you a direction. It helps guide you and gives you an inner compass – helping you decide where to go and what path you might follow. Hell, I might be wrong but I am going to run with this idea – it's been true thus far in my life; if that changes, I'll be sure to let you know.

Given my own set of personal hardships, if I didn't believe in something, I would be one lost cookie. Crumbling fast. This doesn't mean, despite my beliefs, I haven't lost hope at times because I have. It just means that, in my Mary Poppins bag of beliefs, I've always managed to find a pick-me-up – an invisible crane to lift me from the deep, deep hole I sometimes manage to dig myself into.

Without believing in yourself, without believing in someone else, and without having some sort of faith, you can create out of yourself a real mental midget. Good *fricken'* luck with that. You've just made your life twenty times more difficult – and that's being quite generous. So brush off that good cop, bad cop, flick your inner angel and devil off your shoulders. Try listening to your own instincts and see what the heck happens. You may fail. You probably will, once, twice, maybe even a dozen times. The cool thing about believing though is that eventually, something good will happen. **I promise.**

Aim to make your beliefs healthy. That they drive you to become a better human being. So ask yourself: Are these beliefs helping or hurting my chances to maintaining my dreams? Belief forms guidance builds relationships (some physical, some imaginary), challenges the way the mind works and guides you through leading a more fulfilled life.

Remember now, to never pass judgments on others beliefs. Instead, expand your knowledge, gain a new perspective, challenge your own stance. This usually helps you develop more empathy towards others. The reality is – people already believe in anything and everything. Stop being closeminded, expand intellectually, don't look on the superficial pieces people carry, quit being shallow and leave your stubbornness at the door. Belief is not just a religious figure or symbol it is whatever gets you through each day.

Something like the statement "They are always with you..." That's something I've heard more times than I can count. Something I'll continue to hear for the rest of my life. They'll all tell you that the ones you've lost are still there, sharing these moments with you. Not in the flesh of course, but they are there, next to you, watching you, guiding you.

However, the many, **many** times I've heard "your dad is always watching you," I've learned it's true. I finally got off my high horse, and shunted aside my sometimes stubborn personality and ... **I started to believe it was true.** He is here. He is always watching me and always by my side. Yesterday, today, and tomorrow. Every day.

It is all about perspective. About the kind of belief, I've been preaching. About using memories to make all of your senses come to life. To feel, smell, taste and hear the memories. It's closing your eyes and letting tears roll down your face – anytime and every time they want to roll down your face. It's smiling and giggling at memories of an old joke, or licking your lips from the memory of the taste of one of their home-cooked meals, or covering your ears as if you're holding a seashell to your ear, just to their voice.

Despite the memories, something's been lost that will never return. During the times when you need them the most, it will be impossible to listen to their "voice of reason" advice. It'll be impossible to feel them squeeze you tightly, to hug your brains out or to smell their own, deeply personal scent.

But you can talk to them, talk to them out loud, talk to them in your head, or even talk to them on a piece of paper or a computer screen. It may feel silly at first, ***but they will listen*** – in your heart, you'll know they hear you loud and clear.

Without that belief to you sustain you, you'll slowly crumble during your struggles and hardships. You'll become that cookie, just like the one I once was. For this belief to work in your life, it doesn't really matter if you are a religious person or not. My faith has dramatically changed as I have grown as a human being. My soul is different. My views are slightly different. However, I just believe. Believe in that connection which exists beyond death – but only if you allow that connection to happen. It is a pure fact that you can charge your senses and find your ability to achieve that emotional and mental high that comes with reconnecting with someone you thought was lost for all time.

When people pass over, when their time on this physical earth is done, you have the ability to build a connection with them, to create and sustain an unbreakable bond. Those you love are wherever you decide to put them. They can be a face in the sky, or they can be found sitting in the chair next to you. They will follow wherever you leave a trail. Let them in – imagine how they would live if they were still here today, and share that life with them.

Believe in something, anything. Always.

PHIL GLAZER RULES: ABOVE AND BEYOND

Going above and beyond was always about doing more than was asked for. One example that stands out for me is when my dad made his baseball players, throughout the season, do yard work for local veterans. He taught people that it's not just about the game – it's about helping people who may need help. My dad's boys were young and able and to those that supported his team the team supported them in return. They cut grass, blew leaves, plowed snow, picked weeds and they did it all with a smile. In doing so, they also learned to respect the veterans who'd given so much to our country. Imagine, civics lessons from a baseball coach!

Going above and beyond was always important to my dad's pursuit of happiness. His pursuit of happiness was all about making others happy along the way. The more you do for others, the more you get back in return – and that happens without you even noticing. Just as Buzz Lightyear said "To infinity and beyond," that's how my dad lived his life. With small random acts of kindness. Above and beyond doesn't mean getting more money, more materials, more diamonds. It's just doing more than what is expected and asked for. It means don't be mediocre. If you want to be the best, you have to do things that are going to make you the best. You can always do more.

LIFE PARTNERS, SOUL MATES.

"I belong with you, you belong with me, you're my sweetheart"— Lumineers

My mom married my dad at the young age of eighteen. They got engaged after a short six months. Before my dad died, they had been married for twenty-four years. Before my mom was twenty-four years old, they had two beautifully crazy girls. To support this family, mom and dad worked their asses off. They supported us and loved us through tantrums, sibling rivalries and messy rooms, our first periods, heartbreaks, rejection and belly laughs, teen-aged attitude and bad grades, dance and softball, our first cars, college … and always through life's problems. They somehow did all this with grace and love and a lot of laughter.

My parents were hands down the best. Literally. The best for each other. The best of friends. The best of lovers. The best of the best.

I know, I'm biased, but really … They didn't fight where we could see or hear them. They didn't worry us when life got tough.

They were strong, they were happy, they were in love. They did everything together. By everything, I mean everything. They went to the grocery store together. They drove to work together. They hung out on the weekend together. They watched TV together –even when all they watched were reality television shows like The Bachelor or Mistresses. They played Yahtzee together. They came and watched and supported our games together. They laughed together. They told silly knock-knock jokes together. They supported each other. They even played the penny slots together. You name it they did it, but they did it together.

My parents are the standard, the touchstone, what I strive for in a marriage, once I get around to that "day." They set the example that married people should love each other unconditionally. To show that love, they:

Supported one another without flinching. Went above and beyond for each other. Did what it takes to make the other person glow, including dad rubbing my mom's feet at night or mom going to watch a baseball game my dad coached. Laughed every day. Looked at each other and smiled just because they feel so lucky that their life-partners are theirs. Had real conversations with one another, serious or simple. Cared for each other when one is sick, even if "sick" means one of them just got a little too drunk on a fun night out with friends and is now just a little hung over.

Shared the same values. Became each other's "just-right" person by being their best friend first, and their lover second.

"Parented" together and not apart. Made decisions together. Knew everything about one another, even down to the smallest of details, such as how my mom didn't like flowers because:

Mom thought it was a waste of money because they died. Dad's favorite color was green because that was his high school color. Mom drank Miller Lite while dad drank Ketel One. Mom's favorite fast food comes from Taco Bell. Dad would eat anything but cottage cheese.

Needless to say, when my dad died, I didn't want my mom to follow him. I didn't want her to die of a broken heart. I hear that happens. When some people's loved ones die, they die too. They die a little bit each day while they are still alive, and eventually, those little deaths take them too.

It takes them because heartbreak hurts, and there is no prescription that heals that pain. It takes them because the love of their life left them too soon – they weren't ready, perhaps not realizing that if you really love someone, you're never ready to lose them. It takes them because they don't remember how to laugh, and they can't forget how to cry.

It takes them because they are numb to love – there's a gaping hole in their souls, their hearts, their lives, holes they can never fill. It takes them because they don't want to love anyone else, or can't even imagine loving anyone else, ever again. It takes them because they think they know that nobody else's love will match up to the love they lost. It takes them because they are always sad, and being sad is no way to live. It takes them because they miss the one they lost more than anything in the world.

It takes them because they would do anything –and I mean anything – just to talk to, or see, or feel, hear, or smell that person just one more time. Even for a minute. It takes them because they never pictured their life like this. Alone.

It takes their soul because they never pictured their life without their life partner. It takes them because they never pictured their life spent living in a big empty house filled with memories, but without the person there to share those memories with.

It takes them a little bit, every day, and keeps taking them until the day they finally decide they still have a life here. Here on earth. Here in a place where others need them, where others care so much for them. Where they aren't alone, at least not alone the way they feel until they realize that life still offers them more. Where, although their life is different and not at all how they pictured it, it can still be the best of lives.

But for some people, the loss of their life partner takes them for good. They die for real because of their unhealing broken heart. This tragic fact kills me. This really happens, and I thank my dad every day that he wouldn't let my mom die of a broken heart. He made sure that her grief took her for a little while, but finally, dad made sure she has found happiness again. He made sure that her cries turned into laughs again.

For a year and a half, we watched my mom grieve the loss of her best friend. The one person who was her life. Her forever love. Her "he was supposed to be her one-time love" lover. To say the least, this was difficult for all of us because, although we had lost our father, who was our first love, dad wasn't the person we shared a bed with every night. Dad wasn't the person we shared our deepest secrets with. Dad wasn't the person we created children and a family with. Dad wasn't our forever guy.

In this situation, all we wanted, for our mom, was for her to be happy again. For her to not be alone. For her to be with someone, again, because she is still young and beautiful and funny and smart and deserves so much more than a lonely life spent alone.

Long before he left, we had conversations with my dad. Many, actually. These were the kind of conversations that, at the time, you wonder why you're having them because you never expected dad to leave earth at forty-nine years old. These were the kinds of conversations that make you roll your eyes a little because you don't want to ever think about either of your parents leaving this earth. The kinds of conversations where dad begins, "When I die one day ... whenever that day might be. Tomorrow. Ten years from now. Hopefully fifty years from now. I don't want your mom to be alone and I don't want you guys to be sad for too long."

Well, unfortunately, his passing happened much sooner than fifty years in our future, or even ten years. Fortunately, however, no matter how uncomfortable they were at the time, we did have those tough conversations. I don't believe dad had a premonition of his own death – we had those conversations because, to our dad, they were just another part of the responsibility he took for his family. And fortunately, we had those conversations when we could, because –during the difficult times after he died – we didn't have to ask the question "what dad would have wanted?" Unlike most people who are unexpectedly left behind, he already knew what he wanted.

That fact doesn't make the loss of a loved-one, especially a loss that occurs decades too early, any easier. We still weren't ready when the time came – not for my mom to be alone and not for us to (for a time) to not be happy. Eventually, mom wasn't alone, and eventually, we were happy again, but even knowing what dad wanted, the struggle to move on with our lives represented a long, difficult time for us before those positives came to pass. Knowing what our dad wanted, for us – or for you, knowing what your lost-too-soon loved-one wanted – doesn't mean you get there any faster.

There is no shortcut to sanity. No shortcut that will make your feelings feel less painful. Changes like this are really hard to take. Knowing what dad wanted doesn't mean that it's any easier to watch your mom go on dates, to start to fall in love again, to watch her smile at someone else, to watch someone else smile at her – not quite the way my dad looked at her, but close. Sometimes too close.

Despite knowing better, these thoughts still make me feel guilty. The fact that experience mom return to life wasn't easy to watch, or to hear about – that makes me feel guilty, too. Because, despite our denial of what we'd lost, we also knew the time would come when she'd become a woman again, one who loved and who was loved. We wanted the time to come. My dad wanted the time to come, too. But when it came, we still weren't ready. Not yet. Especially because, while she'd found a new someone, that person wasn't a new "someone" for the rest of us. He wasn't our dad; and because we're adults, he was never going to be our step-dad, either. He was just someone who was attached to mom. That scared me.

I was scared someone was going to try to replace my dad, and I wasn't okay with that. I was scared someone was going to hurt my mom, and I wasn't okay with that, either. I was scared someone new was now in our family, but for all the wrong reasons. I was scared this new person wouldn't like us. I was scared he would take mom away from us. I was definitely scared that combining families would be weird and odd. I was scared he wouldn't feel like supporting mom's sorrow during those times when she still had to cry for my dad. I was scared that no matter how "good" this new guy was, she would still miss dad's smile and his deep, abiding love.

I was scared this new guy wouldn't understand her loss. I was scared he would get jealous of those never-ending feelings. I was scared she would enjoy her "new" family more than she did ours. That's really scary! I was scared she would change her last name, move out of our house, sell my dad's car, take our family pictures down, stop wearing her wedding ring and – worse – get a new one.

Intellectually, we all knew this time would come. However, that knowledge didn't make this scary time's arrival any easier to handle. Instead, when this time finally did arrive ...

It made us miss our dad even more.

It made us argue when, normally, we didn't.

It caused hurt feelings, confrontation, and uncomfortable situations.

These are just some of the things I feel guilty about, things which also made it harder for mom, for my sister, and for me. These are things I didn't want (and still don't want) to feel, because these feelings were not what my dad wanted, and not what we wanted, either. But they were and are real, no matter how much we didn't and still don't want them.

When your time for dealing with loss comes, remember that life is a process. Remember that it's okay to feel uncomfortable when someone new enters your life – not directly, but through someone else you love. Remember that when that new someone becomes a huge part of your surviving parent's life, it's okay to not feel good about this, no matter how much joy he or she brings to your still-living parent.

This whole situation was strange at first, because the kids – my sister and me – we, in effect, became the parents. We became protective. We turned from child-mode into parent mode, wanting to make sure that mom didn't get hurt. Just as she hoped our own future significant others had the right intentions, we insisted this new guy had to have the right intentions, too. This was difficult for my mom. She knew what she wanted for her, and felt that we shouldn't worry. But we worried the same way that she, as a parent, had worries for us, her children.

The most important way to deal with these situations is to be open and honest. Which, between the three of us, proved to be difficult at times, if only because we are all stubborn as hell. Here's what stubborn looks like.

My mom has locked herself in her room. She ignored phone calls. We have all yelled and cried and not said anything. What we couldn't say in words we said in "bad" body language, including an eye roll here and there. Bottom line: Life after dad has been a work in progress, for all of us.

For me, I had to physically tell myself to stop being stubborn. To give someone a chance. A chance he deserved and a chance my mom deserved. A chance to let someone new in. A chance to let the feelings happen.

A big step for me happened on December 3rd, 2017. Partially, telling you this date makes me feel a little guilty, a bit ashamed, if only because it took two years for me to get to this point. Still, I got myself to this point, eventually, and that's what is important.

My stubbornness ended with a text message I sent to this man, a text message that I genuinely meant … it just took me a while to get there.

"I just wanted to say thank you for making my mom happy, and for giving her something positive, especially considering she's had so many negative things and people in her life. I appreciate it." His response was nothing less than I expected from him, but still, it was something I very much needed in order to trust his intentions. "That's awesome to hear, and she is my dream come true. She is a one in a million." My final response was "She sure is."

This is all still an ongoing process, but it is one I am willing to take on for my mother's sake. She deserves this, and I want nothing more than her undying happiness to exist again.

What I can say, despite all my conflicted feelings, is that I am grateful that my mom is not alone. That she hasn't forgotten what love feels like. That she has found a new partner, a new best friend, a new love. I know I will never call that new someone else dad. Despite my loss, I don't need to I have one – one Phil-Glazer-as-dad is sufficient for an entire life. I will never forget the standard of love and marriage that my parents showcased for me for my entire life.

As I move forward, I will always strive to have the love and friendship that they had. However, I will do my best to root for the man in my mom's life. I will trust in him to take care of her, protect her and love her. Not just for herself, or for us, but also out of respect for my dad. And no matter how hard I fight it, I will still be protective of mom and her feelings. I will make it a point that she comes first, that she is on my team and that I will fight for her.

That's what dad would have wanted.

If you lose a parent too soon, you'll face these same kinds of issues. You may make the same choices I did, or your choices may be different. The key is to be honest with yourself, and with your surviving parent. Be true to yourself, and be true to the parent you lost.

PHIL GLAZER RULES: LOVE CONQUERS ALL

Love conquers all. At the prime age of 19, this actually became my first tattoo. I still remember reading "Love conquers all" while studying Shakespeare during my senior English class – I instantly fell in love with that phrase. Some people say "oh, so cliché!" However, this is something I firmly believe in, and not just because it's permanently etched across my ribs. Although, because of that tattoo, I better not turn back. From what I have learned from observing my superiors, as well as from my relationships is simple: love is the most important emotion you can ever have and ever will have.

If you're into cold, hard, statistics then you best believe that love is an important emotion. In fact, according to Maslow's classic *Hierarchy of Needs,* Love and Belonging fall right in the middle. Which means you need love to live. Which means ... love does indeed conquer all. Which means y'all need it to thrive.

With that said, if you're not a hopeless romantic like me – hey, stop that eye-rolling over there – this depends on what you think love is. If you think love is only about all that mooshy gooshy stuff, about flower deliveries, teddy bears, and chocolates, well I'm here to tell you that you are losing it.

Love does not only apply when you are in a romantic relationship. It applies to everything life has to offer. People, places, careers, hobbies, animals. Anything. Everything. Love is then followed by passion. To succeed at anything in this life we need love and passion for something or someone.

Love is all about filling your heart with someone or something. Taking care of that someone or something. Keeping it safe. Cherishing it. Trusting it. Not taking any of its heartbeats for granted. Not forgetting what it needs and wants. Love is investing completely, fully, kindly and open-mindedly. Whether you love a person, place, or thing, you put the things you love most on the top of your "this is how I live my life" list.

Through his actions, my dad taught me the importance of love. More times than I can count, his actions directly correlated to his values. His love for my mother was undeniable – he would do anything for her.

His love for my sister and me was through the roof. His love for baseball was stunning, yet he gave it up as a profession because of his greater love for my mom. Moving p
ast family, his love for coaching others was profound and life-long; and in his career, he put his full heart into his work. No matter how busy he was – and he was busy – he seldom passed up any opportunity to help others. His idea of love was to give it to others, confident that love would appear back in his heart in some way. He didn't expect anything from others, but somehow that

love always returned. For all his life, his heart grew fuller and bigger.

Remembering Phil

"I noticed how much he cared for the three women in his life - he loved your mom so tenderly and profusely! He would do anything for her and then do it all over again! She loved him right back and the two of them set up a picture of marriage that seemed flawless and magical"
*– **Niki Tilicki***

*"Not long after he met KimTilicki, the love of his life and they would end up conquering so many things together and bringing into the world my two beautiful nieces, Nikki and Alexa. They are very dear to me and Kim is like a sister to me." – **Diana Cefaratti***

"I was telling Phil how Kevin always has to open my car door or any door I walked through. He always walked me to my car at the end of our dates. He brought me flowers and wanted to hold my hand. He called me every day just to ask how my day was. It was all just strange to me. It actually made me feel uncomfortable in the beginning. I had never had a boyfriend who was so gentlemanly. At the end he looks me right in the eyes and says you are a special person Jessie, "why don't

you think you deserve someone who is going to treat you right?" He was like" no really, why, why is it a bad thing. Don't you deserve to be treated like a lady?" I don't even remember what I answered. I just remember Phil forcing me to think about it. It was his way of giving me advice without really saying much. He was letting me come to my own conclusions with just a simple nudge. He wouldn't lecture with his opinions and beliefs. He would never put you down. He would make you a better person by presenting you a different way of looking at something and then sit back and let you grow and change on your own. If I had to pick a marriage that I was trying to model my own after it would hands down 100% be Kim and Phil's. They just had this mutual respect for each other that was so apparent. They truly wanted be with and spend time with the other person and would go out of their way to do so. I seriously find myself in a situation with Kevin and think to myself what would Kim and Phil have done in this situation." – **Jessie Smith Eshelman**

PHIL GLAZER RULES: "HONEYDEW THIS, HONEYDEW THAT"

This was always a joke on our family dinners. When the four of us would go out to dinner – and my sister and I were still young enough to order off the kids menu, or at least pretend we were young enough – we would. Now, do you remember how, when you ordered off the kids menu, your meal came with a side of fruit? That fruit was always an oh-so-simple melody of grapes, cantaloupe and of course, honey dew.

Well, every time this plate of food came to the table my dad would look at my sister and I and go "did you know that mom's favorite fruit is honey dew girls?"

In our heads, we would say "who the heck's favorite fruit is honey dew? It sucks." But instead of giving voice to our thoughts, we would politely say "No, we didn't know that."

This next part never got old. My dad would quickly fire back with a smile on his face and a wink in the direction of my mom and say, "yeah, don't you hear mom every day talking to me, saying honey dew this, honey dew that?"

I know my dad never took the simple things in life too seriously. He knew there were times to be serious and times to let go. My dad would do anything to make his three girls smile, and in moments that he knew he could do just that he would let go and let be. So take life less seriously in the moments that you're able to. Belly laugh and make others cry (cry from laughter of course).

Remembering Phil

*"That was it. No big lecture. Just simple words that meant a lot. You just felt the love in those few simple words. That's who I feel Phil was. Honest but eloquent in the way he talked. A man who loved his family but didn't smother them. A role model and a wonderful human being. – **Jessie Smith Eshelman**

DO WHAT FEEDS YOUR SOUL

"Everywhere is somewhere" - John Lennon

Just as your body needs food and water, your soul needs fuel as well. Soul-fuel is the type of fuel that, when you add fire, it explodes. Soul-fuel is dynamic. Soul-fuel is beautiful. Soul-fuel is hard to explain but easy to feel.

To feel the heat.

To feel the power.

To feel the change occurring.

This is what happens when your passions collide with your soul. This is what happens when the universe is talking directly to you – when it is saying, "Whatever you are doing at this moment, right now, this is your soul-fuel. This is what feeds your soul. This is what you need in life, to it a life worth living."

The point of feeding your soul is simple: a well-fed soul helps you grow. It gives you opportunities that you didn't know exist. Opportunities that open up your heart to feel things you didn't know you would … or even could … ever feel. Feeding your soul is more than just a physical experience. It changes you mentally and emotionally, as well. It makes you giddy. It gives you a lump in your throat ... or in the pit of your stomach. It does this in the best possible way, a way that makes you smile for no reason. I am feeding my soul right now, just telling you how important it is to feed your soul. I'm feeling giddy. There's a lump in my throat. I'm thrilled knowing that you might decide to try feeding your soul, too.

What feeds my soul, you ask? Here are a few:

Conquering the world.

Traveling the world.

Making an army of dreamers in the world (starting with you).

I've talked about conquering the world before. By conquering the world, I mean that I want to make the world a better place, for you and me. To the best of my ability, I want you to feel like you can dream – then send you out to go achieve those dreams. To believe in kindness and know that it is stronger than hate.

Traveling is definitely something that feeds my soul, and probably yours too. Travel ... While you can. When you can. As much as you can. Wherever you can. Everywhere you can. However you can. But how do you make travel into soul-fuel? Plan it. Do it spontaneously. Do whatever it takes. Do whatever works for you. Just do it.

Listen to the voice of experience here. You will gain so much from packing up some of your favorite things and leaving behind what you think you call "home." It doesn't matter if you're gone for a single day or for a two-month epic journey. It doesn't matter if you jump in your car for a road trip or hop on a plane for a cross-country adventure.

When done right, traveling makes you uncomfortable. It puts you in an environment where the possibility of inconsistencies – things that shake up your daily life – are endless. When you travel, even from state to state, sometimes even from city to city, the cultures, lifestyles, vibes, weather conditions, smells, foods, and activities are different from whatever your norm may be. Even within some cities, you can travel from Little Havana to Little Italy in a half-hour, but find yourself in completely different worlds.

The best part about leaving the place you call home is that having done so, you'll now have a better idea of what you like or don't like about home. What attracts you to, or repels you from, new places? That is what you want to explore. Leaving your comfort zones brings up so many new opportunities. Start getting comfortable with being uncomfortable. Among them are opportunities to *observe* people, places, and things. I strongly advise you, as you considering traveling, to begin by just sitting on a bench somewhere and people-watch. You'll get a kick out of it, and I promise you that you'll learn a ton about other people, too. Then, strap on a pair and go talk to a stranger in the bar, or at the local Starbucks. Go build connections with people you don't know.

My best friend, Moy and I decided we were going to do a Pacific Northwest Road trip. The best part and most exciting part

315

of this trip was how spontaneous it began. We FaceTimed one random night to catch up on each other's lives. I mentioned that I wanted to do this trip and had been thinking about it for a while and by the next day she had dates scheduled and two days later our first flight were booked.

We met each other in San Francisco, rented a car and traveled up the coast to Portland, Seattle, Vancouver and Whistler. Best. Trip. Ever. This trip opened my eyes to the importance of travel for me. A large portion of that is because we wanted to act and feel like locals in each city we stayed in. We went to local coffee shops and posted up doing work for hours. We went to small bars and restaurants. One man and one night stick out in particular. We were sitting at a Mexican bar in Portland to get our fix of chips, salsa, and margaritas (we were having them in each city we went to). Sitting there, we started chatting with the bartender and all of his regulars. This was the best way to know the city and its vibes. We ended up at this bar for a total of five hours and left with so much wisdom.

Wise words from one of our new friends Michael: *"There's four questions: Where did I come from? Where am I going? Why am I here? What is my purpose? Those are the four questions that drive everything in human life. Be it science, be it religion, be it anything. Basically, you have to find gratitude in realizing that you may not answer those four questions but it's really the*

journey in attempting to answer those four questions."
Thank you for this and for making us feel right at home.

I think there are three types of people in the world: Those who go above and beyond, and have the money to travel; Those who will do anything they can to travel, even if they don't have the means; and Those who never leave their state or even their home city ...

If you want to feed your soul, be the person who will do anything to travel. If traveling doesn't suit your fancy do what does and do it whole-heartedly. But ... I'm not just saying this. I truly believe travel is that really valuable ... I also really think you'll love the high you get, and this is the kind of high you won't regret later. So what are you waiting for? Bring this book with you and hit the road.

Life lessons are everywhere. There is so much wisdom in our everyday lives. So much more than we even need to look for – after all, what we need is just a conversation away. Perspective is a key to traveling as soul-fuel – expanding your own perspective, especially with help from others, is a must-do. But don't just set out to meet people – make friends while you're at it. Connect with people. And trust me, you'll never know what you have in common with the stranger standing across from you at a bar or in a park until you reach out and find out.

I love traveling to places that make me forget how tiny my problems – and I –really are. Now listen, folks, because this is a key that will open a magic door. To places and do things that make you forget your problems. Places that seem bigger than life, and situations that make your problems seem minuscule by comparison.

In the past three months, I have done just that – traveled to places that are much bigger than I am. This is the kind of travel that inspires me the most. Seeking to fuel my soul, I've gone to places more beautiful than I ever imagined, as well as to places so crowded you actually feel like you don't matter. I've traveled to smack dab in the middle of nowhere – places, where you could dance around naked and not a soul, would know. I've been to places where it's so humid it constantly feels like you just wet your pants (this is the worst).

At first, I felt like I was traveling to run away from my problems, or just running from life in general. This may seem weird, since I have said – repeatedly in this book – to not quit at life, and shit like that. For me though, it's not quitting if you walk away from a fight that you no longer need to win. In that kind of situation, you've already given it your all – and I mean your all – only to see that you've given enough. You don't not work hard here, not when you reach the point of quitting, only to realize that it's not about quitting – it's more or less just time to pivot and start a new adventure. That's not quitting – that's freeing yourself from worse possibilities than you face going off in a new direction.

This running thing I am talking about, running away from your problems, that's the kind of feeling you get when you really just want to get away. In reality, sometimes running away makes you run head-on into new opportunities, into eye-opening experiences. Instead of running away from life, I discover I'm not letting life run away from me. I'm making the most of each new experience.

Now my last portion of soul-fuel is all about this "make an army of dreamers in the world" ... this soul-fuel really lights a fire under my ass. An army is a group of people who all stand for a purpose. The very idea feeds my soul tremendously. Making an army of dreamers is all about encouraging you to tell your story whenever you can because you never know who is listening. You never know who you are inspiring, or who you may be helping. Creating an army of dreamers is all about creating a movement, a team of believers. Of people who grind till they die. Of people who become family without the blood. Of people who believe so much that they make things happen on their own.

Find your soul-fuel. Run a marathon, or start with a half. Read books and lots of them. Join a club, even if that club is your Wednesday Wine Night with the girls.

Do what lights your fire. Try new things. Meet new people. Don't get discouraged when at times you can't find your soul-fuel, it'll come to you. Don't get discouraged if and when others don't understand or agree with your soul-fuel. The best part about finding your soul-fuel is that no one needs to understand it besides you. No one feels the fire inside you. No one else feels the lump in your throat, the giddiness, the freedom you feel when this all happens. But when you really feel it, you'll know you're enough.

November 6, 2017—Time to sink or swim.

What do you do when you stop liking what you liked to do?

You do not stay complacent because you're scared to like something else and fail. You pivot. You find your passion. You grind and thrive under all conditions. You start liking something else and you like it full heartedly.

PHIL GLAZER RULES: DON'T QUIT

Growing up, we didn't quit things once we'd started. If we asked to play basketball, then halfway through season decided we didn't like it ... too bad. We played until the season ended. Lesson learned.

If I asked to take a night off from dance to go to hang out with my friends ... " too bad, Alexa. We paid thousands of dollars a year to let you dance, so you're going to dance. You made your choice, now live with it." Lesson learned.

If we worked but decided we didn't like our job ... too bad. Suck it up until you find a new one. You took a job to make money, and this job is what you signed up for.

Basically, we were taught that if you start something, you damn well better finish it. Quitting is for losers. So try harder. Do more. Give things a chance. Make things happen. Shock the world. You didn't come this far to only come this far.

Remembering Phil

*"He coached baseball (and I am sure softball) to teach life lessons. Thankfully I was lucky enough to have two boys (Danny & Nicky) play for him. He taught them to finish what they started, NEVER, EVER quit. One of my favorite baseball stories is when every kid in fall ball was on a 50 pitch count. My son Danny didn't realize what it really meant. He walked the bases loaded and then hit a batter. Coach Phil walked out to the mound. My son thought he was coming out to give him the hook so he handed him the ball. Coach Phil gave him the ball back and said "you're on pitch 23, you have 27 more pitches to go.. You better figure it out." What a great life lesson, figure it out. Bear down. Focus. Life is not always going to be easy but keep putting one foot in front of the other and you can figure it out." – **Dan Stewart***

"I remember when we were in fifth or sixth grade and altar boys at St. Mary's. We needed a ride to school at like 6:15am … his mom was always there to take us before going to work at Bonnie Bell. The demonstrated

*work ethic and did not go unnoticed. Your Grandpa Joe was always working. My father worked seven days a week for many many years to provide for us nine kids … we had big families. Parents worked without bitching to provide for their kids" – **Terrance Kane***

PHIL GLAZER RULES: IT'S NEVER ABOUT THE MONEY

Salary didn't matter. Winning the lottery didn't matter. Having the money to go buy a big fancy house or car didn't matter. Wanting money to grow on trees didn't matter. My dad focused on experiences rather than on money.

Of course, money helps buy some of these experiences, because sometimes experiences include vacations and adventures. And while big fancy houses and cars aren't necessary, houses and cars are necessary, and those take money. However, my dad knew that when you focus less on making the money, winning the money, having the money … you stress less and you become happier and the experiences come. My dad taught me that focusing on money makes people greedy and that when you get more than enough of it when you hit it big, you only want more and more. This makes people lose out on life, relationships, and refreshing moments. Money fills your pockets, but experience fills your soul, and that's what life is all about, people. Money buys things, it doesn't buy happiness or kindness.

HAPPINESS

"If the hurt comes so will the happiness." - Rupi Kaur

Our Founding Fathers got it right:

*"We hold these truths to be self-evident, that all men ... are endowed by their Creator with certain unalienable Rights, that among these are ... the pursuit of **Happiness**."*

Happiness is both a state of being and something to pursue every day of your life. You'll be able to more effectively embrace happiness when it's there and pursue happiness when it's not once you realize that happiness has four components to it.

You need to choose **happiness**. You need to allow **happiness** to be contagious. Let your **happiness** spread to others like the chicken pox, because why not? You have to accept that embracing happiness is a life-long pursuit – just like a fine wine, happiness only gets better with age.

Whether my dad chose happiness by, every morning, by telling his image in the mirror to have a good day, or by going to coach a baseball game, or by telling my mom a silly joke, or by sending someone across the room a smile, his happiness vibe was contagious. His happiness spread like the chicken pox. For example, my dad taught me the power of positive thinking, the power of happiness as something to have and something to pursue. After he died, these lessons helped me to cope, to overcome, to move forward with my life despite having an aching emptiness inside that nothing could eliminate.

I do my best to choose happiness each morning. On the days that it's hard and that I don't want to I try to give myself some form of perspective. That people have it worse than me. That if I am not happy because I didn't sleep well, well at least you have a bed, Alexa. At least you have running water to shower or a stove for a hot breakfast. That's my reality. My reality tells me that I should never be unhappy because, in a world that I don't really believe in luck, I am so "lucky." Happiness should be easier to get to. I shouldn't have to fight for it.

Now although my reality set in terms like this is "lucky" sometimes it is hard. We feel unlucky. We feel stuck in a rut. We don't want to listen to perspective and we want to wallow in self-invited pity parties. I get it. I do it too. I hate to admit it but I am also human. I try to choose happiness but sometimes it's really hard to get there. What I can say that at times you have to try harder. Try harder to be happy because you can. Because the lives we live in terms of where we live, what we have. We are "lucky."

An important thing about happiness is how you define it. Happiness isn't a one-size-fits-all concept. You get to define what happiness is to you, and that definition can change from day to day, or even moment to moment. You get to decide what happiness is and how it is fulfilled. You get to decide to go for it. Please go for it. You get to decide for yourself that when you're feeling moody, go shake your booty? Isn't that happiness? At least a little bit of happiness?

However, happiness will not come to you – real happiness has to come from you. A wise woman named Alexa Glazer once said: "screw this bullshit." Now she has all the happiness in the world. She found her *happily ever after* fairytale lifestyle even after suffering from losses that should have plunged her into unending misery. While she's not there yet, she's at least on her way to that fairytale ending. She started on the path to her own *happy ever after* when she stopped sweating the little things, and taking life less seriously, this is when she started thinking about and dealing with only about the things she actually had control over. Now she dances in the kitchen, eats ice cream straight from the carton, sings in the shower and is a spontaneous "wanderluster." Those are her keys to happiness. Find yours.

ALEXA GLAZER

IT'S A BIRD. IT'S A PLANE.
NO IT'S A SIGN.

"Sometimes you will never know the value of a moment until it's a memory" - Dr Seuss

In this next section, I need you to buy into where I'm going. I want you to do this so what I've got to tell you will actually make sense. Frankly, the topic is not something everyone believes in. In fact, if you don't believe where I'm going, I don't blame you. If what happened to me hasn't happened to you – yet – it's going to be difficult to believe in it. But it's important that you believe – or at least to suspend your disbelief. So please, try and stay open-minded.

OK, here it goes.

I believe that in this life, people and things give us "signs." This is important, because, at least for me, these signs tend to keep me afloat. They keep me eager, alert to life and waiting for more. Because I'm still here on this earth, those signs keep me connected to a world – or to a heaven – that I don't know anything about, at least not yet. These signs connect me to that place "somewhere between heaven and earth". This element of faith in things not seen goes back to the concept of believing. Belief can be something as small, commitment-wise, as believing in believing in something. That something can be anything. It should be anything.

You know what you believe in. I happen to believe in signs. Because I think this is really important, I'm going to take you through the "why" of my belief, including:

Why I believe in signs

Why I believe in dreams

Why I believe that my dad is not just some face in the sky

Why I believe that people who have passed still have the ability to connect with each and every one of us

There are reasons for all of these beliefs, as well as your own beliefs, but I'm here to tell you that you can't fake it. If you try to fake the belief, you'll wind up waiting forever for something to happen, not realizing that this something won't happen because you don't believe in it. Not really. If you don't believe in something, you'll miss it. Trust me on this.

However, if you do believe in believing, those somethings you believe in will happen, and they'll happen smack dab right in front of your face. When one of those somethings does happen, you might be tempted to think it's just one of those coincidences we all experience in life. But once you believe, you will feel it when one of those somethings happens to you. You will know it.

Sometimes you will hear it, taste it, touch it, and sometimes you'll even see it.

I'd like to think that people who cross over still want – and are still able – to communicate with us in some way, shape, or form, just like they did before they died. I believe that something like this will happen after you've been through any really major struggle.

I'm talking about a sign. I can almost hear you asking me: A sign? Like what? … An angel? A miracle? A vision? Yes, maybe one of those. But whatever your sign is, it will be personal to you – so personal you won't doubt it, even if your rational mind tells you that you don't believe it. If you're heart and mind are in the right place, you'll look at your sign as some sort of blessing. Bring on all the feels like goosebumps feelings.

If you open your mind, I'm going to make you believe it. Right here. Right now. So let me take you on a little ride.

Let me take you back to a very vulnerable time for me. As I stated earlier, I'm from a Catholic family that believes in "viewing" someone after they've passed before they're buried. I realize this isn't common for everyone – perhaps this sounds foreign to you based on your own experience – but this viewing was very important to me – I had to see my dad one more time before the funeral and this was it.

Anyway, this sign took place the night before my dad's wake, and let me remind you that he died when I was half-way across the continent, so I hadn't seen my dad yet. I wasn't able to

329

go to the hospital with mom and Nikki because I was still flying across the country to get home. So the first time I would have even been able to see him in person would be while he was lying in the casket with his eyes closed, wearing some makeup intended to make his body look more like he did when he was still alive. He'd be dressed in nice clothing, waiting patiently for all of his last good-byes.

Talk about feeling overwhelmed.

I get the same feeling in my gut writing this section right now that I did when I'd just arrived back home, leading up to that moment. This was tough for me. The first time I was going to see my dad was at the funeral home, in front of the rest of my family. Not exactly a private moment. Believe me, I felt the pressure. To say I was *not* looking forward to this "all eyes on me" experience was quite an understatement.

The night before my dad's wake I was up to the wee hours of the morning looking at pictures, watching videos, editing a memorial video, listening to music, and watching motivational speeches (anything from Eric Thomas, because my dad and I both loved him). Honestly though, who can actually close their eyes and shut off their brain the night before one of the biggest days of their lives, anyway? No one. Certainly not me.

Well, eventually I fell asleep. For maybe an hour or two. At most. Then, when I woke up, I was confused. Very confused. Looking up, I saw my dad sitting at the end of my bed with his arms crossed and his head resting on them. He said nothing. I said nothing. How could I? My dad was dead, yet here he was, sitting in my room. I rubbed my eyes to make sure that this was really happening, and sure enough, it was. He was still there, present with me for a moment, looking right into my eyes! This was no dream, no illusion. Sitting there, he was as real a person as he'd ever been in life. He was not some ghostly figure, some angel with wings, or just some bright light hovering at the edge of my bed. He was Phil Glazer, my dad. Age 49, stocky and tough and confident-looking, just like he always was.

When my sister Nikki woke up, I instantly told her what had happened. "Nikki," I said, "dad was in my room last night. I saw him sitting at the edge of my bed, just looking at me. I know it sounds kind of weird, but he was there. I swear."

To my surprise, her response was "He was in my room too. Just staring at me." When we saw our mom, we told her the same thing. She also responded with, "He was there for me, too, sitting right at the edge of the bed"

Right now, I'm getting emotional just thinking about this experience. It was the most surreal moment of my life. Nothing quite added up. Clearly, it's a moment I can't fully explain. A moment so raw and dreamy. A moment I will remember for the rest of my life.

This was the first sign that my dad gave me. With no words from either of us, that was him telling me, "I can now be in more than one place at a time. I promise that no matter where you, Nikki, and your mother are, I will be with all of you."

From that instant, I knew that dad would forever be by my side, watching over me, just like the angel he now was. But that was just the first sign.

The next sign occurred the night of the funeral. This was the first time my family and I were alone – no one besides the three of us was at our house. All our well-wishing visitors had finally left, giving us a little peace and quiet. If you don't know anything about big Catholic family funerals, when someone dies, people bring food to the house. Lots and lots of food. Sandwiches, cookies, lasagna, pizza, cheese platters. You name it, we got it. In the immediate aftermath of a funeral, you'll find a bunch of family and friends at the house doing everything they can to lend a helping hand. Mostly, they're doing their best to keep your mind off what just happened.

This is all truly a blessing. Trust me. No one wants to cook at a time like this, and nobody who's just lost someone precious to them wants to be completely alone.

After days of getting ready for the funeral, however, followed by five straight hours of people standing in line at the wake, and another full day of being at the funeral home, church, and the cemetery, you're ready for a break. You feel relieved when you can finally be alone when you can finally begin to take in what actually just happened. It all feels like a nightmare – not at all like your normal reality. That's the first moment when the definiteness of death finally starts to soak in. When the big stuff is over, and it's back to what you're used to. Now you're supposed to get on with your life.

We went home, we turned on the television and didn't say a word to each other. Until ... all of the power went out at the house. The lights, the TV, everything. It was off for probably a total of 5 very slow seconds, then everything turned back on. However, this power-outage wasn't anything like it usually is when the power goes out. You know, your TV resets, your clocks are wrong and flashing, and of course, all the lights at the other houses on your street go out, too. No. Not this time. This was different. The TV turned on, back to the channel we were watching. The lights switched back on, as with the click of the switch, but only the ones we had on originally. The clock wasn't flashing, demanding to be re-set. Then, of course, on our street, no one else's power went out.

You might think this is a bit of a stretch, but it isn't. One thing I learned growing up was that my grandpa – my dad's dad, who passed away when I was in 4th grade – always used to turn the lights on and off just to tell us "Hey, I'm here." He'd always been a trickster – it was his way of him reminding us to not forget that he was here with us. This same kind of thing happened time and time again after my dad passed. The lights would turn off and we knew grandpa was there to say hello.

This single lights-off lights-on instance was much more than just a one-time oddity. When it happened, there was just the three of us here alone in a finally-empty house. Just us girls ...

and then, there was my dad. He showed up! We were a family again. For those incredibly slow five seconds, we were a whole family again, just sitting around in the living room enjoying each others' company. Day made. Sign read. Message sent.

When the lights turned back on, my mom, Nikki, and I just looked at each other, with shocked faces and grateful smiles. We said, in unison, "That was dad!" Again, some would – some will – say it was just some glitch, and for those of you who feel that way, to you I say, "just let us have our moment." It's moments like just like this one that people can't take away from me, no matter how logical or persistent they may be.

These are those moments – when they happen to you – that you'll actually feel it. It is, at one and the same time, the most real and the most unreal combination of events you'll ever experience, but if and when you allow yourself to believe in them, you know they're real.

Another sign comes in dreams. My first dad dream occurred about five months after his passing, in June of 2014. That June was the first time I'd gone back home to Ohio since his funeral. Please try to imagine the intense anxiety I was feeling right before this trip.

I was anticipating walking into our now empty-feeling home. I honestly expected it to feel like someone else's home, not ours. When I came home my dad was gone, of course. Nikki and Mindy had, at least for the time being, moved in to be closer to my mom. My mom was still sleeping in the room where she had to watch her husband collapse. My old room – now my room again – was still right across the hall.

When I went to bed that first night, I talked to my dad, just like he was there again, sitting on the edge of the bed. I told him all of the thoughts that were running ... no, actually full-on sprinting ... through my head. I said my piece, had a good cry, drank some Ketel 1 on the rocks and fell asleep.

This time when I woke up, I woke up from the first dream in which my dad had made his guest appearance. Instantly, I began crying happy tears. Tears of joy. My vivid dream took place in the kitchen of our home, there on Timberlake Drive. We were sitting on the high tops at the island, just talking the way we always did. Simple and easy conversation. It was so normal, and it felt so real.

The last question I asked my dad before I woke up was, "Can you really see us? Can you see everything we are doing and really be anywhere we are?" Then before he could respond, I woke up. Initially, I was upset because I got no response. "Thanks a lot, dad!"

But that dream and how it ended made me think. My last one was not a question you're allowed to ask, and it's not a question people who cross over are allowed to answer. Some things have to be taken on faith. If you believe, then you already know the answer. The answer is, "well DUHHHH, why do you think I am here right now, Alexa? Stop asking such silly questions you silly girl."

Following another dream I had which featured my dad. I woke up in full-on tears. Tears because I had asked him yet another question and either I didn't remember the answer or he never gave it to me. Tears because I tried so hard not to open my eyes – with all my heart, I wanted nothing more than to go back into this dream. But we all know these kinds of "sign" dreams don't work that way. You can't just snap your fingers and hop back into a dream, no matter how hard you may want to. So there I was, tears streaming down my face from seeing my dad's face in a dream one more time. That particular dad-dream was my third in three years. Dad-dreams are far and few between, which is another reason I got so upset to have left it before it seemed to finish.

A few days later, I talked to my sister on the phone – by this time I was back in Vegas and she was still in Cleveland – and it turned out that she'd had her own third dad-dream the very same night that I did. On the same night, we had both seen our dad in our dreams. Think about that, skeptics. Nikki described her dream-like dad is in the army. He knew he's already gone and felt bad when he had to leave, but he knows he will see us again, and we'd see him. In each of our dad-dreams, he always has a smile on his face.

Back to those lights again. Maybe because his dad had done it to all of us, my dad used to flicker my mom's light in their bedroom. He hasn't done that in a while, but I think it's because he knows we're doing better. But anytime my mom was having an extra bad night, or on a night when she was talking about my dad while sitting in her room, or times when he would get brought up on the phone while she was talking in the bedroom, her lights would flicker. Again I know some people think just a coincidence, and that's okay, but I continue to beg to differ. I'd heard my mom talk about the flickering lights time and time again, but I'd never witnessed it … until the day I finally did. That particular moment made me beam. I was in her room and upset about my dad when their lights went a-flicker. I think this moment became so special for me because it really turned our feelings and our moods around. We went from being sad to being happy, all because we felt him there with us.

The second time I witnessed this flicker was the day before Father's Day. I was alone in my apartment, feeling very anxious about this upcoming "holiday." This was a time of transition. My roommates had already moved out and I was set to move out the next morning. My ex-boyfriend at the time was already long gone for the baseball season, so he just got my end of anxiety text messages. This is one of those nights when I decided to write some of this book, to let out some anxious thoughts. Suddenly, in that moment, in my empty apartment, with me tormented by my sprinting mind, the lights flickered. Dad was there, telling me to not be stressed. To stop the anxious thoughts. To slow down my heart rate. It worked.

I mentioned earlier that ex-boyfriend number two and I had a difficult start. By difficult start I mean we were a secret from the rest of the world for about six months. Let me tell you, sneaking around is zero fun. It adds a ton of stress to the already-stressful starting of a new relationship. At this time, we would hang out behind closed doors, or out at our secret spot, listening to music, talking, and even laying in the street watching the stars. We'd talk about things the way you see relationships evolve in the movies, but we were a secret and felt we had no other choice. Anyway, during this period we went through a bit of a rough patch. A decision needed to be made, either to continue on or to stop what we'd started. So we agreed to meet at our spot and talk it out. I got their first and was laying in the street trying to think about what was about to happen.

Then I said these words out loud: "Dad I need a sign. Please give me some sort of sign. Please tell me this is worth it because if not, the secrets and the stress aren't worth it. I need something here to tell me if we should continue, to know that we are good for each other."

Boom, just as my secret boyfriend pulls up in his car, a shooting star streaked across the sky. This was only the second shooting star I'd ever seen. Significantly, the first one I'd seen was also with this boy. We'd seen it here, at our secret spot, one of the first times we hung out together.

Needless to say, that was a sign for me. Still, I know what y'all want to say ... well, he's ex-boyfriend number two ... Meaning he dumped me eventually. Meaning it didn't work out. Meaning that wasn't a sign after all.

But you'd be wrong. For the time we were together, he is everything I needed ... while I had him. Most importantly, he did his absolute best in helping me through my "dad moments." For that, I am grateful. That shooting star was a sign. We were together for another two years, and in those two years, that relationship taught me a lot.

There have been other small signs ...

Obviously, as you go through your day-to-day life, you ask people a lot how they are. For me, when they respond with dad's all-time-favorite saying, "just livin' the dream ...," it instantly reminds me of my dad. When this happens, I think that he's just stopped by to say "hi."

Cardinals. Whenever the bird flies around, mom, Nikki and I associate that with my dad. For no other reason we could imagine, we had this one bird sit in our backyard the entire time I was home for the funeral. So when I see a bird – especially a cardinal, and especially at a time and a place where I'm not expecting to see a bird, I feel dad's just dropping by to say "hi."

Other times nothing happens at all. For these kinds of sings, there's just a feeling that overcomes me. Suddenly, the sense of dad is very strong, very close. These are the moments I look forward to the most. They remind me that he is still there for me, and for us. That he wants to be in my life, and in our lives.

I know what some people say because I've heard them say it. Alexa, you can twist around any scenario to make it seem relevant to you and your story. And while that is true, theoretically, that also isn't what's happening.

I promise you, there is no twisting going on. All of these experiences give me a sense of closeness. Fullness. A hole in my heart is slightly refilled for at least a second, a precious moment. If you're open to such signs and experiences, you'll come to know what I mean.

However, if you don't believe in signs, I feel bad for you, but to each their own though. But if you don't believe, be nice to those of us who do. It costs you nothing to be nice, so please, never ever not ever downplay mine or someone else's moment of bliss. Give us that, regardless of how irrational you insist we're being. These so-called "made up" scenarios and signs, they strike a memory we once had, and when they do, they have the remarkable ability to create new memories, even as they keep old memories alive.

Here's the bottom line. When a death happens, many people assume that the door on that relationship closes, and in a sense, it does. But if you can start imagining this relationship as more than just a single room, if you can visualize the relationship as a hallway with many other doors to open, then that relationship, in another sense, continues on in the present. The possibilities of maintaining what seems like an unmaintainable relationship do exist, at least they do when you embrace this line of thinking. As long as you're willing to believe.

Sometimes you might feel like you need to search for these occurrences to happen. Don't search, they will come. They will come and fall into your lap like it is no one's business. Embrace them, remember them and feel the bliss.

How do you take the invisible and make it visible?

Dreams are invisible. Taking action is what takes the invisible from being a dream to making it into your visible reality. The process begins with your invisible moments and the end result is your visible moments. The wow I did it moments.

January 28ʹ 2018 – Every year on my dad's anniversary I spend some time on a baseball field. As soon I take that first step on the dirt I get a rush of emotions and a chill over my body. When I look at third base I can imagine him standing there in his short coaching shorts with some seeds in and his sunglasses tanline. I always pour some Ketel at home plate and hit him an imaginary dinger as I run the bases. This splash of Ketel on home plate. It magical turned into a heart when I looked down. Some people says it's a reach, I call that a sign. Thanks for meeting me at the field Dad.

Remembering Phil

"Hey Alexa, I just wanted to tell you this. On Saturday, I played in my last baseball game. It was emotional, but as a senior I started the first game, got taken out, and then didn't start the second game. It wasn't unusual, I had a bad year, sucked a lot, couldn't hit, basically sucked. My coach put me in to pinch hit in the second game, we were playing against the 4th ranked team in the nation and I looked into the sky. I was down 1 ball, 2 stikes and called time out. I stared at the sky and said outloud to myself "coach I don't care about whether we win or lose, I don't care the outcome. Can you please be with me, help me have fun like I did with you and just help my team." The next pitch I ripped a single to right field that tied the game and we ended up winning in the 13th inning on my senior night, last game I ever played. I just wanted to tell you because I feel it was because of you dad."
— **Logan Thomas**

LOVE YOURSELF

"Until you value yourself, you won't value time. Until you value time, you will not do anything." – Unknown

Think on that a minute. There have been many self-worth and confidence quotes like this one that has hit me close to home. The reason is simple. Many times in our lives we face unknown moments that make us question whether or not we can make it. Moments when "just do it" isn't enough. Moments that make us wonder: Are we good enough? Should we keep going?

We get these thoughts because there are "less than" moments when we think we are below the standards of God, or man, moments when our ideas and creativity seem below par, moments when we feel we're "beneath" all of our peers.

Recognizing this saddens me on so many levels. It saddens me because I have been there. Because sometimes I still go to these low places. Because I know I'm not alone – other people go through times like this, too. Perhaps you do; if not, I guarantee you know someone who does, maybe someone who's there right now.

The difference between then and now is that now I am now able to recognize when I'm in a "less than" moment and, knowing that, I'm now able to get out of that damned rut much faster.

When I first started thinking about confidence, I asked myself what the definition of confidence was. I defined it as *to be confident*. But then it hit me. I think you and I are both sufficiently educated to know that you can't have the word being defined in its own definition. It just doesn't work like that. However, it was eye-opening to me that confidence is one of those words we all just assume we know what it means, but until we are asked we can't seem to find the correct, defining words. So ... I looked "confidence" up in the dictionary. I wanted to know for myself what it actually means. This way, knowing what it means, I could actually use that knowledge to become a more confident person.

con·fi·dence: ˈkänfədəns/ *noun*

1. the feeling or belief that one can rely on someone or something; firm trust.
2. the state of feeling certain about the truth of something.
3. a feeling of self-assurance arising from one's appreciation of one's own abilities or qualities.

adjective

1. self-assured, assured, self-confident, positive, assertive, self-possessed, self-reliant, poised.

Suddenly, a word I'd thought knew the meaning of all my life now has so much more meaning to me. Considering "confidence," trust sticks out to me, as does "to be certain about the truth of something," about "having self-assurance from appreciation."

I can now say I know what confidence is, and in knowing confidence, I now know what I need to strive for, and that confidence is not about faking it till you make it.

When it comes to your own self-worth and confidence, believe me, you actually want to feel it. You want to believe it. You *need* to believe it. So love yourself. Trust yourself.

I think many of us forget that confidence isn't something just for yourself. Having confidence in yourself is important, but you also need to have confidence in other people. Business partners, friendships, intimate relationships, teachers, investors in your dreams or in your business – these are some of the people in your life who you need to have confidence in – and vice versa. Having confidence in others builds their confidence as well your own. Your trust in them gives them a great case of the warm and fuzzies, and it inspires them to be more trustworthy. It makes them thrive.

A lot of times people confuse confidence with cockiness. These are two totally different things. Confidence is self-assurance, while cockiness is arrogance. Confidence has you building up people; cockiness means putting others down to make yourself feel better. If you ask me (and even if you don't), I think that everything about ego-driven cockiness is just lame. Instead of living a cocky attitude, try to focus a little more on the kind of positivity you need in your life to make you confident – to be confidence-worthy.

Frankly, I associate cockiness with an ignorant, self-praising, love-for-yourself-but-not-others kind of attitude. To me, cockiness means walking around like you have a stick up your ass, or like you can walk on water. But, that's just personal opinion. It's time to say "enough with the self-praise." Time, instead, to try to humble yourself. So take that stick out of your ass and try walking with ease and grace. I guarantee you will be approached more often by others who are drawn to your self-confidence, just as they'd been driven away by your cockiness.

Since I have been at a self-confidence low point, not once, not twice, but frequently and for years at a time, I have a good deal of practice with trying to build myself back up. Growing up a dancer, I stood in front the mirror for 40-plus hours a week, constantly trying to perfect one graceful dance move after another. In time, the perfection I reached out for moved past just my dance ability. As I sought dance perfection, I also began to notice a lot of things I liked about myself, and a lot of things I didn't like. Striving for perfection in one area of my life, I began picking apart all of the small details of my body, and my mind. I was brutal with myself. Too often, I thought I sucked at dance, which was at odds with my wanting to be nothing but the best.

Soon, no matter what I did, I always wanted to be better. Instinctively, I picked out all of the flaws. I reached out for success, and in doing so, I began to build my confidence.

But I had a long way to go. Sometimes I thought I was too muscular. Most dancers have a tall, slender, slim body. You know, the look you picture when you think "dancer" – which forms in your mind because you automatically think "ballerina." When I looked in the mirror, I decided I was short and stalky, with quads of steel. What I saw in the mirror wasn't quite the dancer ideal. Not the dancer body I'd been hoping for during my adolescence.

Other times, I thought I was too fat. I worried that the cottage cheese I couldn't get rid of – that ugly-to-me stuff that lurked on the back of my legs and on my butt – was going to stop me from doing anything great in my life. Of course, as a dancer, I had to wear those tiny, revealing costumes and uniforms. I had to squeeze myself into them, then go out and perform in front of strangers who – because I was a competitive dancer – were really there to judge me. Having all eyes on me, and I literally mean having eyes scoping out the majority of my body – along with my dance moves – was always extremely intimidating.

My lack of self-confidence wasn't just about dance, either. Remember, I live in Vegas, a town filled with all those flashy lights, all those strippers and professional dancers and hostesses, and all those other beautiful people. Now, at least sometimes, I can look back and realize that what I see just means they are beautiful people on the outside. Beautiful, too many times, in the sense of having beautiful plastic implanted within their skin. But of course, regardless of how they got there, they still look beautiful. Believe me, being a twenty-something lady in a town where most females are professionally gorgeous is not for the faint of heart. Living here, women like to:

Leave the house with a face covered by makeup. Drive a flashy car with shiny rims and a rhinestoned license plate. Own some thousand-dollar Gucci designer bag to rest on our shoulders and five-grand Jimmy Choo spikey-heels on their feet. Have the kind of white teeth that actually really do blind people when they smile. Pay for lady lumps (yes, boobs) that are upright and perky (to say the least). For me, living in Las Vegas with all these ego-crushing self-expectations was a challenge. Before I moved to Vegas, I was just Alexa, a twenty-something student, and competitive dancer from a reviving Rust-belt town the Midwest. Most days, I wore no makeup. My car had only two hub-caps because the other two got stolen and I didn't have the time – or the self-conscious worry – to order new ones. My Target $29.95 purse did just fine. The Louis Vuitton bag I received as a gift typically stayed in the closet. My size-B bra was the last of my worries. My wardrobe was all about comfort.

So you can imagine how my confidence was rocked a bit when I first got here. However, despite the social pressure of living in a city where it seemed like everybody was conforming to some impossible-to-achieve beauty ideal, I didn't want to let that change me. As it turned out, that was exactly the right decision. It works for me, and – if you believe in yourself if you have self-confidence – it will work for you. You shouldn't want to change just because others "expect it" of you. Instead, try being confident in the real you. Embrace and cherish the things that make you beam. Things that make you happy when you're alone with yourself.

As you set out to be (or build) confident in yourself, it's important to understand that some people really are more confident with those enhancements – so judging them by your own self-confident standards isn't fair to them, and, remarkably, judging them doesn't help you, either. Just because you don't want those artificial enhancements, from bold makeup to Gucci's purses and Jimmy Choo's shoes to professional saline boobs doesn't mean that those other people shouldn't want those things either. It doesn't mean that they aren't good people. It just means that, at this stage in their lives, they need a little bit of material, name-brand help with their self-confidence.

They do what works for them. So you should do what works for you. To get you started on figuring out what works for you, these are a few of the things that I do that help me get "out of it," that makes me feel comfortable and confident – and frankly, that's all that matters:

Set intentions. Every day. Positive affirmations can do wonders for your mind, body, and soul. Change your mental diet. This means put on the brakes on all that self-hate, and slow down on all that consumption of negative influences. If something (or someone) tears you down, walk away from it, or them

Stop focusing on what others look like. Enough with the comparing. Things in life can be competitive, but life itself isn't a competition.   Understand that, thanks to Photoshop and plastic surgery, what you see on the TV, in magazines, and on social media is altered. Rarely is what you see really that pure

You do not need validation from anyone   THAT. IS. SO. FREAKIN'. IMPORTANT. In my eyes, it also the key to your success ... and mine ... The only validation you need is that extra heartbeat your body pumps, or that stomach-drop feeling you get when you want to do something wholeheartedly. Your own self-validation matters.   Listen to your body, it's usually right Remember that no one is perfect. Including you. Fight your perfectionist tendencies

Surround yourself with support. People who are "Team You." People who will be your hype when you need it. People are that there for you at the drop of a hat. Love yourself the way you are right now, not waiting to love what you imagine yourself to be, once you get there

You might think this next thing is a bit cheesy, but I beg to differ, and after you read the examples, you might differ, too. So here it is. Affirmations work. That's right, affirmations work.

Either write down these affirmations (below) – or, even better, write down your own affirmations. Then say them out loud, to yourself. Every day. And especially say them every day when you're somewhere deep in the pits. Note that the first part of each of my affirmations applies to everyone. However, the part of the affirmation that comes after-the-... applies to me. You can use the after-the-...s I provide, or you can create your own. So as you think about YOUR own affirmations, plug in YOUR own after-the-... answers.

✓ I like myself and love myself because ... I have a heart filled with pure gold.

✓ I'm an expert at ... dancing it out in the kitchen, eating a full pint of ice cream at one sitting, taking action about my dreams and goals

✓ I feel good about ... where I am and who I am

✓ I'm loved by ... my family, my friends, and by strangers (including some of the people reading this book) who admire me and who expect me to make a difference

✓ I've been told I have pretty ... eyes

✓ The persons I admire most ... my dad, Eric Thomas, Magic Giant

✓ I laugh when I think about ... the dork I typically make of myself in public

✓ People compliment me about ... my will to inspire others

✓ I feel peaceful when ... I read, when I am in a bath filled with bubbles, and when I drink hot chocolate

Go ahead, try it. You might feel silly at first, but trust me, you will get to that place where you actually start to feel better. To feel more confident. To feel more alive.

So stop looking for self-worth from the eyes and mouths of others. The only one you have anything to prove something to is yourself, and what you need to prove is that you love yourself and know you are worth it.

SOUL-KEEPING

"Minimalism as a lifestyle is the art of letting go. Clutter is not just the stuff on your floor, it's anything that stands between you and the life you want to live" – *Unknown*

It's called doing a little housekeeping. Or better yet, *soulkeeping*. When bad things happen, or instead of the best you wind up with the lesser of the good, it is at those times that you realize what and who are the most important people and things in your life. What serves you a purpose and what doesn't.

Soulkeeping challenges you to re-evaluate your current relationships and goals, to define whether those things which seem so important are actually helping – or hurting – the ultimate goals in your life. However, *soulkeeping* is not an easy task. It's not the same as housekeeping. It's not like cleaning your room or your car, separating stuff into "Goodwill" and "trash" piles. Unless you are like me, something of a hoarder, throwing away miscellaneous things that you can buy again if you need to should be an easy task.

For those of us who hoard things with attached memories, not so much.

Housekeeping yourself – instead of housekeeping your house – means making hard decisions. It means removing people from your life who were once a blessing – realizing that, over time, people and relationships can and do change. Similar to my ride or dies. It means that one chapter in your life is over – the time when you needed them, or they needed you, has passed Similar to break-ups. It can be difficult to understand that it's time to either forgive and forget or to hold onto that grudge as you move on with your life. Ultimately, it's time – to regret, or not to regret – the decision you just had to make.

When you close a chapter in your life, you can't help learning from it. Most importantly, though, you discover deep and abiding truths. You slowly start to shift away from those people or things that filled your life with nonsense, distraction, frustration and bad advice – or who were emotional vampires, always too needy, always ready to suck your soul dry. Instead of continuing on as you've done before, you stop doing the things that don't excite you.

As you turn to a new page, you find the truths that make life worth living. Truths that bring you the happiness that you deserve – that we all deserve. Truths that make you thrive like never before. In this search for everlasting happiness, you find those moments that mold you, not break you. You hold on tighter to people who fill you with love, not hate. You finally realize what fuels your passions instead of destroying them.

Removing your soul's clutter gives you the room to see clearly. That, in turn, gives you the room to feel both uncomfortable and vulnerable – feelings which can be scary, but when these feelings come along, suck it up. Not for me, but for you. Remove the dust, brush aside the piles of dirty laundry, stack up the dirty dishes and give yourself the chance to breathe again. Cleaning is never fun, whether it's your house or your soul. A thorough top-to-bottom cleaning is rarely something we look forward to doing, and for good reason. It's a daunting task. But, if you want to move forward with your life, it's a task that still needs to be done.

Though it took a horrific loss to open my eyes to it, my theory to *soulkeeping* doesn't focus only on losing people to death. That is why it relates you – to every other single person reading this. You may have never lost a parent, child, grandparent, or other close relative but you probably have lost a lover or best friend. If not to death, then to a break-up that feels as permanent as death.

Losing people is process survivors of loss have to cope with on a daily basis. In short, life moves on, and so do we. Which means we find new things that bring joy to our hearts – but we also lose things – friends, relationships, even jobs or houses – that once seemed more important to us than life itself.

Soulkeeping involves taking action to move forward, and in doing so, to leave behind everything you may have lost, or just lost touch with. It's about realizing that every relationship and experience had a purpose in your life, those that you keep, and those that you lose or move on from. All in all, *soulkeeping* means evaluating your own personal experiences, then finding out what caused those experiences, good or bad.

PHIL GLAZER RULES: IT'S ALL ABOUT RELATIONSHIPS

Gosh, I can't even begin to count the number of times my dad said this to me growing up. Especially during my teenage years, the years when we're all trying to find out who we're meant to be and what it is we're meant to do in our lives. My dad was Mr. Social – a social butterfly everywhere we went. He knew at least one person everywhere we went – but if he didn't, he'd spark up a conversation. Somehow, some way, he would find something interesting about whomever he opened up to, something to tie them together, something to form a connection and forge a new relationship.

I will always envy this trait about him, as well as in others I meet who have this amazing gift. It's honestly quite the rare and wonderful talent. Although I think – as I'm getting older – I am getting better at this whole relationship and network thing, I'll never match up to dad, or to those few others who have a real gift for social relationships. They have the gift of talking to complete strangers and turning them into new best friends. They're able to continue a new conversation even when it seems there is nothing left to talk about.

This kind of networking is truly a gift, one in which I need to work on. Perhaps you do, too. If not, you're blessed. If you do, then roll up your sleeves and join me. Dad's point is actually quite simple: when you start networking, you never know who you are going to meet. How they can help you. How you can help them.

This kind of social relationship is about networking yourself, and not just your business self, either. Business networking is all about what you can get for yourself. Social networking is all about creating mutual relationships – two-way friendships. Social networking recognizes that relationships are important in life. Whether a relationship becomes a long-term friendship or a short-term casual acquaintanceship – one that doesn't last past that first conversation – doesn't really matter. All relationships teach us something – about others – and, if you look closely, about ourselves as well.

The majority of the time, it's not your best friend who gives you your best new opportunity in life. That new job, that foot in the door for your big break you've been waiting for, or even that introduction to your future husband. Typically, the person with that kind of influence in your life is a person you just met in passing.

He might be the man sitting across from you at Starbucks – who, for me, was the man who gave me my first conference speaking gig. Or he might be the man who sat in the audience at my first speaking gig, who is now the editor of the book you are reading right now. You get my point. This theory fits my life's story. I believe it fits everyone's life story – if you give it a chance.

PHIL GLAZER RULES: NEVER BURN BRIDGES

Burning bridges does you no good. Instead of solving problems, burning bridges creates a crushing weight on your shoulders. That weight ruins any future relationships, future plans, future possibilities. The truth is, you never know what someone can do for you in the future. You never know how people are going to change. We aren't psychics, so it's impossible to see what good this person could do for us one day.

Yes, I know this all seems a little self-centered. It must feel like I'm only focusing on what possibilities this person could "do for me" one day. Well, the truth is, it's more of the weight off your shoulders over what you might have lost rather than about "what's in it for me" sometime in the future. Doing unto others does unto yourself, too.

So kill people with kindness instead of hate. Kill them with love when they may not deserve it. Kill them with soft words when you want nothing more to cuss them out.

The hate, the cuss words, the drama, they do nothing positive for you. Maybe when you give vent to hatred or anger, you actually feel better for a second (literally, maybe for a second). But, that visceral relief doesn't solve anything. Worse, what happens when that person or the situation never disappears? Your moment of release and relief can lead to a lifetime of hostility and confrontation The negative chatter is always something that can come back and bite you in the ass when you least expect it to.

FROM THE OLD ALEXA TO THE NEW ALEXA

When you go through life, especially as you make transitions, you'll find that it's time to say goodbye to the "old" you, then reach out and embrace the new you. It works like this:

From the old Alexa:

The old Alexa was naïve.

The old Alexa believed in luck – she believed that there are such people as the "lucky" ones, and then there are the rest of us.

The old Alexa didn't think she would lose her dad when she was just 21 years old.

The old Alexa didn't have perspective on the hard parts of life. She didn't know that the hard parts are also the good parts because they make you grow. She didn't see life that way.

The old Alexa never asked for help. Never.

The old Alexa chased the boys who'd left her, who'd her hurt her, and she did so because she was afraid to be alone. She was afraid to be uncomfortable.

The old Alexa always put others before herself. She didn't have sufficient self-love to say "no" when somebody asked her, or to do things solely for her.

The old Alexa never confronted anyone or anything. She always wanted things to be perfect. She thought perfect existed somewhere in our reality.

The old Alexa didn't know it's okay to not be perfect.

The old Alexa never learned from her mistakes.

The old Alexa stressed out over the little things.

The old Alexa was a homebody who never wanted to leave her comfort zone.

To the new Alexa:

The new Alexa started giving herself more credit in life.

The new Alexa discovered she'd been too hard on herself, and backed off.

The new Alexa chose to ease up and breathe a little more.

The new Alexa decided to meditate a little more, to self-reflect a little more.

The new Alexa realizes she can lose anyone at anytime.

The new Alexa keeps working on not stressing over the little things.

The new Alexa focuses on letting go of that naïve side of herself .

These are a lot of transitions. That's what this is. As you make them, cut yourself some slack. These things will take time. So, as you move from old-you to new-you, work on your patience, and trust in your process. Keep learning ... knowledge is wisdom, and wisdom is the only kind of wealth that really matters.

As you make this transition from the old-you to the new-you, never stop perfecting your crafts. Keep thinking outside the box, and always keep striving to become an expert at whatever your gifts or crafts or skills may be – you'll never know when you'll really need them.

As you make this transition, hold onto the thought that you are the perfect combination of being sensitive and being a savage. Feel when you need to feel and grind when you need to grind. Exist on your own damned terms – don't be afraid to go wild for a while. Create your own reality – and never forget that you're the only one that can actually make it happen.

Remember that life has a lot of rules, some of which you're going to want to break. But read those rules before you break them – you don't want to break all the rules (some of them have real consequences). However, if all you do is obey all the rules, you'll never have fun, and never transition from the old you to the new you. Along the way, have some fun. Never let the rebel in you die.

You don't have to transition from the old you to new you alone. Find someone who sees the fire in your eyes ... and who wants to play with that fire. Don't settle for anything less. Don't chase boys who don't choose you (this works for guys, too). Your expectations may be high but that man is out there somewhere. Don't search, let him come to you. Until then, be okay being with just you.

Becoming the new you means learning to love being you – and knowing that being you pisses off all the right people. Self-love is the greatest middle finger of all time. Here are a few other rules you can follow (or break, but learn them before you break them):

Kill people with kindness (not hate) but if they deserve killing, kill them anyway.

Logic gets you from Point A to Point B, but imagination gets you anywhere you want to go: imagine, dream, and wander far, because the places your imagination is going to take you are the places people write about in books. Places you see in movies.

Chase your dreams, not your Ketel One – no matter how good whatever you use instead of Ketel One tastes going down, some things in life just aren't worth chasing.

Be consistent in your endeavors. Chase the things that mean the most, the things that you have control over.

And never forget: if you're passionate enough about something, people will want to join your army. As you build your own army, keep the movement moving. Move with me – and move to the beat of your own drummer.

Your step-count always matters, so step away.

Share your story – you never know who's listening and who it may help. Everyone is connected in some way, shape or form, which is why anyone is a potential recruit in your army, in the movement we now share. If you walk in enough circles you are bound to find your way

Never give up. Yet that doesn't mean you have to keep pushing toward a goal that no longer exists. As I've learned, sometimes running from your problems means running into new opportunities. When you feel stuck ... run, and run fast. You never know what you might run in to.

If you know you're a good catch, then dammit, let yourself fall. It's okay to be caught if the person who catches you is the right one for you.

Sometimes it's okay to be the right kind of selfish. Learn to do things for you. Your sanity is important.

Be ready for the next big struggle, but always remember, no matter what you're struggling for (or with), in the end, you'll be okay. This life you have was meant for you.

As you become the new you, never forget the old you – never forget where you came from. Your past is the driving force that made you who you are today. Always believe in believing in something, anything. Believing in your dream is something special.

Keep livin' the dream. In any moment of unease, always go back to your dream – always remember that this dream of yours is the only thing that matters. This dream is what fills your heart with so much joy. It's what makes your heart explode with kindness and love.

When in doubt, first recall your old self, then, from that perspective, write your new self a letter. Point out just how far you've come, so far, and how much fun it will be to get to the next step on your journey. And when you finally become your new self, that becomes the next "old self" on your journey to a newer and even better new self.

This is a journey, not a destination.

December 31, 2017— "Who needs a hype girl when I have me?" — alexa to alexa

PHIL GLAZER RULES: CHASE YOUR DREAMS NOT YOUR KETEL

My dad always had his head on straight, but he never let that get that in the way of living life and having fun. Ketel One on the rocks was his drink of choice. Yes, I mean Ketel One vodka over ice. That's it, that's all.

However, I'm not trying to get the point across to go drinking Ketel One every night.

My point is, even though my dad had this level-headedness, he still managed to indulge when the time was right. With that, as with everything else he taught us, consistency is key, and consistency is exactly what I learned from my dad's drinking choice. When one drink works, drink that drink. I'm not saying don't expand your horizons. I'm saying if something works time and time again, then it's time to be consistent.

"Chase your dreams, not your Ketel." This is another tattoo of mine. One which, when people see it, they don't know whether to smile or wince, if only because they are unsure if I was drunk when I got the tattoo. Then they wonder if I am an alcoholic, or if I lost a bet.

All of those are wrong. I was sober. I thought about the tattoo and phrase for some time and, for me, it is actually quite meaningful. It's actually one of my favorite tattoo's to date/ It makes me smile every time I manage to get a little peek at it.

"Chase your dreams, not your Ketel," means that some things in life aren't worth chasing. It means that the things which are worth chasing are worth running full force, head on, sprinting for them until your lungs want to explode and your heart is burning. It means that with that consistency, anything is possible. It means that if you chase your dreams and take action, those dreams will, in fact, come true. Finally, it means that if you let go of the things that aren't worth chasing, you will have a weight off your shoulders that will let you run wild.

Remembering Phil

"During the summer I had enlisted in the United States Air Force, there would be times where we'd go to a sports bar. I was not 21 at the time I might add, and somehow with his way with words he always got me a drink. He believed that "If you're old enough to serve our country you're old enough to enjoy a beer," and I can promise you that we, in fact, did enjoy plenty of beers together. There had been some events that took place over vacations that I will not share (so my mom doesn't kick my ass), but they were all very memorable. Phil was a champ, the man drank straight vodka, and that was his drink of choice. Phil loved to have a great time just like the rest of us." – Zack DePalma

FULL CIRCLE MOMENTS

Does what goes around really come around? Yes. Like when the boomerang surprisingly comes back to you, when you catch it with your own two hands. When what going around comes back around – that is the moment when your life moves past those "everything happens for a reason" moments to a time when you actually start to see the purpose of it all.

Of everything that happens.

It's when you start to not only feel more grateful but to actually **act** more grateful. You might not know the reason for the struggle itself – for the moment that knocked you on your ass a time or two – but regardless of the reason, you start to open up to what that whatever-is-coming-back-around may have actually done for you. Maybe it brought you closer to the purpose of your life, or maybe it opens your eyes to the fact that your struggle, or your many struggles, were just key components – puzzle piece to your ultimate "why." This happened for me. I mean it took a little while for the boomerang to come back ... but it did come back.

"Your WHY is the purpose, cause or belief that inspires you. ... at work and at home, that will help you find greater fulfillment in all that you do ... This is what it means to find your WHY ... Fulfillment comes when we live our lives on purpose." – Simon Sinek

I think Simon Sinek says it best. That's probably why he has written a book on this topic and why he delivered his famous TED talk on this topic ... This idea has always resonated with me, but now more so than ever. Face it, it's important when an idea fits your own purpose ... that's when you need to. Run. With. It.

I have always known that I have it in me to be something or someone who lives for other people. To not just live for others, but to go above and beyond what most others do for the rest of those others. To be: A **leader**. Ears for people to talk to. Arms for someone who needs a hug. Motivation for someone who is feeling a bit too lazy for his (or her) own good. Family when they have none. A friend when they need one.

The not just one, not just two, but the many struggles I have endured have only proven to me that I am, in fact, supposed to help people. I was put here on this earth to serve humanity in some way, shape or form. That is my purpose. My destiny is:

To love selflessly. To spread kindness on post-its. To write letters of wisdom. To make videos about what living life to the fullest really means. To speak perspective. To write my story. To share my heart. To show people what my definition of livin' the dream means.

I can remember the first time I had that "aaa haaaa" moment. That "holy shit, I think I know what my dream job is … kinda" moment. That "one problem I have is that my dream job doesn't have a title you can look up in the classifieds or find on Indeed.com" moment. That "it's "up to you, Alexa, to be" moment when I become:

A difference maker. A storyteller. A world conqueror.

So this may have not only been when I finally had my first "aaa haaa" moment, but also my first "haha! Good luck, with that, Alexa, your job doesn't exactly exist on planet earth" moment. Since you've read this far, I think (I certainly hope) you know me better by now, my friend. You know I don't tend to listen to the voices in my head or to the little angelic and devilish guys sitting on my shoulders. Whenever I hear one of them, I turn that noise off real quick. Instead of listening to all that laughable nonsense, I said to myself, "Difference maker. Storyteller. World Conqueror. Any one of those will look mighty good on a business card."

So I did just that. I actually made those business cards. Let me tell you, they look beautiful. To top it off the confidence of writing those "job titles" on them, they proved to be quite the conversation starter, too.

What happened next? I'd finally figured out my dream job, but what the hell did that entail? Rather than sit and wonder, I started to develop a plan or – to be more accurate – many, many

371

plans based on all the ideas I had jam packed in my brain. Some that made sense, while others didn't look good on paper, not at all. The more ideas I came up with, however, the more excited I got. At times, all those new ideas also had me feeling more than a bit overwhelmed. Still, I like to say that I have entrepreneur blood pumping in my veins. I was born to start and build an empire of my own. Which means that the more ideas I have, the more opportunities I have for success.

Currently, I am in the process of trying to create something larger than life. To create a movement that actually moves. To create something much, much bigger than this 5'3," fun-sized Alexa Glazer. To create something that I want the entire world to grasp on to. To create something that sticks, roams, and adventures.

I want to not only have an entrepreneurship mindset, with that special kind of blood type pumping in my veins but to actually become an entrepreneur. To say, "I created this. This is my baby." To say "I am the boss, and I am a boss babe." The life guided by the idea that my "why" has become exceedingly important up to this point in my journey, and for all my future endeavors. Without that oh-so-special "why," what do you really have? Not much.

That "why" has become vastly important because, in moments of fear, moments of chaos, moments of defeat, or moments when I've reached a plateau and don't think I can go any farther, I have to be able to go back to my why.

So do you.

Your "why" should become your happy place. Your safe haven. Essentially, it is and should be your bible. This is the beginning of your full circle moment. Realizing that typically your "why" came from you "when" moment. The moment that changed your life and then created your life's purpose. This is why it shall become your safe place.

This is the case for everything in life. All aspirations begin with that very special "why." This is true in your career, your relationships, your family and everything "life" has to offer you.

Then there is the follow–through, whatever that means to you. Keep your mind in check for that purpose. Don't get lost in the end all, the be-all, the possibilities of large success, huge money, or the shiny aspects of being an entrepreneur or being whatever your heart and soul is set on fire from. Instead, know what your "why" is and live that "why" for today. Tomorrow will come, or it won't, but you can't live in the future, and shouldn't try.

Knowing your "why" means knowing your values. It's one thing to know and understand your values but it's another thing entirely to actually value them. Seems a bit contradictory, but many people don't put this thought into account. Valuing your values is all about following through with them. Your values shouldn't just look good on paper. They should be active in your life, daily. They need to be a part of you, to be one with you. They should all look good on you. When will this happen for you?

It's one thing to know and understand your values, but it's another thing entirely to actually value them.
Practice what you preach. If you value family, do you – on random occasions – ask them how are they are? If you value religion, do you practice your faith every day? If you value time, do you take advantage of every moment? If you value money, do you save or spend? If you value passion, do you let your passions drive your life? Many people value what looks good on paper, but don't actually act on them.

When you stop worrying about what can be. When you stop stressing about the little things. When you stop wondering how to get there. When you focus more on why you want to get there. That's when your "how" prayers will be answered.

In time. One day. In the future. Maybe that day is today. Maybe that day is tomorrow. Maybe that day is three years from now. You'll never know until it arrives, but it will arrive if you never give up on your "why." As long as you always believe in your purpose, as long as you base your "why" on trust. **Trust the process and the process will trust you.**

I truly believe that I was put on this planet to change lives. And I truly believe that you were put on this planet for your own cosmic purpose. You may already know what that purpose is, but perhaps not … yet.

We don't always figure out what we were meant to do until our minds think it's too late to actually go for it. Maybe that's how you're feeling, right now. If so, let me tell you a little secret … it's never too late to do what you were meant to do. So I challenge you.

I challenge you to change that mindset.

Whether you find your own particular "why" at age ten, age 25, or age 85, as long as you're alive and open to new possibilities, nothing is impossible. To me, very little is unrealistic. I think – no, I know – that you have all the time in the world, and all the power you need, to build the empire you were born to create, and to leave behind the legacy you were meant to show the world, regardless of time or age.

Write down your thoughts. Create ideas. Lots of them. So many that some seem silly. That's what makes the really good ones stand out. Make things happen. If you don't, someone else will – not for you, but for themselves. So it might as well be you. Life is way too short to continue talking about your ideas – or worse, only thinking about your ideas and then watching someone else make your ideas their reality. That's bullshit if you ask me.

Instead of thinking your ideas are too big to cultivate, think about how big of a difference you can make in the world. Never limit yourself or your mind. When you know your "why" the "how" will come. Just trust.

PHIL GLAZER RULES: GIVE RATHER THAN GET

To give to others rather than to receive is quite the simple concept – at Christmas time, for instance, you hear "it is better to give than to receive," an idea foreign to children but more reasonable for adults. I think this is something you start to understand as you get older, and eventually, it's not just about receiving presents on your birthday or at Christmas.

Instead, "giving" is all about watching the faces of others when they receive something from you, something that they least expected and most wanted. This also happens when you surprise someone, again, when they least expect it. Now, this surprise doesn't always have to be a present you spent a fortune on. Sometimes the best gifts are the ones you spent nothing on it. Giving is giving anything. It's giving your soul. Your heart. Your everything.

June 23, 2017— I can remember a few months ago day dreaming about the time that I would be grinding through all hours of the night to ship out whatever my first move would be for this movement of mine. So now, that it's here, and the first orders are out, it's a very surreal moment for me. I try my best to do things for others that I forget what this process is doing for me and the experience so far has been overwhelming in the best way possible because it has touched me in every way. Emotionally, physically and mentally.

August 21, 2017 – Dreams became reality this weekend and I am still dancing on cloud nine. The beauty of taking chances and making moves.

__January 5, 2015__ — I think in life we all have moments of realization. When realize that literally nothing else in the world matters. That nothing matters outside of your wildest dreams that have literally become your wildest reality. Tonight, I had that moment. Tonight, I sit here pinching myself as I sit on cloud nine watching pigs fly.

I'm currently having that moment of jaw dropping realization. That moment of pure bliss that goes beyond what I have daydreamed about and further than I thought my imagination could even travel. This moment is giving me the chilliest of chills and the highest of highs (no this isn't the pain pills talking, either).

This feeling, these emotions, it's like what they talk about in the movies. It's what you see on the big screen. It's what you hear in those feel good folk songs. It's what you read in those famous poems. It starts to feel a lot like you're literally living in your very own fairy tale. I know, I sound a little crazy. Well maybe and probably a lot crazy. Butterflies, chills, highs, fairy tales ... Alexa you're nuts, girl. I promise though t is is the realist of feelings.

Tonight, I sat on the couch staring - literally just staring - at the manuscript of my book. I printed off all of the final edits of my sections, stapled them together, put on a cover page (Livin' the dream... today because tomorrow is not promised. Written by, Alexa Glazer) and had hundreds of pages of words I wrote, sitting on my damn lap. Holy shit, Written by, Alexa Glazer. I am a damn author. Of a damn book. That people are going to read. Wow. Reality check, friends.

This book, this moment, is four years in the making. It's allowing complete strangers access to my deepest and darkest secrets, thoughts, and it's a VIP ticket into my heart. The heart that is so full right now.

I began writing as a coping mechanism. It was a way to have physical proof of my feelings. To have my thoughts leave my jam-packed mind and go into the universe once and for all. I wrote this book as a way to never forget moments I shared with my dad, because that's the scariest thought to have when someone leaves you. You never want to forget. Forget the smile, the laughs, the conversations. You fear losing memory. I wrote to never forget moments I thought I wasn't going to make it, but here I am standing tall, chest out, feet planted. I wrote to simply just write.

Tonight, as I sat on the couch staring and holding my book like a baby, I began reading section after section to my roommate, Jenna, one of my number one advocates. With tears streaming down my face (and hers), belly laughs (coming from both of us), sarcastic Alexa remarks, followed by more giggles, and I can honestly say I have never been prouder of anything in my entire life. I can't wait to share this story of mine with the entire world. **The. Entire. World.**

The realization I am having once again is that this is exactly what I am supposed to be doing with my life. That me, Alexa Glazer is exactly where she is supposed to be. With exactly the right people around her. That somehow, someway the worst moment of my entire life has selfishly given me some of the best moments. It's the realization that I NEED to help people, that I love - love, and that nothing is impossible. Literally nothing.

I like to joke that I am a small human with the biggest heart in the world. That if you gave The Grinch my heart, he would change. He would love everyone, and everything and be the kindest soul out there. So back to this heart of mine, I believe that my heart is as golden as can be and my biggest goals is that I want to give every person I encounter a piece of it.

Now, I was very excitingly telling a group of youth students this, that I wanted each and every one of them to leave the day with a piece of my heart. One boy raised his hand and so genuinely said "Alexa, I can't take a piece of your heart?" and I said "Yes of course you can! Why not?" he responded with "If you give everyone *a piece of your heart ... what are you going to have left for you?" My heart stopped. It was the sweetest thing, and it also gave me another one of these realization moments. A moment I hadn't thought about before. I responded it with ... "I can give everyone a piece of my heart because you all have all given me a piece of your heart without even knowing it. It's like an even exchange."*

This is everything. *Throughout my entire process of "livin' the dream," these moments give me life. They keep me going. They are what make my heart beat, my blood pump, and my lungs breathe. I try so unbelievably hard to spread this movement and to literally make it move from human to human, over state lines, across bodies of water, and soaring across the entire world, that I forget what it is doing to me. It's changing me for sure. It's making me the best human being that I can possibly be.*

So, thank you world for sincerely accepting me. Accepting my values and ideals. Accepting my movement and creating waves. Accepting that I am just a human trying to help other humans. Accepting that everyone is entitled to their feelings, that they are valid and that they are real and that not enough people tell others that. Accepting that I am far from perfect but embracing every flaw, embracing my perfectly in perfect life. Accepting that I want to break the rules and color outside the lines. Accepting Alexa for Alexa, and accepting you as you.

Here I am, in that moment, and I can't stop grinning from ear to ear. The moment that my heart is beating so fast and that I feel as the person next to me could hear the thumping going on inside my chest. The moment I all of a sudden became very hot and bothered. The moment I began sweating a little, that my palms are sweating and I think you could squeeze out some sweat from the armpits of my shirt. It's like the world stopped but I am still going, just in slow motion.

Here's not to my moment of realization but to yours. Whenever that time comes. Whenever your heart is filled with the amount of love and passion that you feel like it may actually explode ... honor it. Remember that life is unfair to everyone and that is what makes life so fair. So, my friend, you are exactly where you need to be. I promise if you are in a low place it will get better and I promise you if you are at a high point it will still get better. Trust your journey.

January 7, 2018 *— Some people may call me crazy I would just say I have a lot of character Yes, I make myself laugh. Yes, I actually buckled the manuscript of* *my book into my passenger seat of my car. Yes, I am a huge dork just geeking out over one of the most surreal moments of my life. Judge me it's okay. Don't ever apologize for being you because there is no one else in the world as cool as you.*

January 17, 2018— *The amount of full circle moments going on in my life right now is insane. Life is so scary but life is so damn good all at the same time.*

PHIL GLAZER RULES: THE IMPORTANCE OF FUNDAMENTALS

The basics set you up for success. Never forget where you started, because that is what gets you to where you want to be. Don't lose sight of the simple things.

This rule came about because my dad talked so much about this rule when it came to baseball, and as "Coach Phil," a lot of his life-rules came out of baseball. Rules like: use two hands, watch the pitch go in the catcher's glove, run through the bag, slide whenever you're unsure if you're going to make it in time.

These are the things you learn when you start out playing baseball. They are the basics. And as basics, they also apply to life. I learned these rules applied to more than baseball when I started dancing. Ballet is the background to every style and technique in dance. Whether you are doing tap dance, hip hop or jazz, you are always using the basic fundamentals of ballet, the ones you learned when you were starting out at three years old.

Later, I learned that these basics work in life as well. Life's basics are the ones you learned when you were little. You learned to be kind. To smile at people. To be polite. To say "please" and "thank you." To not roll your eyes. To shake people's hands and give them eye contact. These are the basic fundamentals of civil behavior that do not go unnoticed. They are what set you apart from those that think these things don't help you achieve success. The importance of fundamentals, what Coach Phil called the basics, is simple: they are what help you perfect your craft, including the "craft" of living well. They make you bright and shiny. They make you an expert in your field. They give people an experience.

Remembering Phil

"I was about eight years old or so going to my sisters softball game. Unfortunately, Alexa couldn't come, so I was all alone for this one! (Very rare Alexa and I weren't together at these games) So being me, I was wandering around with a baseball on another field. I started to throw the ball against the fence when I saw Mr. Glazer walking my way. I was a little confused but went with it. He came onto the field and said "Big John, what you doing?" I said

"just messing around." So he said "want me to teach you some things?" I didn't think twice. We began to play catch and he starting to teach me how to throw change ups and some other pitches that were safe for my age to throw. I'll never forget those pitch grips! When the game ended and I say "shouldn't you go shake hands and stuff? " he replies " I would, but the umps aren't very happy with me" The funny thing is he got thrown out of my sisters game, so he came down and continued to teach the game he loved. I'll never forget that day and that funny smirk he had when he told me about the umps. LIVIN THE DREAM! Miss you Coach Phil." – **John Sabolik**

*"My memories kick in more when I was about 4 and Phil 6 and a half. He made me a baseball T to practice hitting. I used to tease him all the time that I was his only friend. I remember him making me play ball with him all the time and this goes on for years. We would be out in the yard practicing – hitting, catching, grounders and running bases. In the end, as I grew, I ended up playing ball like a boy! He must have always wanted a little brother. We had many of years of that and many other things that filled in the blanks." – **Diana Cefaratti**

WHAT I WOULD SAY TO YOU ...

Some of us are lucky enough to live a very full, vibrant lives with our dads. To have an unbreakable, unforgettable, undeniable father-daughter bond. To have someone there who's always ready to show you the ropes of life. To be there for you during every accomplishment – as well as every heartbreak, failure, and each one of those never-to-be-forgotten "get your shit together" moments.

I am not one of those lucky ones.

OK, for my first 21 years, I did have that unbreakable, unforgettable, undeniable father-daughter bond. I did have some of those "show you ropes of life" courses jam-packed into the first years of my life. I had my dad there for some of my stand-out accomplishments (unfortunately, not the reeaaallly big ones), some of my heartbreaks (but at least he got to witness the rest of those heartbreaks from his place there in heaven), some failure (but not quite my biggest), and at least a few pivotal "get your shit together" moments (we all have these, usually too often).

As for a full vibrant life … absolutely not. I got 21 years. Which might sound like a lot, but it isn't – not by a long shot. And my heart shudders to know others get even less time with their dads. My dad's passing happened out of nowhere, in the snap of someone's fingers. One instant he was vibrantly alive. The next moment, no. He died when he was only 49 years old. Dealing with his death, and with the rest of my life, I learned to mature and grow as a human being. I grew up real fast.

Dad, while you've been away, these are the things I have learned. *These are the things that I want to say to you.*

You gave me unconditional love, and I still feel it. Never stop giving us signs – they get us through each tough day. You showed me the meaning of love in every sense of the word. You showed it in your marriage, in your parenting, and with everyone you encountered. However, I do wish you made more appearances in my dreams, and I wouldn't mind feeling more love. So if there is any way that you can jump into them a little more often … more than three times in three years … I would jump for joy every morning. But that's just a suggestion.

You showed me how a woman should be treated. How small gestures go a long way. How fighting doesn't resolve problems. How important it is to find a best friend to your life-long partner. Any man in my life has a tough act to follow, but that's okay. You are the standard, and that standard is sky high. I hope to find the man who can live up to your example one day, but until then I'll try not to worry about it.

You made it clear that we should figure things out on our own. You've always been a helping hand, an ear that would listen, and a voice of reason. However, you never once told me what to do. I thank you for this. Having been told to figure it out for myself, I now know what it feels like to be an adult (kind of). Thanks to that life-lesson, I can hold my own. Thank you for leaving me with others who can be that hand, ear, and voice, but a bigger thanks for giving me the courage to make a decision for myself.

You taught me resilience. I've only really learned what this word means more recently. While you were here, I wasn't always aware that you were teaching me this particular lesson, which is a good thing. Your resiliency lessons helped me find within myself the ability to bounce back. More important, you taught me to never give up … and resilience is a gigantic part of that. I take this lesson to heart because, now, after you left this physical part of the earth, I have been through the most difficult thing in my life. I have been through the worst but because I knew giving up wasn't an option, I am still here and still striving.

You became a best friend. Sure, you're my dad, but the bond we shared was like no other. It wasn't just this biological link, the genetics we share, or the last name you gave me. It was the fact that you would sit and wait for me every night after work just to talk. It was the fact that you would stop anything for me at any given moment in time, and I would do the same for you. It was the fact that you were my number one fan, and I was one of your many fans. We can't choose our family, but we do choose our friends. How lucky am I that I got you for both?

I miss you. Every. Damn. Day. That feeling will never go away. I don't want it to go away, either. There is no limit to the things I would do to have another conversation with you, whether I got the chance to have another day with you or just five uninterrupted minutes with you. Every day I wish I could snap my fingers and have you magically appear before my eyes. But if you did appear, I know I wouldn't believe it. I'd rub my eyes and pick up my jaw from the floor, but if this could actually happen, dad, my heart would be so full

I'm mad at you. I'm mad because you left us way too early. You left without saying goodbye. You left, and we're all still here, each of us with a dad-sized or husband-sized hole in our hearts. I'm mad because you couldn't come to my college graduation. I'm mad because you'll also miss joining me for countless other future monumental life moments. You won't be at the launch party for this book I'm writing and, from your place in heaven, you're reading. You won't be at my wedding – the father of the bride won't be attending. I won't have you to walk me down the aisle or join me in that father-daughter dance that you requested to be choreographed. That's something I'll never get over and I'll probably continue to hold a grudge over. To say the least it really chaps my ass. But you also taught me to express myself honestly, enabling to tell you I'm still mad, and probably always will be.

I forgive you, though. I forgive you because I know you didn't want this. I forgive you because you would have said goodbye if you could have. So even though I might still be a little pissed at you, in my heart I know it's not your fault.

I promise you that I will keep your legacy alive.

Phil Glazer was the dad of a lifetime (and trust me, before I'm finished, everyone will know this). The man, the myth, the legend. I promise that I will use what you taught me to inspire others, to kick ass and take names, to grow a pair when I feel like wallowing in self-pity, to always catch the ball with two hands, to make you more proud than ever, to run super diamonds around a baseball field for mental errors, to stay true to the woman that I am, to remain Glazer Strong, and to always keep on *"livin' the dream..."* day in and day out.

I love you. Forever and always. To the moon and back. There really isn't anything more to say here.

I can't wait to see you in heaven one day. I believe that this reunion day is going to be years and decades from now – while it's in the hands of some greater power, I plan on living a long life, and I'm going to keep trying to go on livin' the dream. Since you didn't get the chance to do so, I plan to live that life for the both of us.

Sure, I know plans don't always go as well … "planned," hence you not being here, but I'm aiming for a full life ahead. But I want you to know I look forward to whenever this reunion day comes to pass, and on that day, I look forward to seeing you again. Until then, I will continue drinking Ketel One for you, hitting imaginary dingers all the way up to my angel in the outfield, and dancing with you in my dreams.

LIVIN' THE DREAM ...

"To live life through sacrifice, the grind, small victories, humility and happiness." -- Alexa Glazer

PHIL GLAZER RULES: Livin' the dream ⋯

Livin' the dream!

This was my dad's absolute number one rule in life. His absolute favorite saying and his life-long motto. The statement itself is broad, as it should be. It is a rule up for interpretation and the basis for pure bliss in all of our lives.

At first thought, many people seem to think that *Livin' the dream* means being extraordinary. To an extent, they're right. *Livin' the dream* does have a lot to do with being exceptional, even extraordinary. But it's not about being extraordinary in ways most people seem to think. It doesn't involve being extraordinary in terms of power, money or fame. If you are inclined to doubt me, just look at the lives of people who won a massive lottery. For many, if not most such winners, their lives turned into train wrecks. Still, don't believe me? Google: ***The aftermath of winning the lottery***. You'll see what I mean.

Livin' the dream doesn't have to do with all the shine and sparkle of life, although shine and sparkle could be part of it, and yes we all love just a little bit of that glitter. ***Livin' the dream*** is also about life's struggles, too, the dirt and the grunge. It's about proving that, regardless of what gets thrown at you, you are still living. Right now, if you want to live your own dream, you have a chance. Find it! Take it! Don't waste it!

Phil Glazer's spirit was undeniably rich. I may be biased, but this is what I know about him. Phil Glazer had the kindest soul. He was the best father, husband, friend and coach anyone could ask for. He was truly the man, the myth, and the legend. He was *livin' the dream* – his own dream – day in and day out, right up to the day he died, and his legacy continues to live that dream in those who he'd touched in life. He was fulfilled and thriving, not because of the materialistic extremities of life – he wasn't rich and didn't want to be – but because of his three girls, his commitment of service to others, his passion for life, and baseball.

This wasn't always the case. Until his family came into his life, Phil Glazer's dream was to play professional baseball. To play in the big leagues, to be an All-Star, to help his team win the World Series. To have people wear his jersey, one with the name GLAZER written across the jersey's shoulders. To be a role model to so many others looking to reach their wildest dreams.

The statistics for those who want to live this particular dream are daunting. The percentage of really good high school and collegiate players who make it to the big leagues is incredibly low. So there my dad was ... not quite good enough, not quite tall enough, not quite fast enough ... which meant that he was not drafted. Dream crushed. Well damn. For Phil Glazer, *Livin' the Dream* of playing in the majors was out of the question now right? Wrong.

While making a team didn't happen, Phil Glazer's next big dream was to be a scout for the bigs ... and guess what? He got that opportunity. He got that call from the New York Yankees, who wanted him to be a full-time scout. Dream achieved, right? Or so you would think ... but despite this once-in-a-lifetime chance, Phil Glazer didn't take it. By the time the offer arrived, he had other priorities, other dreams.

Let me tell you that when I found this out, just five months ago (as I write this), from my grandmother, I was actually upset with my dad. *Practice what you preach*, I thought. You reach a dream ... you get the dream ... go after it ... *what the heck, dad.*

The truth is, my dad didn't fail at making his dreams a reality. By the time the Yankees came calling (to which I've got to say, "thank goodness," because who really likes the Yankees anyway?), those dreams had simply changed. Because of that dream-change, he had to make a decision to pivot. He had to forget his childhood dream of being part of the major leagues and look at the bigger picture of what his actual dream had become.

My dad turned down this Yankees position because he found out my mother was pregnant with my sister. Setting aside his life-long dream, he realized that he didn't want us to go through the professional baseball lifestyle. Which by no means is all butterflies and unicorns like people like to think. Instead of living on the road, scouting out players who might make it in the bigs, his family became his dream. His idea of *Livin' the Dream* shifted. His priorities shifted. He didn't let his downfalls and fears control him. He found his *why* – his real purpose in life.

What Phil overcame in his early 20s has become a major problem with society today. We put so much thought into the idea of fear, we have become obsessed with the fear of failure. This fear doesn't allow our dreams to be fulfilled. When that happens, when we don't take steps to realize our dreams, those dreams merely become wishes or fantasies. This is what happens when no one wants to work harder than the person next to them. When no one wants to grind, to lose sleep, to sacrifice social time or to spend money from their own dang pockets. Wishing instead of working, we wait for our Fairy Godmother to wave her Disney-sparkling wand and turn our pumpkins into carriages, the mice into horses, and our rags into designer gowns.

In our screwed up, trophies-for-everybody because everybody's-great-just-the-way-they-are society, we find ourselves petrified at the very thought of having to feel those feelings. I was talking about earlier about how you feel those fears in your entire being. We are scared to fail, even though the only person who truly decides if we're failing is ourselves. Having forgotten that we can actually change for the better, we are scared to change. So my dear friend, stop being scared, stop fearing failure, stop conforming to society. Embrace change, and let change happen.

After changing his dreams, my dad still was an All-Star, but instead of being an All-Star baseball player going to the World Series – or even an All-Star scout finding the next Babe Ruth for the Yankees, he became an All-Star in life. Phil Glazer was still playing in the big leagues, but instead of playing in Major League Baseball, he played in the big leagues of marriage and parenthood. From the moment he pivoted, those passions surfaced every day of his life. His new big-league team wasn't a group of men with really nice looking butts in their tight baseball pants. No, his team was us, the woman who he married, the two kids he helped create with his own blood.

Livin' the Dream should be focused on the now. *Livin' the Dream* is something you do TODAY because tomorrow is not promised to anyone. No matter how much you might wish it to be otherwise, TOMORROW is not promised to you. Nor is it promised to me – not for anyone reading this book or living in this world. This idea of *Livin' the Dream* is here both to prove to you, and to remind you, that you are lucky enough to be here, to be alive, and to be present, TODAY – for you to stop just dreaming and actually start doing something to live that dream. To fully understand that the best part of living is to actually go out and live. Too many people live like they are already dead, and unless you actually do something about your dreams, you might wind up being one of those walking dead.

So go out and gain wealth – in terms of experience and perspective – then go out and live your dream. Live. Don't just survive – just surviving is a cop-out. That's you numbing yourself to the endless possibilities your dreams have to offer you. Do not be numb to your dreams. Do not stumble blindly through life. Run. Run fast. Go on, sweet child, live. Live your dream.

Livin' the Dream is not your end all and be all. It is not your final destination, the end of your journey, or the glitz and glam of life. *Livin' the Dream* is also about the grind. *Livin' the Dream* encompasses the highs and lows of life. It's all about the celebrations, as well as the darkest of days.

You are alive – I know this because you're still reading – and as humans, we have the opportunity to make something of ourselves, day in and day out. Big or small. Skinny or fat. Lame or extravagant. It's your choice – to make an impact and thrive under all conditions … or to hide from life and wait, quietly, until it just goes away.

Livin' the Dream is all about finding happiness and purpose in your everyday life. It is about always pushing yourself past the limits your mindsets for you. It's about having dreams: big, small, imaginary, and infinite, then going out and reaching for them. But *Livin' the Dream* is also about:

Loving the process of getting there

Pushing through the struggles

Waking up and grinding

Accepting failures and embracing victories

Pivoting and finding new solutions, yet keeping a sense of self along the way

If you get anything from this book, it is the concept of this theory. The concept that you need to wake up, Every. Single. Day. And be *"Livin' the Dream ..."* Good day or bad day **you keep Livin' the Dream.**

Keep the illusion in mind. You have to believe in your dream before you can truly understand it. Believe in the fact of that dream, even though you wake up each day to go to school, followed by waiting on tables at a Ramen restaurant for not the best tips in the world (if you haven't guessed, this was me). Despite all that, if you are *Livin' the Dream,* then you are exactly where you need to be **right now.** Do that and you are quite definitely *"Livin' the Dream ..."*

That dream is your yesterday, your today and – though it's not promised to you – your tomorrow. *Livin' the Dream* means you are going to:

Thrive under all circumstances

Be the champion of your own destiny whatever that may entail

Discover that the grind is worth the reward

Realize that life is based on contradictions after contradictions

I believe that our dreams are what make the world go round. Our dreams prove that everything we face in life is situational – that there is a gray area and nothing is black and white. Our dreams prove that rules are meant to be broken, that everyone should believe in something, anything because belief shapes our lives and allows us to live our dreams.

Believe in believing in something, anything, maybe even in *livin' the dream*, because that right there is believing in positivity. That belief is adding kindness in your days. Believing in *livin' the dream* is hope, gratefulness, heart, passion, and resilience.

Remembering Phil

"Livin' the dream as said by my husband of 26 ½ years … what does it mean to me? Hmm … this is hard. I've tried writing this for years and could never finish – its time now. After Phil passed, it was hard to hear, because I wasn't "livin' the dream…" in fact, my dream was gone. Everything I thought our "empty nest" life was going to be – gone. I cried every day for over a year. It was a very difficult to live in a house where we shared so many memories. There were many days I would just want the pain to stop. But how? I knew I would have to pull it together – this is what Phil would have wanted. I thought about our kids, Nikki and Alexa, and said I have to do it for them. I have to figure out how to move forward. How to "live the dream" again. The dream would be different without Phil. This would be a step by step process. I started smiling again when someone would say

"livin' the dream ..." I would start having good feelings about hearing it again. I know there will always be ups and downs but Phil would have wanted us to be happy and move forward. So for now, Livin' the dream means we need to live a life, share memories, savor the memories and make new ones. I will always love and miss him. Phil has left us physically but his love for life will remain with all of us. He touched so many people in so many ways. We will continue to live his legacy and hope that when you head or say Livin' the dream you think of Phil and remember the smile on his face every time he said it.." **–Kim Glazer (Wife of Phil, Mother of Nikki and Alexa)**

"Livin' the dream to me means enjoying your life, and not stressing about people who do not care they are stressing others". **– Nikki Glazer Stoicoiu**

"He would ask them, "Men, what could be better than walking between those white lines and playing a game? And what are we doing here today?" The players would all reply **"LIVIN THE DREAM!"**. *He coached with the same heart and enthusiasm as he played the game."* **–Scott Haborak (Habo)**

"What it means to **"live the dream."** *This phrase made its way into my vocabulary shortly after beginning my softball*

career with Coach Phil. Regardless of life's circumstances, you make a choice to be happy with your life. If your life is going a direction that you don't want it to or if you see something that you would rather do you are courageous enough to make a change. You appreciate every day as a gift. Most of all, you appreciate the process. **Livin' the Dream** *is showing gratitude for opportunities to get better and embracing the less glamorous components of the daily grind in exchange for the opportunity to be great.* **Livin' the Dream** *means that you don't complain but rather have a grateful heart for early morning workouts or late night studying because you understand that the reason you have to do these things when you'd rather be doing something else means that you are working toward a greater goal, something great." –* **Patti Mariano Kopasakis**

"It means that you need to live every day to the fullest. When you have an opportunity you need to take it and you need to put your whole heart in it – and work your ass off to achieve your goals. To me, it means to do something that you love. Phil was a teacher of baseball, the game we all love so much, but he was also a teacher of life. Baseball ends for everyone at some point, and when it's over you have to find another passion. You need to ask yourself when you open your eyes in the morning and close them at night, can you say "I am **Livin' the Dream***?" That is the only way*

Phil would want us to live. Chase goals and achieve them, work your ass off, be loving and caring to all, find a passion and pursue it, do what makes you happy, and always remember ladies and gentleman to keep "Livin' the Dream!"
– Zack DePalma

"Livin' the Dream - your dad said this in response to anyone who questioned how he was doing - it definitely made people listen more as the usual response would be - fine... I loved his enthusiasm for life! And his response made me look deeply at that dream - he had a beautiful wife and two incredible daughters! He knew that the dream was about all of you - not winning the lottery - for what he had was so much more! It made me realize that I too am livin' the dream for I have an amazing family and married into such a spectacular group of people." **– Niki Tilicki**

*"It reflected your Dad's fun-loving, humorous personality ... He was not rich, not playing in the Major Leagues, not living a carefree life. That life might have been something we all dreamt about, but his reality was enough. He was happy and fulfilled. His family; your Mom and your sister and you, were enough for him to want to tell everyone he was **"Living the Dream"!** – Terrance Kane*

*"I think that Uncle Phil was one of those rare people who had it in them to be happy. To me, "livin' the dream" embodies the meaning of living with purpose and again, being actively happy. I have realized that you cannot wait to be happy. It does not just happen and you have to make it happen. I don't know if this is what he meant, but this is what I have thought." – **Nick Glazer***

*"Living the dream to me always meant being grateful for your talents and the results of your hard work. Your Dad never once complained about anything. Always seemed to have a humble and thankful heart" – **Bob Strebelow***

FROM THE DREAMERS OF THIS WORLD

"Stepping into your faith, surrendering and actively pursuing your dream"

"Doing what you want to do, whenever you want to do it without having to face the pressures of life."

"Being happy with yourself. It's simple. If you don't enjoy what you're doing and respecting yourself then that is not life and that's not the dream to me."

"Livin' the dream is being able to do what you love to do whole heartedly."

"Embracing the freedom that is inherently ours and that we forget we have sometimes. Knowing that you're never done, there's always the next step the next thing you're always advancing."

"Living the dream is being able to prosper and go beyond your dreams and accomplish your goals number one. Number two, be able to help others while you're at it and number three, succeed in life no matter what. There is no one stopping you, no one able to stop you."

"Having a good friend. Not a whole lot like Facebook. Just a few good friends. Like one, four or five. Not more than 50. I'm not impressed by people who have 700,000 likes."

"It's actually peace. Satisfaction, in going for it in your endeavor."

"Living on your own terms without inhibition"

"Small victories and big success."

"I think Livin' the dream I means being authentic I think it means doing things despite what others think of you. Whether you're doing good or bad someone's going to hate

your guts.. Whether you're doing good or bad someone's going to love you. Livin' the dream is #doyou. The number one component to livin' the dream is serving others. There's no greater sacrifice than to make someone's life better than yours. That's f*cking livin' the dream. Do you, be you."

"I was totally focused on aspects of what I thought was livin' the dream but isn't actual what livin' the dream is.. I now make a living "saving the planet". I save the world. That is livin' the dream. Being in a situation in which you are around positive people. You wake up and feel good about what you do and wake up and feel good about your job."

MY FINAL WORDS ...

To my dreamers, my movers, my difference makers. I hope this book serves you well. I hope that it has and will help you as much as it has helped me. I hope you know you found a genuine friend in me and I can't wait for your journey ahead. I hope you now feel that you are *livin' the dream* and can embrace each sacrifice, love the grind, stay humble, find the small victories and be on the pursuit to happiness in each day. It's your turn. C'mon, go now. Close this book in your hands and take it from here. Keep the movement moving and move with me! Cheers to **livin' the dream ...** today because tomorrow is not promised.

PHIL GLAZER RULE LIST

Livin' the dream⋯

Livin' the dream means being focused on the now. Livin' the dream means living for today because tomorrow is not promised. Livin' the dream means being alive and present in life and to gain wealth in terms of experience and knowledge. Livin' the dream is all about the process and our journey.

Strap on a pair

Strap on a pair means to buy-in and suck it up. Holding your head high and not between your legs. Accepting fault and not throwing blame.

Love Conquers All

Love does not only apply to you in a romantic relationship. It applies to everything life has to offer. You thrive on love. Love means filling your heart with someone or something. Taking care of it. Keeping it safe. Cherishing it. Trusting it. Not taking any of its heartbeats for granted. Not forgetting its needs and wants. Love is investing completely, fully, kindly and open-mindedly.

Family first

Family comes first, but this family doesn't have to be biological family. You have the opportunity to choose some of your family. Choose wisely and forget the ones who forget you. Members of the family are the ones who stand by you without flinching when all shit goes to hell.

Chase your dreams, not your Ketel.

Some things in life just aren't worth chasing. Chase your passions – whatever leads you to your dreams. Anything that does not serve you and your life a purpose does not deserve to be chased. Be strong enough not to settle, to form a consistency and do things in life wholeheartedly.

Glazer Strong

Glazer Strong means kicking ass and taking names. It means being a believer in kindness. It means defending love over hate. It means having an open heart and an open mind.

The baseball field is where you learn your life lessons

Sports teach you a lot of what you need to know for your future. Sports are more than games, they are lessons. They teach your discipline, work ethic, passion, and teamwork.

Do things with passion ⋯ or don't do them at all.

Passion motivates you to get things done – to actually go all in or go all out. Passion takes you to another level. Passion is what sets your soul on fire. Passion frees your mind and lets your adrenaline set you free.

Discipline

This is the bridge between goals and accomplishments. With discipline comes freedom. You either choose the pain of discipline or the pain of regret

Give rather than get

Getting a sense of comfort when giving to others, without worrying about getting anything in return.

Never burn bridges

Cross the bridge, don't burn the bridge. Instead of solving problems, burning bridges creates a crushing weight on your shoulders. That weight ruins any future relationships, future plans, future possibilities.

Two hands

Two hands is a baseball term that means do things right. The first time, the second time. All the time. Don't take shortcuts, because, in the end, this will only hurt you and the things you are trying to accomplish. Go all in, or you might as well go all out.

You'll figure it out on your own
On your own time, you will figure things out. By learning from others. Gaining experiences. Growing from your mistakes and accomplishments

It is what it is
It is what it is. It was what it was. It will be what it will be. In these moments, learn to pivot. It's the moments that come after the "it is what it is" that really count. It's what you do next and how you take control of the endless possibilities.

"Let me get out my financial calculator"
When you know you have the answer to something, use it. When you are able to figure out something complex more simply, do it. When you know how to get from point A to point B get yourself there and don't second guess it.

It's all about relationships
You never know who the person next to you is. How they can help you. How they can hurt you. So love and be loved. Network the hell out of yourself. Tell your story, because you never know who's listening.

The importance of fundamentals
The basics set you up for success. Never forget where you started, because that gets you to where you want to be. Don't lose sight of the simple things.

Go above and beyond

Don't be mediocre. If you want to be the best, you have to do things that are going to make you the best. You can always do more. Ask yourself, how bad do you want it

Learn from those who have experienced more

See it. Understand it. Learn from it and change what needs to be changed. Do it with courage so that you don't spend any more moments with regret, guilt, fear, or anger.

It's never about the money

Money fills your pockets but experience fills your soul, and that's what it's all about. Money buys things, it doesn't buy happiness or kindness. Become wealthy in terms of experience and wisdom not how much money you have in your bank account. Money doesn't come with you on the other side, do things and spend it while you can.

Don't quit

Quitting is for losers. Try harder. Do more. Give things a chance. Make things happen and shock the world. You didn't come this far to only come this far···

Super diamonds

When you have a mental error, run for it. When you lose, run for it. When you aren't where you want to be or are supposed to be, run for it. Hold yourself accountable.

"Honey dew this, honey dew that"

In life, not all things should be taken seriously. Have fun in all situations. Laugh when you shouldn't. Smile just because. Be free-spirited.

"I don't want to see your face anymore"

If there is no need for confrontation ··· cool off and walk away.

CONTRADICTION LIST

Life isn't that unfair if it is unfair to everyone. That's what makes life so fair.

Rules are made to be broken.

Maintain an unmaintainable relationship.

Be comfortable with being uncomfortable.

Live in the moment. Embrace it. Focus on the now.

What goes up must come down.

"When people ask about love, they tell you about heartbreak."– Brene Brown

How do you take the invisible and make it visible?

Why the things we fear most often stop being fears when you accomplish them.

Secure and safe isn't always secure and safe.

The key to success is laziness.

How do we build a stable future in a world of instability, when the only consistency is constant change?

What do you do when you stop liking what you liked to do?

Turning pro is free but not without a cost.

"You can't ask others what you have to do in order to be authentic."– Simon Sinek

When you are young, you say I love you because I need you. When you grow up, you realize I need you because I love you.

Be positive in negative situations.

Being selfish isn't always selfish.

Perfect your creativity.

Be perfectly imperfect.

It's one thing to know and understand your values, but it's another thing to actually value them.

ABOUT THE AUTHOR

Just a girl, just an ordinary girl with an extraordinary dream. Hey there friends, my name is, Alexa Glazer, a 25-year-old girl who is on the road to living out her dreams. Dreams of passionate endeavors and mind-blowing experiences. I'm all about life changes and bold moves. I dance it out in the kitchen, shake my booty when I'm feeling moody and think that chocolate ice cream is always the answer. I think you can, in fact, be the perfect combination of sensitive and savage, cute and sexy. I have the purest of hearts and want to give everyone a little piece of it.

I believe in believing in something, anything. I believe that life is based on contradictions and that everything we face is situational. I believe in adventures and being a collector of experiences. I believe in forever love, superstitions, the fact that rules are meant to be broken and that the key to success is to be *livin' the dream* ... and that involves –

SACRIFICE. THE GRIND. HUMILITY. SMALL VICTORIES. HAPPINESS.

Let me fill you in on the background to my madness. My dad, the greatest dad of all time, passed away when I was 21 years old. He was a best friend and a mentor to me. Now, this portion of

410

my life doesn't define me. Instead, it has molded me into the woman that I am today. It has knocked me off my feet, put me at my worst and has also pleasantly surprised me by giving me the perspective to make me my best. It has evolved, matured, changed and motivated me to try and *conquer the world*. By conquering the world I mean making it a better place for you and I me and putting a positive light into people's lives.

"How can one girl conquer the world?" you ask.? Well shit, I'm asking myself that exact same question. I'm quite aware this will not be easy, but I plan to make it happen anyway. How? Aspiring to inspire all walks of life, all shapes, all colors, all sizes, all ages. Helping people understand that our struggles are what mold us into becoming better human beings. Life happens, shit happens, but what you do next is up to you.

My goals – in this book, and in my life – are to give you content (i.e., information) that you can relate to. I hope, as you read on, you can hear an honest- to- goodness real person talking to you. A gal just trying to give perspectives on real life. Because there ain't nothin fake about what we go through on the daily. I want to challenge your mind, and in turn, for you to challenge mine. I **love** a good challenge. I'm here to give you a spark, maybe even a firework blast of hope, inspiration, and a sense of gratefulness. This is your personal invitation to my *livin' the dream* party. Believe me, it's a party worth attending. Join me for the party of a lifetime.

ALEXA GLAZER

CPSIA information can be obtained
at www.ICGtesting.com
Printed in the USA
FFOW03n0014090318
45552652-46330FF